I0813048

IMAGES
of America

AVONDALE

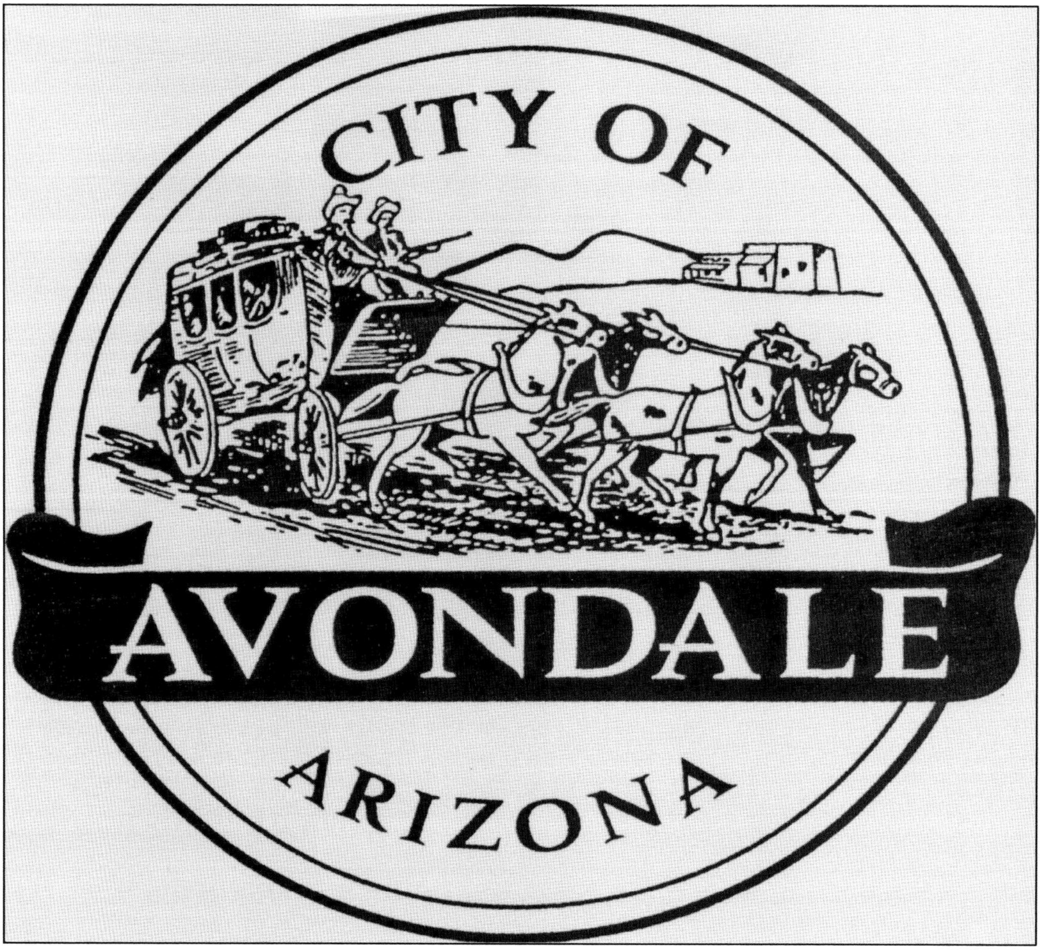

The Avondale symbol represents the hardy pioneers who had the foresight to see that a stagecoach stop was needed in order to serve the westward movement of streaming immigrants. The West was full of discoveries and wonders not yet realized, and rugged men and women who were the first settlers needed supplies for their stock and families and a safe route to their destination. Stagecoach stations had to have a source of water, which on the Agua Fria was a hand-dug well; you couldn't just turn on the faucet and let it rip. Billy Moore provided cool water and a resting place for the teams of horses and later lodging for weary passengers.

ON THE COVER: An array of Avondale and Goodyear city officials worked together on the Waste Water Treatment Facility at Lower Buckeye Road and Fourth Street in Avondale.

IMAGES
of America

AVONDALE

Jerry Squire and the City of Avondale

ARCADIA
PUBLISHING

ISBN 978-0-7385-4843-2

Published by Arcadia Publishing
Charleston SC, Chicago IL, Portsmouth NH, San Francisco CA

Printed in the United States of America

Library of Congress Catalog Card Number: 2007935842

For all general information contact Arcadia Publishing at:
Telephone 843-853-2070
Fax 843-853-0044
E-mail sales@arcadiapublishing.com
For customer service and orders:
Toll-Free 1-888-313-2665

Visit us on the Internet at www.arcadiapublishing.com

*I am dedicating this book to the younger generation
so that they may peer into our past and discover Avondale's pioneers,
who were hardworking, inventive, and determined to succeed
for their future generations to come.*

CONTENTS

Acknowledgments

I would like to thank the City of Avondale, who partnered with me on this unique volume of Avondale's photographic history, and especially Linda Farris, who is Avondale's city clerk. For years, Linda has treasured and preserved hundreds of vintage photographs of Avondale, many of which are featured in this book. A special thanks goes to Sally Schulkie Marcotte, the Collier family, *West Valley View* newspaper, Carolyn Taylor, Mike Taylor, Angel Nandin, Nancy Brant, Pier Simeri, Ruth Clark, Ken and Sally Kiko, the Tri City Chamber of Commerce, and my own family and friends who donated photographs and have supported my historical labors of love for Avondale's history. And finally thanks to Arcadia Publishing's very own talented acquisitions editor Jared S. Jackson, who encouraged me every day along the way and made it a joy to work hard.

INTRODUCTION

Avondale was established by hardy pioneers, but there was another Avondale long before the Spanish and European settlers arrived. The Hohokam were a thriving society with agriculture as the center of life; they were believed to have been the ancestors of the present-day Pima Indians. Canals still used today by local farmers were cut through the earth to water ancient crops.

The first Europeans ventured into Arizona in 1536. A latter expedition was led by Fray Marcos de Niza in 1539, followed by Coronado's expeditions, which arrived in 1540. Around 1687 and 1704, Father Kino discovered and recorded many Native American encampments from Mexico to the Estrella Mountains on his way to California.

In 1848, there was a war between Mexico and the United Stated in which the Treaty of Guadalupe Hidalgo was established—a line running down the middle of the Gila River became the northern boundary of Mexico.

The Arizona Territory was not to be just yet. Mexican land that was in dispute was later bought by the federal government in 1854, thus the Gadsden Purchase. This immense part of the earth needed to be surveyed as per the 1848 Treaty of Guadalupe Hidalgo, but neither side was in agreement. After much debate, the Mexican and U.S. governments came to an understanding and the surveying began. Andrew B. Gray, U.S. surveyor, and Lt. A. W. Whipple, astronomer and surveyor, were hired to do the job. They arrived at the confluence of the Gila and the Salt Rivers in 1851. In 1865, John A. Clark, surveyor general for New Mexico and Arizona, made the decision to establish an initial point—the beginning of surveys in Arizona and other southwestern states.

The original monument for the "Initial Point" was commissioned by John R. Bartlett and the U.S. Boundary Commission. Fifteen years passed before William H. Pierce erected a permanent marker of native rocks stacked in a cone figuration eight feet in circumference and eight feet high with a six-foot pole protruding from the top. The commission designated the "Initial Point" of Arizona as 33 degrees, 22 minutes, 37 seconds north latitude and 112 degrees, 18 minutes, 20 seconds west longitude; the summit is 1,158.63 feet above sea level.

William H. Pierce finished the job 15 years later. He erected a permanent marker for the Gila and Salt River Base Meridian used for surveys today. The job was finished after much government red tape, Native American uprisings, long bouts of boredom because of the terrain and weather conditions, and even episodes of drunkenness. It is rumored the crew became weary and wanted to return home so they cut the survey short, and Arizona never got its ocean port off the Sea of Cortez.

Anyone who owns property in Arizona has a deed, and the legal description starts at Monument Hill, the "Initial Point." The monument was and is still important to establish boundaries between Mexico and the United States. Almost every plot of land in Arizona and other border states is measured from Monument Hill, located on the eastern edge of Phoenix International Raceway, nestled at the base of the Estrella Mountains in Avondale, Arizona.

Gold was discovered in Wickenburg and Prescott, which created commerce between Tucson and northern Arizona. Shipments of supplies and people were carried by stagecoaches that needed places of rest for the teams of horses and refuge from marauding Native Americans as well as to get a little shuteye and some grub to eat.

The Tucson, Prescott, and San Bernardino stage companies ran weekly service from Tucson to Wickenburg, where connections could be made to Prescott and from there on to California. This stage route followed the trail leading from Maricopa Wells to the Wickenburg trail. The alignment of the trail passed through present-day Avondale, which would be known as Coldwater Stage Station.

Billy Graham Moore, born in Cheraw, South Carolina, in 1849, became a blacksmith and at the age of 16 served as a member of Quantrill's Raiders, a company of Southern outlaws and partisans with a reputation as unsavory or courageous, depending upon which side you were on. After the infamous massacre of Lawrence, Kansas, by the gang, as well as numerous other atrocities, the surviving members of the Quantrill outfit, which included Frank and Jesse James among its alumni, began to disperse. Billy laid low for awhile, using aliases until he received a pardon from the governor of Missouri.

Billy joined a wagon train going to Prescott, Arizona. He then showed up in Chloride. Moore farmed and worked as a cowboy and bartender for a number of years. He established a bar at Gillette, a ghost town now north of Cave Creek. A bar he owned near what is now the Black Canyon Highway is the source of the name for Moore Canyon near Rock Springs. Later he became justice of the peace at Agua Fria.

In 1880, "Uncle Billy," as the locals called him, established a stage stop along the banks of the Agua Fria River; maybe he saw some need for a way station for stagecoaches and freight wagons that traveled from Tucson to Wickenburg and Prescott.

Moore married Bicentia Galaboize or "Cynthia" on January 17, 1884. She supposedly nursed him back to health after he was ambushed by Apache Indians in the White Tank Mountains; he then fell in love with her and they married. Billy and Cynthia later adopted a daughter who was accidentally trampled by a mule. "Aunt Cynthia" was never the same.

Avondale's growth can be largely credited to the Goodyear Tire and Rubber Company's cotton farms and the Naval Air Base—yes, there was a navy base in the middle of the desert. Both facilities came into their own during World War II: Goodyear Farms grew cotton for the fibers in tires of that time, and the weather was excellent to train pilots and house obsolete planes.

As often happens in history, small towns are consumed by larger municipalities. Cashion and Littleton are two of these. Today they are part of Avondale's past.

Dr. S. D. Little, a dentist, settled on the west corner of Avondale Boulevard and MC 85 where Littleton School exists today. A small store, a few homes, and an office were built. Dr. Little tried to petition for a post office but was unsuccessful. He ventured on to Bisbee. Jim Cashion of the Cashion Ranch just east of Avondale Avenue succeeded in establishing a post office in 1911. Cashion Ranch raised beef and later ostriches. The feathers were used for ladies' hats, but when the automobile appeared, the feathered hats would not stay on women's heads, so they fell out of favor. As a result, the ostriches were to be sold. Dr. Chandler bought the birds and had them moved to Chandler, Arizona. Cowboys herded the large birds as they would cattle, not knowing ostriches would act differently. The uncontrolled foul caused a death when a team of horses driving a wagon reared up and threw its owners.

One

The Early Years of Coldwater

Avondale was christened Coldwater by William Graham Moore, not the first white man to the West Valley—since Kit Carson, Fr. Eusebio Kino, and others passed down the Gila River on their way to California—but Moore was the first Anglo to settle the area.

Known as Billy Moore to future generations of Avondale, he hand-dug a well that not only was the beginning of his stagecoach stop but also launched the beginning of a growing city. If he could gaze upon the future, he would have seen dramatic changes to come. The dusty trail to his store was altered, renamed, paved, and then paved again. The population went from 1 to 69,356 in the span of 115 years.

The water well Billy established was the beginning of all the agriculture in the area. Without his meager undertaking, others would not have recognized the potential of the desert landscape. The crops Billy reaped opened the eyes of the others.

As passengers of the stage and cowboys watering their horses looked upon the field of hay and herds of livestock, they knew of this town's potential and came to settle here.

Billy did not want growth. A recluse of sorts, Billy had a colorful past that he possibly wanted to keep hidden from the public eye. But here in Coldwater, others could not resist his little place of isolated paradise. Billy must have taken the inevitable changes in stride because he expanded his stage stop to a general store.

Chased by his past, Billy was always looking over his shoulder. He had a rifle handy in case of marauding Native Americans, and everyone in town knew that if you came looking for Billy, you had better announce yourself in advance. One man forgot this unwritten law, and Billy Moore shot through his front door, killing the unannounced individual instantly. Area residents then warned newcomers of his disagreeable ways, and no one made the same mistake again around Coldwater's first household name.

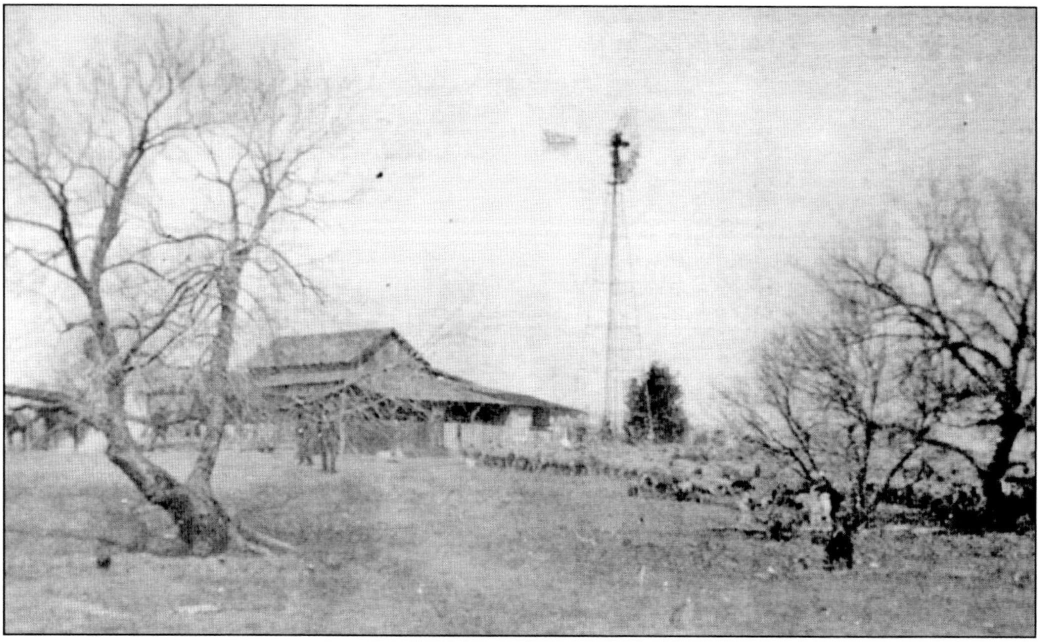

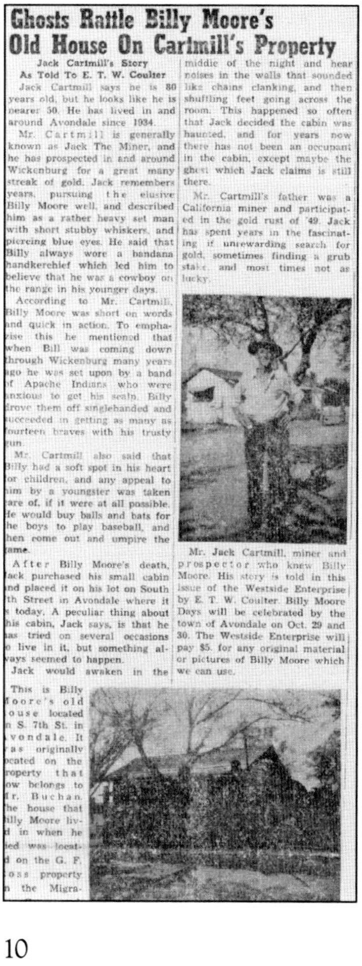

Ghosts Rattle Billy Moore's Old House On Carlmill's Property

Jack Cartmill's Story
As Told To E. T. W. Coulter

Jack Cartmill says he is 80 years old, but he looks like he is nearer 50. He has lived in and around Avondale since 1934.

Mr. Cartmill is generally known as Jack The Miner, and he has prospected in and around Wickenburg for a great many streak of gold. Jack remembers years, pursuing the elusive Billy Moore well, and described him as a rather heavy set man with short stubby whiskers, and piercing blue eyes. He said that Billy always wore a bandana handkerchief which led him to believe that he was a cowboy on the range in his younger days.

According to Mr. Cartmill, Billy Moore was short on words and quick in action. To emphasize this he mentioned that when Bill was coming down through Wickenburg many years ago he was set upon by a band of Apache Indians who were anxious to get his scalp. Billy drove them off singlehanded and succeeded in getting as many as fourteen braves with his trusty gun.

Mr. Cartmill also said that Billy had a soft spot in his heart for children, and any appeal to him by a youngster was taken care of, if it were at all possible. He would buy balls and bats for the boys to play baseball, and then come out and umpire the game.

After Billy Moore's death, Jack purchased his small cabin and placed it on his lot on South 7th Street in Avondale where it is today. A peculiar thing about this cabin, Jack says, is that he has tried on several occasions to live in it, but something always seemed to happen.

Jack would awaken in the middle of the night and hear noises in the walls that sounded like chains clanking, and then shuffling feet going across the room. This happened so often that Jack decided the cabin was haunted, and for years now there has not been an occupant in the cabin, except maybe the ghost which Jack claims is still there.

Mr. Cartmill's father was a California miner and participated in the gold rust of '49. Jack has spent years in the fascinating if unrewarding search for gold, sometimes finding a grub stake, and most times not as lucky.

Mr. Jack Cartmill, miner and prospector who knew Billy Moore. His story is told in this issue of the Westside Enterprise by E. T. W. Coulter. Billy Moore Days will be celebrated by the town of Avondale on Oct. 29 and 30. The Westside Enterprise will pay $5. for any original material or pictures of Billy Moore which we can use.

This is Billy Moore's old house located on S. 7th St. in Avondale. It was originally located on the property that now belongs to Mr. Buchan. The house that Billy Moore lived in when he died was located on the G. F. Ross property on the Migra-

Billy Moore homesteaded 280 acres along the Agua Fria River on March 6, 1895, under the laws of the Territory of Arizona for $600. He must have seen the potential of the land. He may not have seen the future growth, but the area suited him and the many settlers who were to come. Pictures are hard to come by depicting Billy Moore's life; this picture came from an old article from the *Westsider* newspaper. (Courtesy City of Avondale.)

After Moore's death, his cabin was purchased by Jack Cartmill. Cartmill moved the cabin to South Seventh Street, where he claimed it was haunted. Cartmill reported that he could hear chains clanking and feet shuffling across the floor as he tried to sleep at night. He finally gave up the thought of occupying the small dwelling. The cabin was at this location until recently, when an Avondale renewal project was put in place and new homes were built on the very spot. (Courtesy City of Avondale.)

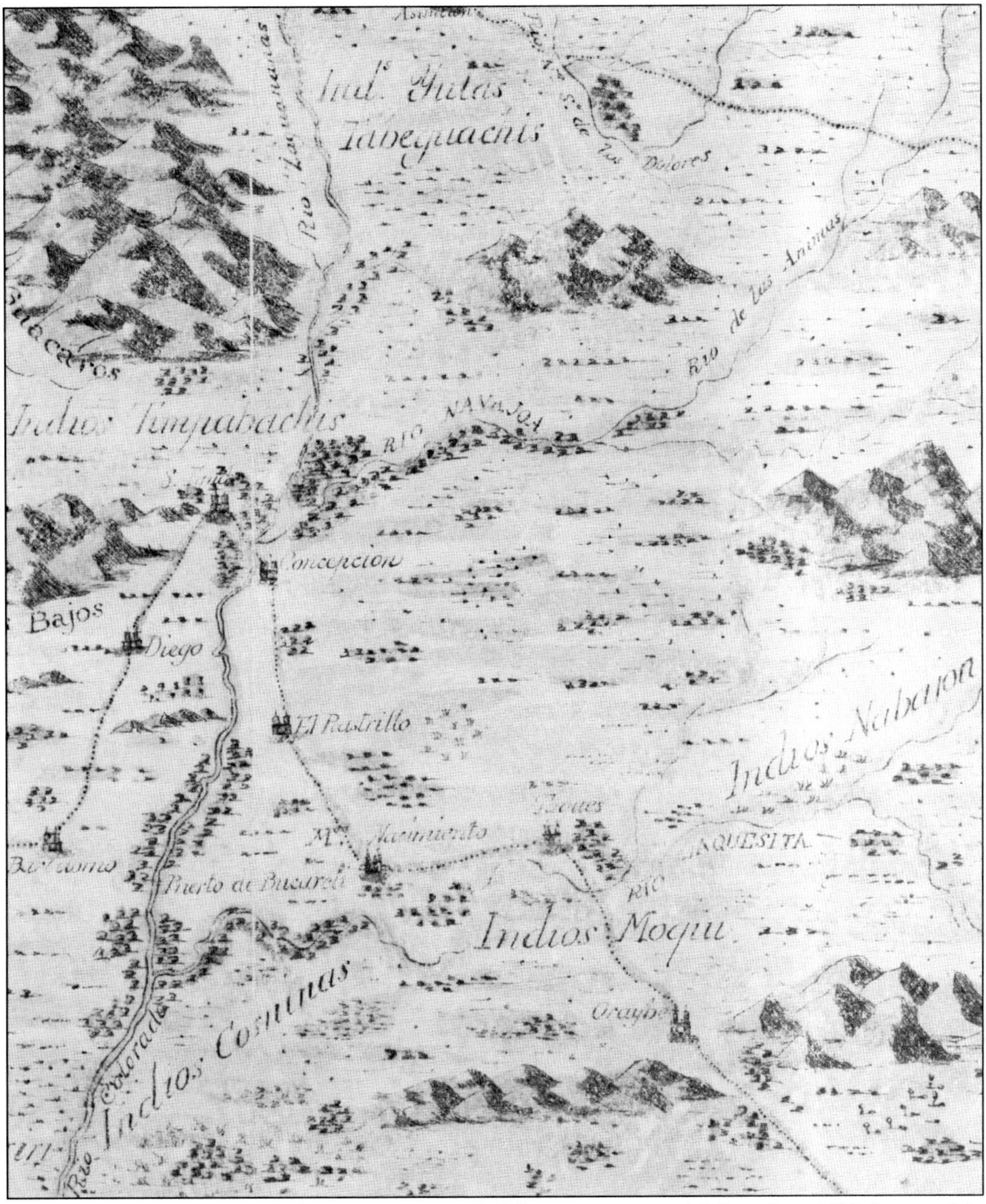

Father Kino followed the Gila River west to California twice, in 1697 and in 1699. It is widely believed in Avondale that Kino was the first European to see the Estrella Mountains. Since he was trained as a mathematician and cartographer, the records and maps of his travels through Arizona are much more reliable than many of the early explorers. Father Kino explored and mapped several of the Native American encampments between the Estrella Mountains and the current Mexican border. (Courtesy City of Avondale.)

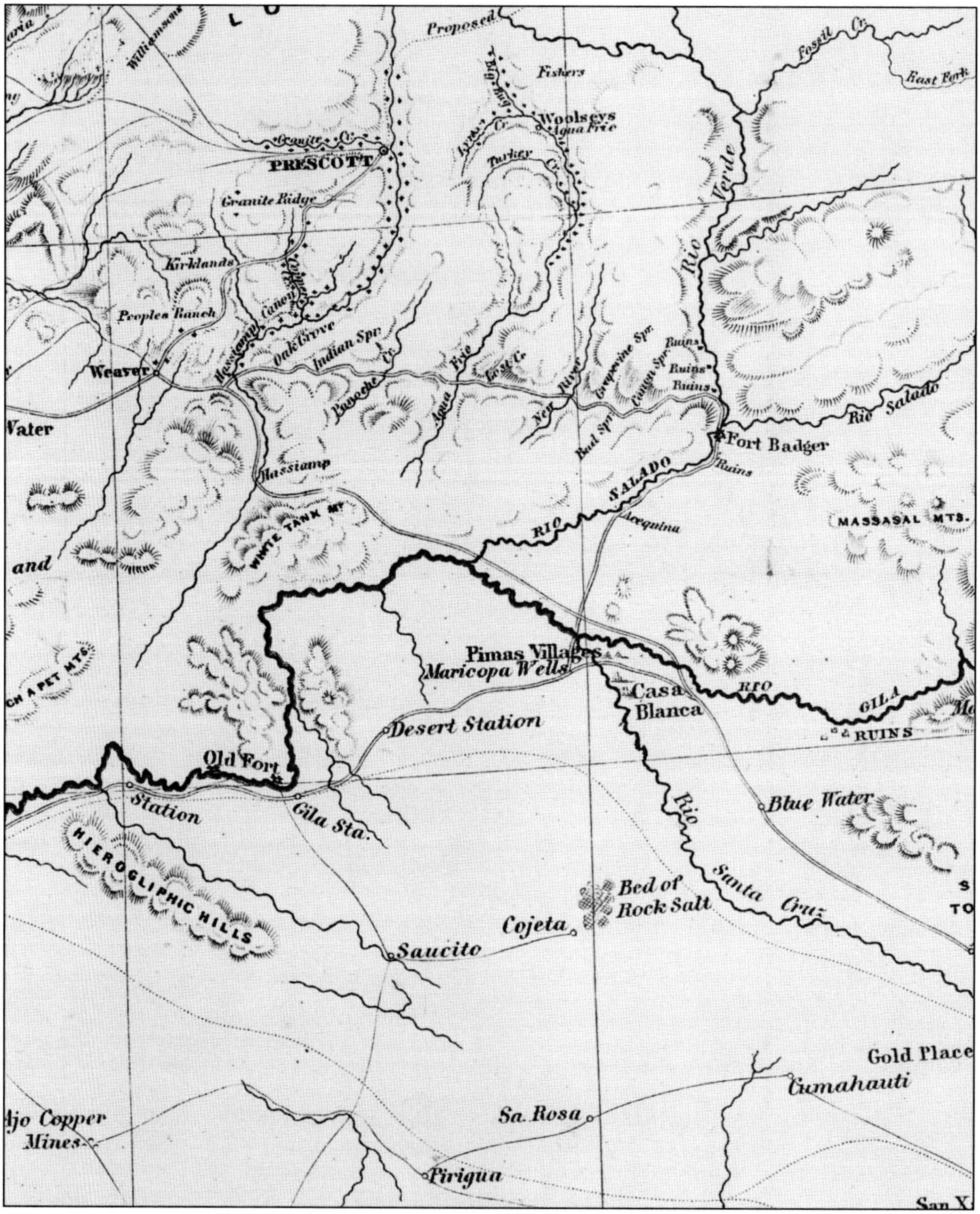

After the war with Mexico, the Treaty of Guadalupe Hidalgo was drawn up, calling for new boundaries. There was a dispute as to where the lines should be charted. The U.S. government contracted with William H. Pierce and his crew in 1867 to follow previous markings of Andrew B. Gray, U.S. surveyor, and Lt. A. W. Whipple, an astronomer and surveyor who 15 years earlier had climbed and charted Monument Hill, the Initial Point of all land to be surveyed as per the Gadsden Purchase. Pierce used such instruments as a Burt's Solar Compass to determine direction and a metal chain 33 feet long with 55 links to measure distances. (Courtesy City of Avondale.)

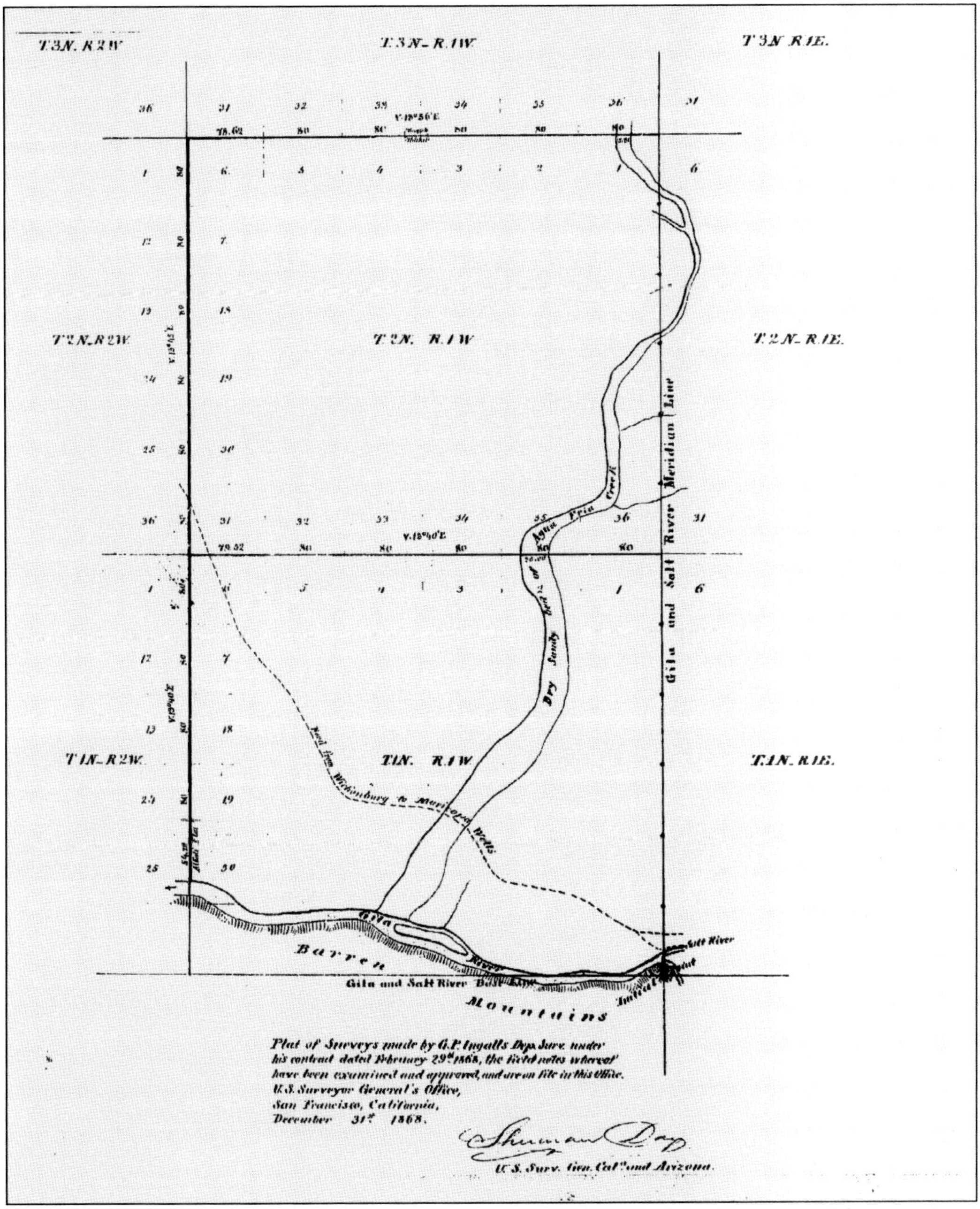

A map of the Gila and Salt River Base Meridian officially marked the Territory of Arizona, land purchased from Mexico per the Treaty of Guadalupe Hidalgo. Hard feelings surrounded the treaty as it was the result of the Mexican-American War of 1848 and interpretations of where the border lines were to be abounded. After much deliberation, the U.S. government hired a crew to mark the beginning of the southwestern part of the United States. G. P. Ingalls actually built a monument in 1868. The Initial Point was to become the most important indicator between Mexico and the United States. (Courtesy City of Avondale.)

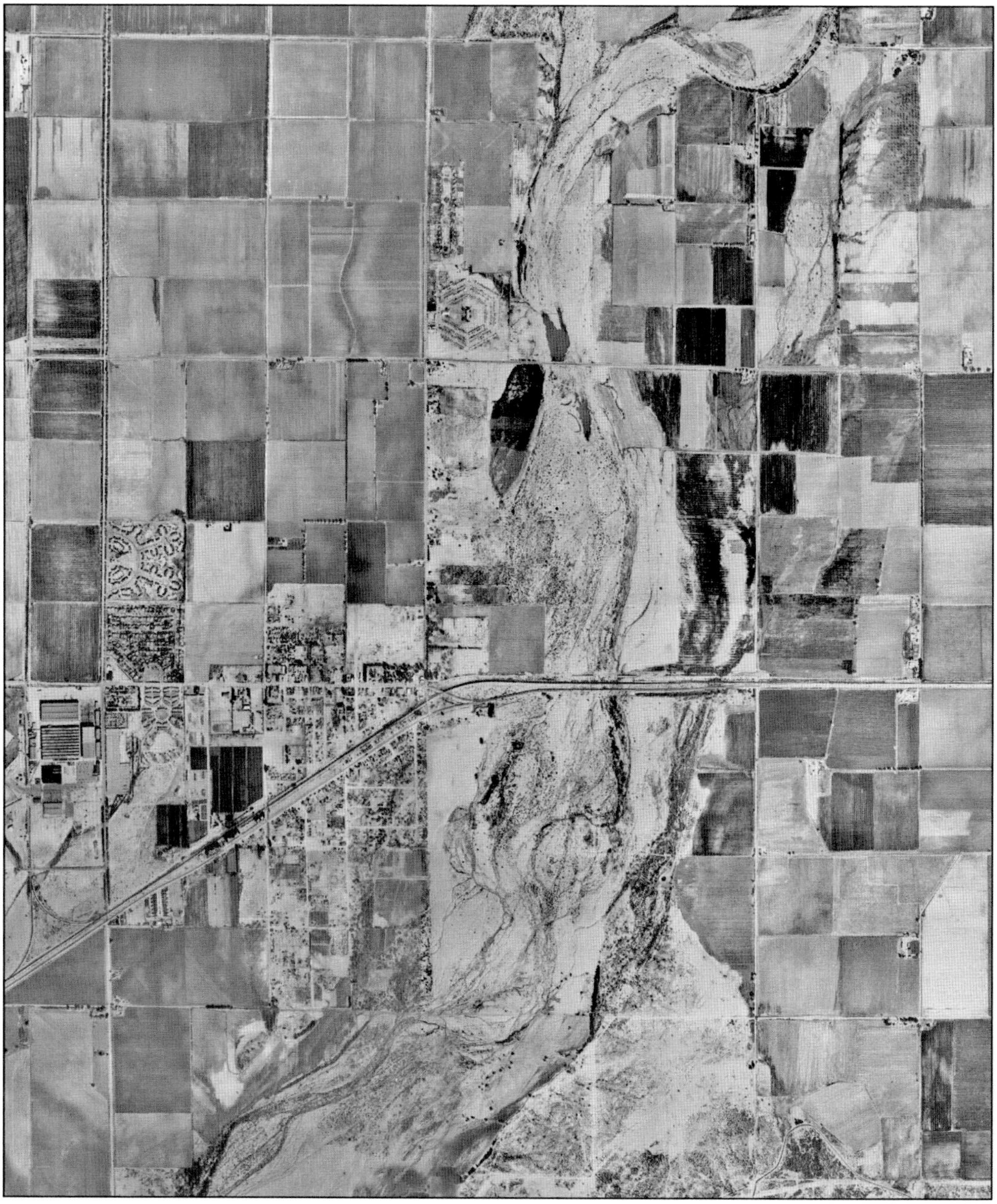

This 1949 aerial photograph features sparse housing developments in Avondale's early community. At this point in time, local residents still called this diminutive town "Coldwater." Western Avenue, the major drag through town, was diverted to a street called Main, or today MC 85; the road curved a little south of the old route to prevent traffic problems. The highway became the major traveled road from Phoenix to San Diego, and both cities were experiencing rapid growth. There were no freeways in those days but lots of automobiles scurrying through small towns on a major route. The roads were narrow and treacherous and made from cement with spacers every so often that would buckle with the extreme heat. As you traveled along, there would be a noise where the slabs of cement met, followed by a loud thump as the road buckled. It all made for an almost musical sound. (Courtesy City of Avondale.)

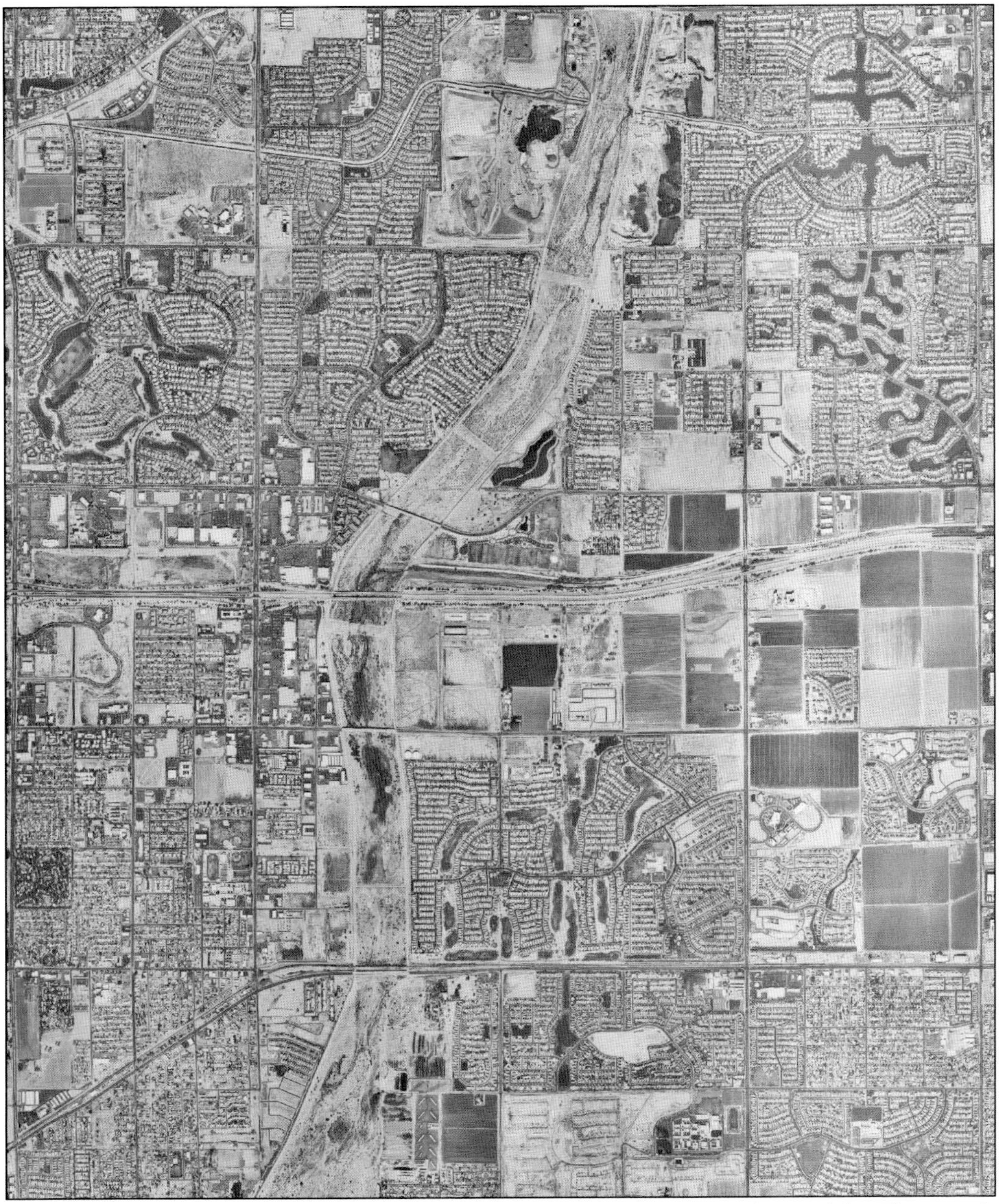

Change is obvious when one looks at the maps, such as this 2007 map of Avondale. The growth has been breathtaking. You can pass an empty lot one day, and the next time you visit the area, it may be under construction. Avondale had to provide infrastructure to the vast area, and roads, utility lines, sewers, and the like were to be constructed throughout the city. This was no small task, and credit should be given to the public works department, which in the early years worked with sheer muscle power and little machinery. Large plots of earth needed to be moved; mule power was the machine of the day. Mule teams were attached to large planks of wood that scraped across the desert, and after many passes, the land would be somewhat flat and cleared of desert vegetation. Later steam-powered equipment evolved and was used, and as technology progressed, gas engines appeared; today diesel power is the ticket. (Courtesy City of Avondale.)

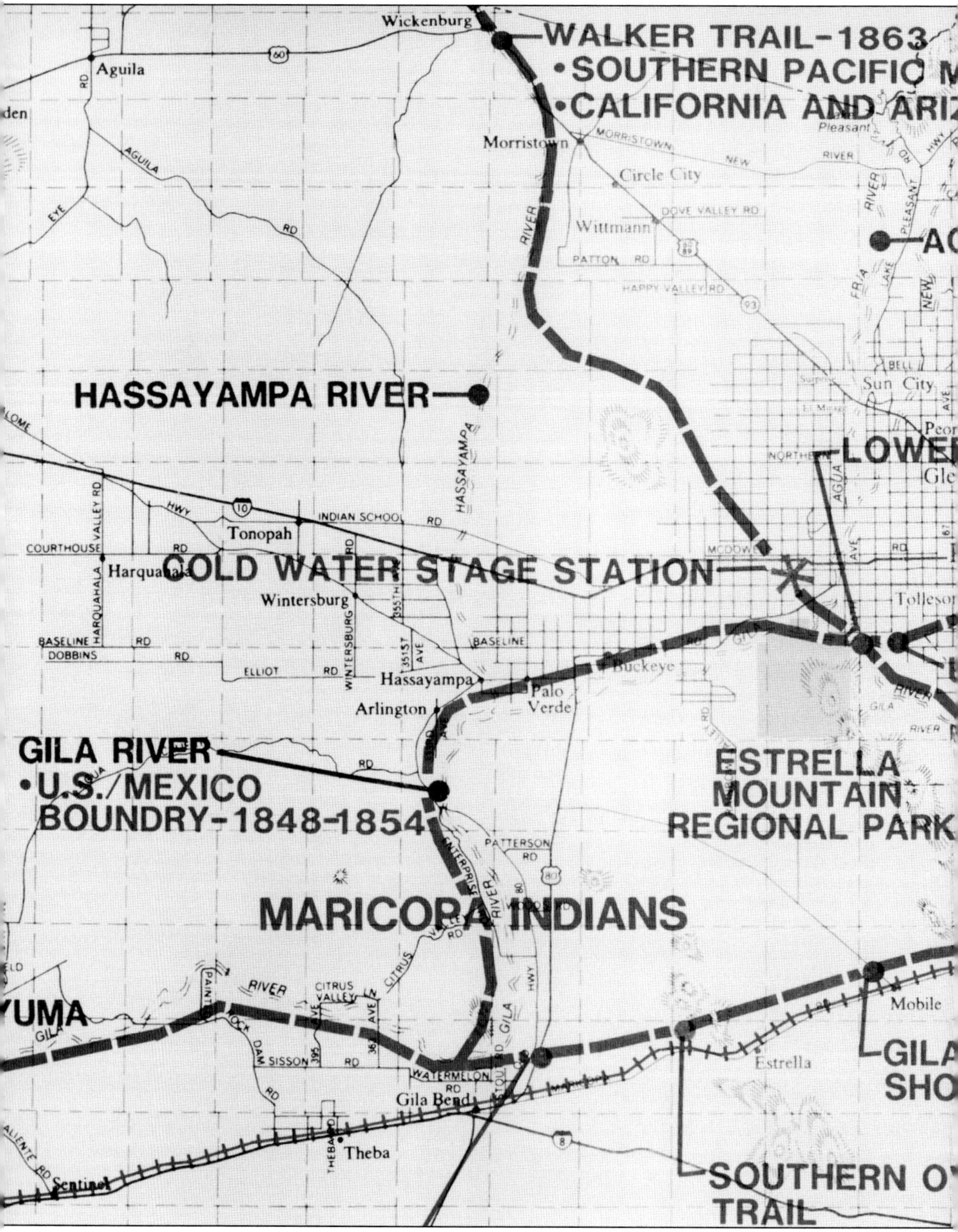
WALKER TRAIL-1863
•SOUTHERN PACIFIC
•CALIFORNIA AND
HASSAYAMPA RIVER
COLD WATER STAGE STATION
GILA RIVER
•U.S./MEXICO BOUNDRY-1848-1854
ESTRELLA MOUNTAIN REGIONAL PARK
MARICOPA INDIANS
SOUTHERN
TRAIL
Wickenburg
Aguila
Morristown
Circle City
Wittmann
Sun City
Tonopah
Wintersburg
Hassayampa
Arlington
Palo Verde
Buckeye
Mobile
Estrella
Gila Bend
Theba
Sentinel

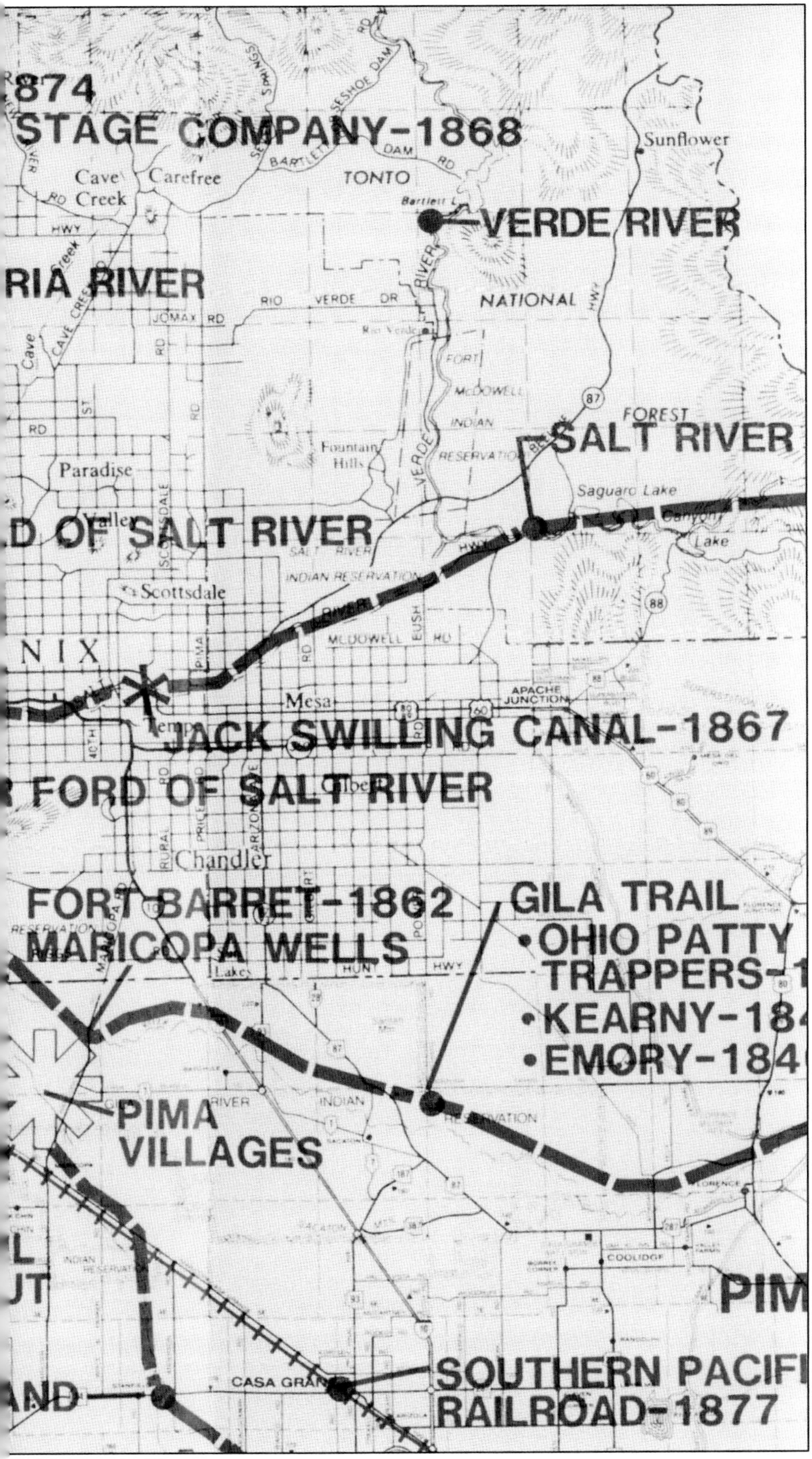

Notice the old trails and the distance between encampments on this map. Billy Moore saw the potential of a good blacksmith and a watering hole and decided Coldwater Station could provide services to weary travelers, two- and four-legged ones. As with many old-timers, Billy later had a change of heart when the name Coldwater, Arizona, was altered to Avondale, Arizona. Billy decided progress wasn't all it was cracked up to be; he wanted to keep the slower pace of a small community. Change was hard for Uncle Billy; he didn't trust new inventions like the automobile. The horseless carriage never knew the way home after he was done kicking up his heels in town, but his reliable horse always got him back to the barn. (Courtesy Maricopa County Parks Department.)

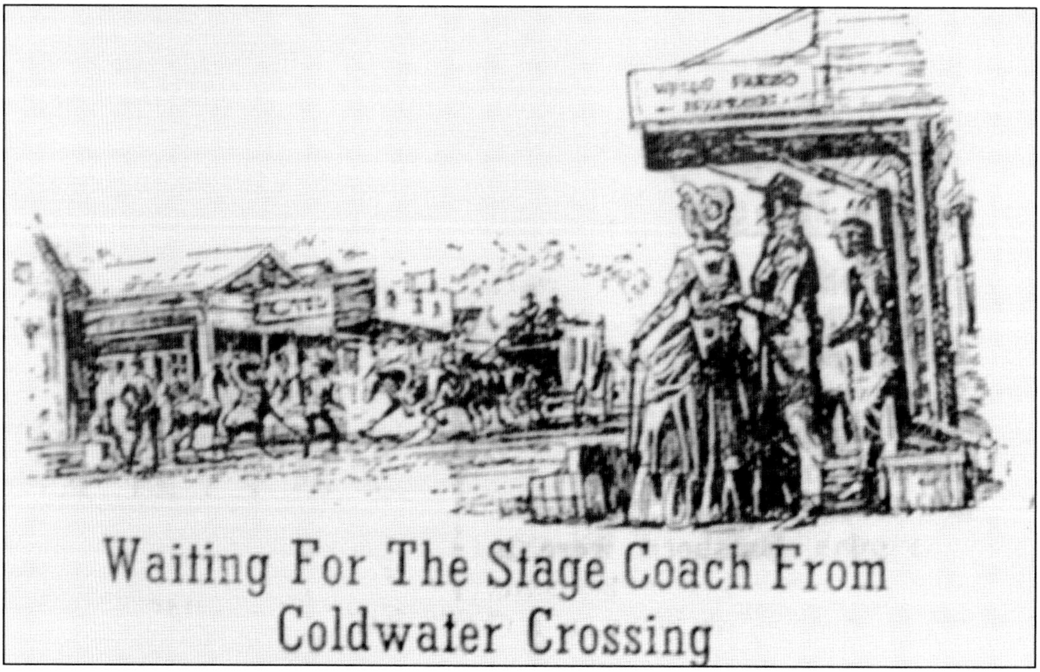

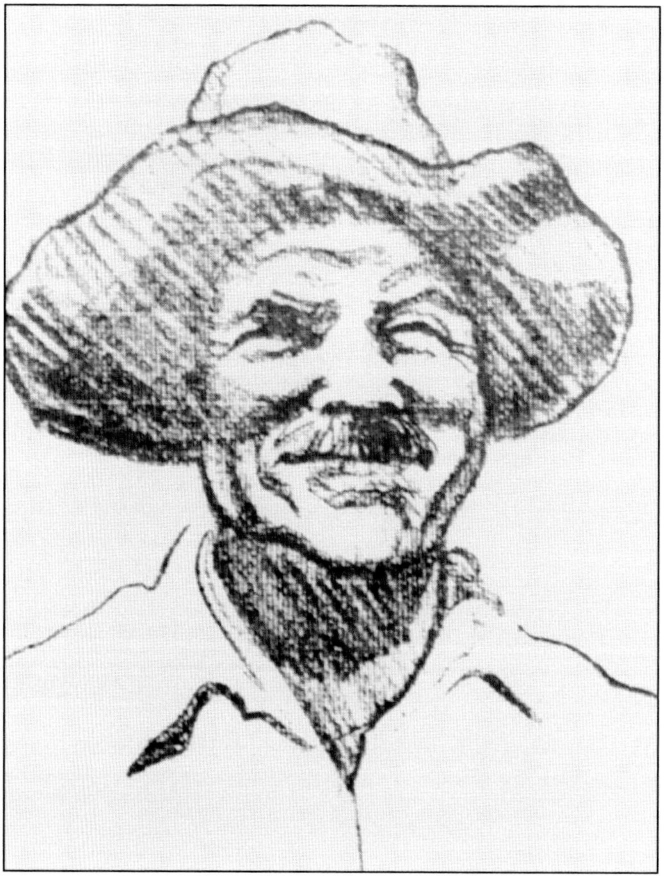

Both local newspapers, the *Westsider* and later the *West Valley View*, annually print historical stories highlighting the celebration of Billy Moore Days in Avondale. They kept the Billy Moore spirit alive, for without this information, people who arrived yearly wouldn't know where Avondale's roots originated. Children especially needed to know about Avondale's rich history and that a community doesn't appear from the desert; hardy pioneers had to endure hardships we today can only read about. There was no mass transportation, air-conditioning, electricity, or grocery stores. Nearly everything had to be made either from hand or imagination. Can you visualize a generation with no television, electronic apparatus, or pop celebrities? (Courtesy City of Avondale.)

Two

Avondale Begins

The name of the town was to be changed from Coldwater to Avondale because of an argument Billy Moore had with the U.S. postal inspector. Moore was selling homemade liquor at the store where the post office resided. Because it was illegal to sell liquor where U.S. mail was delivered, the postal inspector became upset and an argument between the two caused the inspector to move the post office.

Avondale truly got its start during the Great Depression. Transformation was on its way. Midwesterners had little hope for their crops because of a long drought and poor farming practices. Farmland was literally being blown away. Farmers' crops failed, and great dust storms blew topsoil into the atmosphere. People left by the droves as they were starving and had no other alternative. The desperation of leaving behind homesteads they farmed for generations took its toll on Avondale's residents. The added burden of the stock market crash of 1929 had everyone looking for hope.

A discouraged nation headed west for the land of milk and honey. Many travelers packed only what they could fit into their cars, and Arizona was the state most had to pass through on the route to California. But the traveling fold was turned away from California if they did not have cash in their pockets, so they settled in Arizona.

The major route to California passed through Coldwater, Arizona, on Buckeye Road. Often money had run out by this time, so men stopped and tried to get work locally doing anything they could to scrape together some traveling money.

As they became accustomed to the growing city, they liked what they saw and decided they had reached their land of milk and honey in the desert landscape of Avondale.

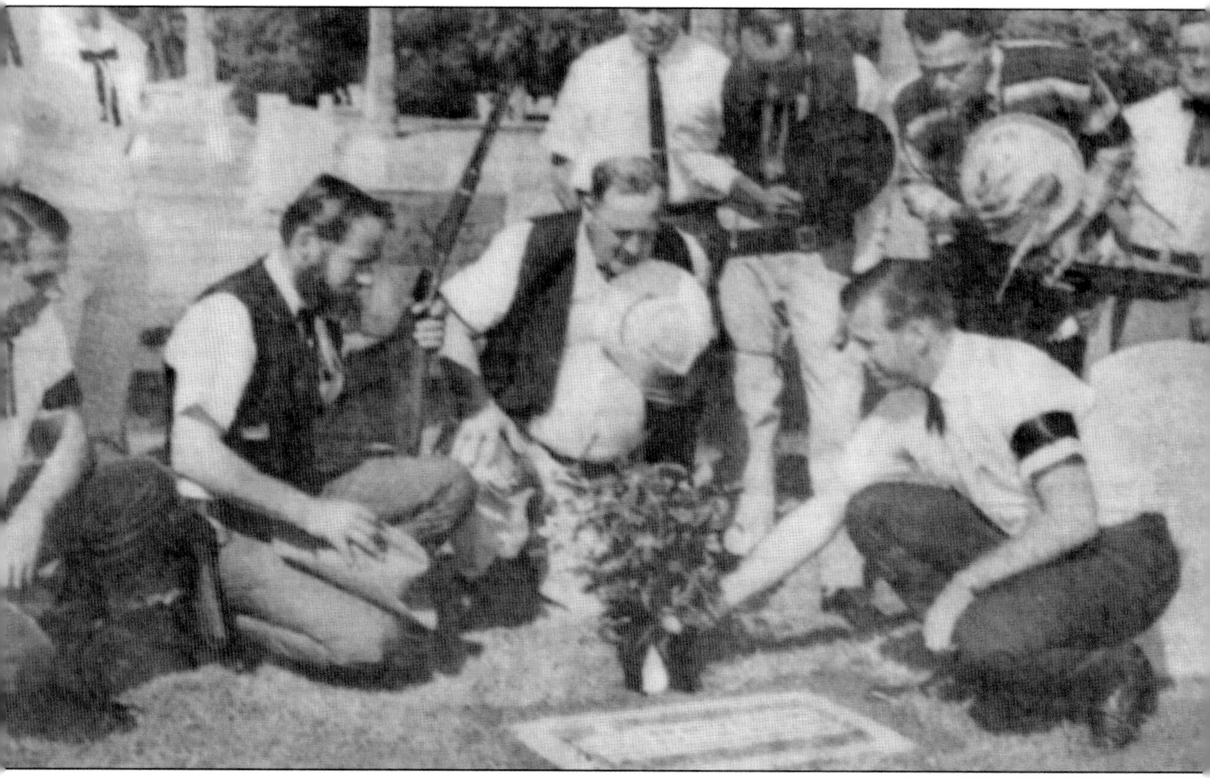

Citizens realized there was no headstone marking pioneer Billy Moore's grave and brought it to the attention of the chamber of commerce. Together they provided the marker assuring Uncle Billy's place in history. Moore's grave is no longer unknown. Uncle Billy's resting place is in Greenwood Memory Lawn Cemetery, located in west Phoenix. Residents were not only caring but were known for their community action and a neighborhood spirit. The civic-minded community would give of their time if money was scarce when called upon or money by those who could donate. Community awareness was an ingredient of the pioneers. (Courtesy City of Avondale.)

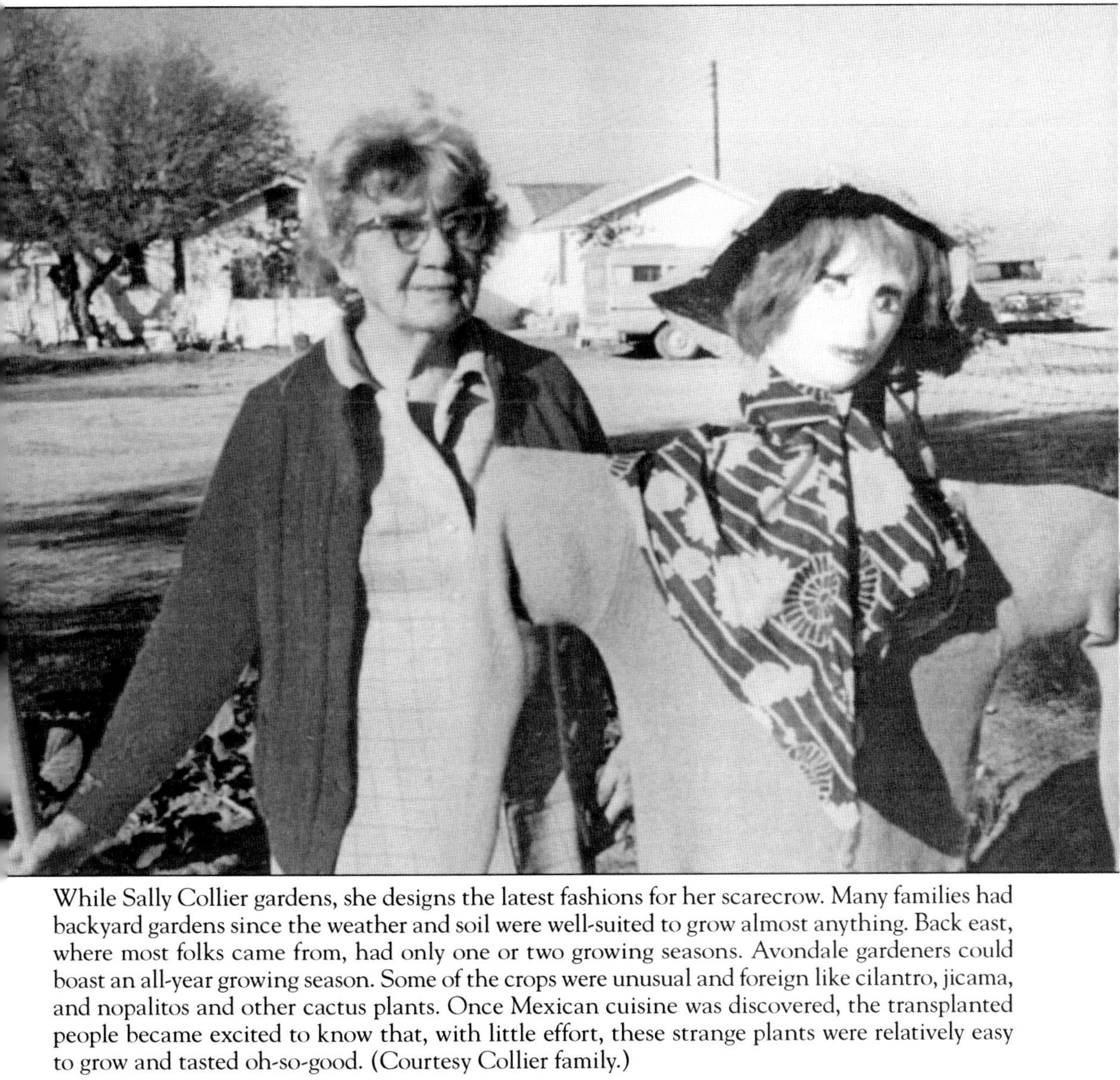

While Sally Collier gardens, she designs the latest fashions for her scarecrow. Many families had backyard gardens since the weather and soil were well-suited to grow almost anything. Back east, where most folks came from, had only one or two growing seasons. Avondale gardeners could boast an all-year growing season. Some of the crops were unusual and foreign like cilantro, jicama, and nopalitos and other cactus plants. Once Mexican cuisine was discovered, the transplanted people became excited to know that, with little effort, these strange plants were relatively easy to grow and tasted oh-so-good. (Courtesy Collier family.)

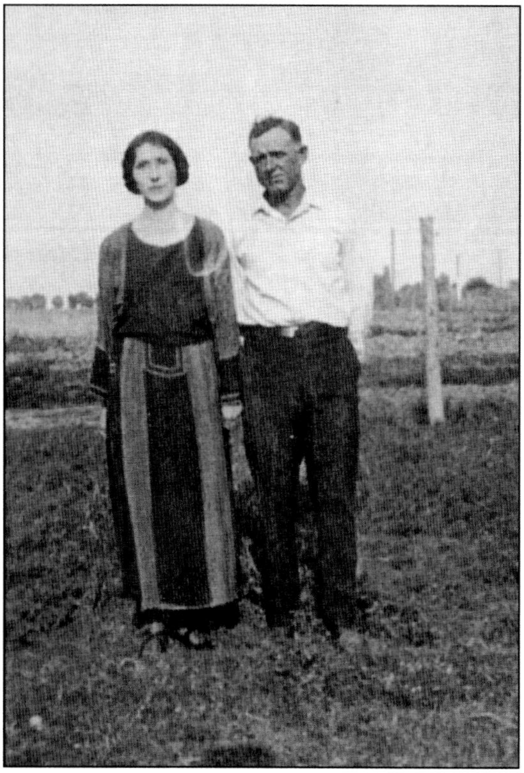

Thayer and Pearl Jackson Collier were married in 1915. This picture was taken in 1918 on the Collier Ranch. The couple had one daughter and raised two nieces and one nephew after the children's parents passed away young. Thayer was a productive, upstanding citizen who had children's education in his heart. (Courtesy Collier family.)

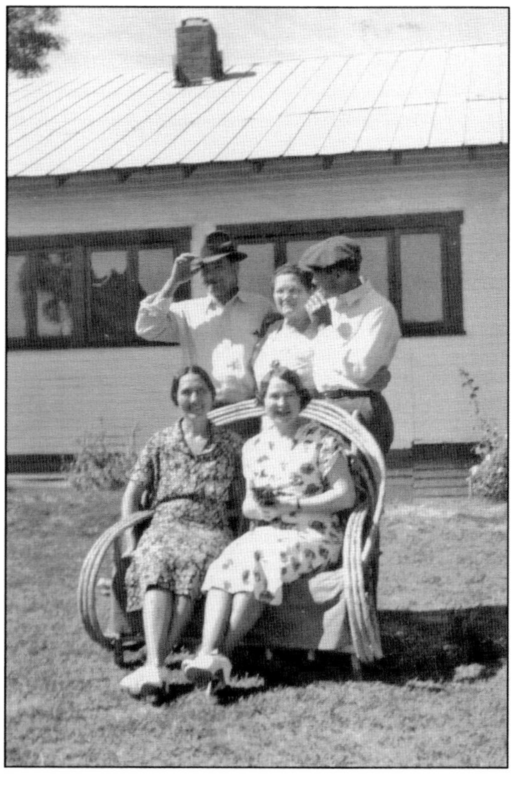

Pearl Jackson Collier sits with family in front of the Collier Ranch house in the spring of 1940. From left to right are (seated on a willow chair) Pearl Jackson Collier and her sister Gladys Jackson; (standing) Pearl's brother Winfred Jackson; Pearl's mother, Alice Jackson; and Pearl's brother Leonard Jackson. Pearl Jackson loved to tend her rose garden and cook for all the men on the farm. Pearl often took a cook stove in the field just to make home-cooked meals for the hired hands. (Courtesy Sally Schulkie Marcotte and the Collier family.)

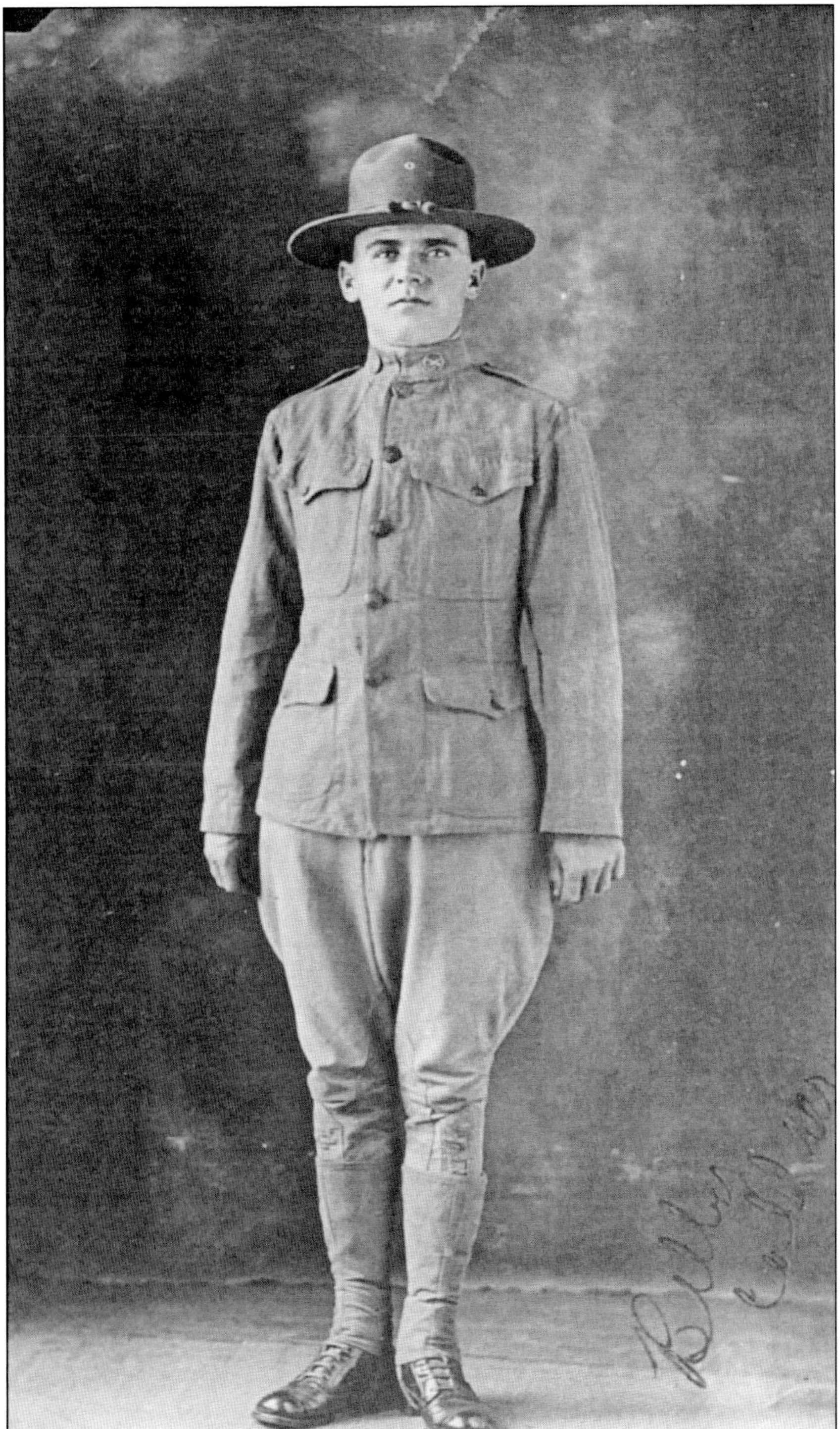

William "Billy" Collier was a soldier in the First World War. The picture shows him in his snappy uniform. After Billy was discharged from the military, he moved to Vera Cruz, Mexico, where he built homes for workers in the oil field. (Courtesy Sally Schulkie Marcotte and the Collier family.)

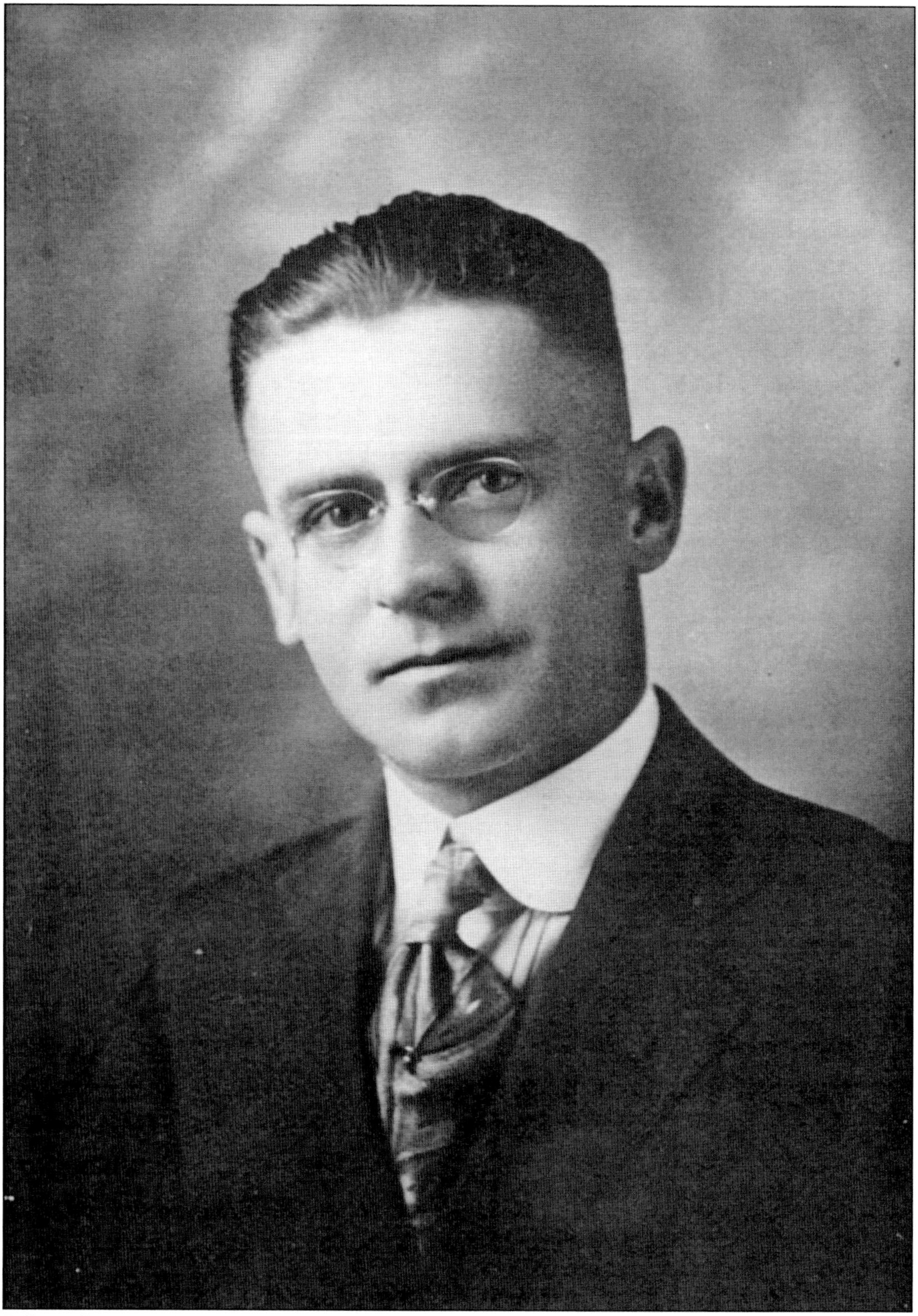

Billy Collier retired and purchased a small farm next to his brother Thayer, where he and his wife, Molly, lived until end of their lives. (Courtesy Sally Schulkie Marcotte and the Collier family.)

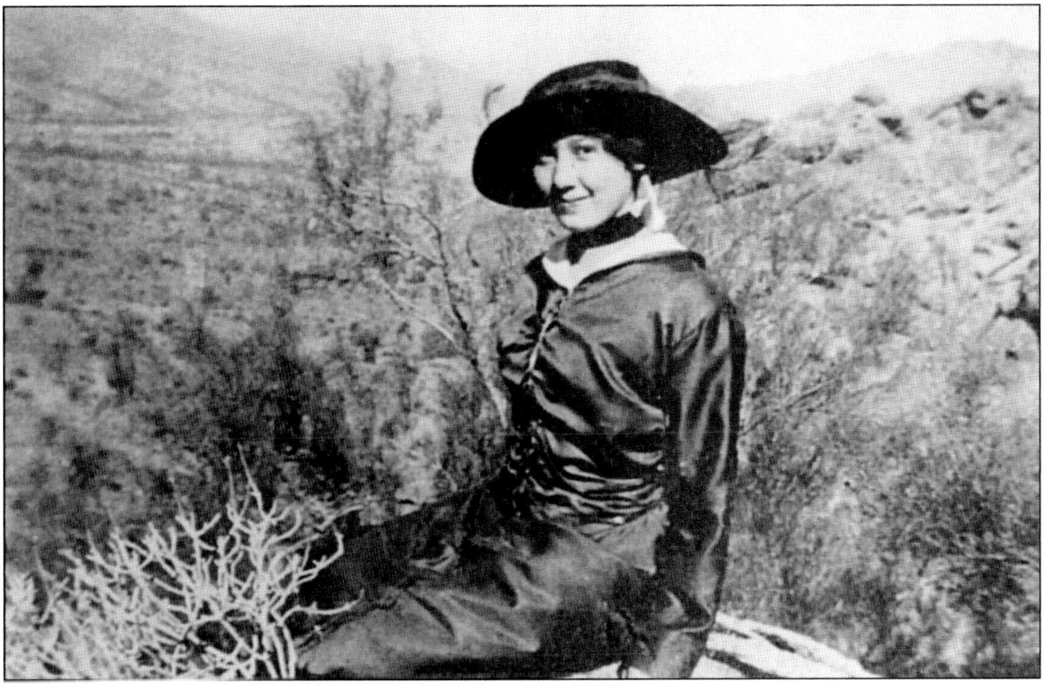

Pearl Jackson Collier married Thayer Collier in 1915 and become the matriarch of the family. Pearl was an Arizona native born in Phoenix in 1896. This picture was taken in Kirkland, Arizona, where she was visiting her family. (Courtesy Sally Schulkie Marcotte and the Collier family.)

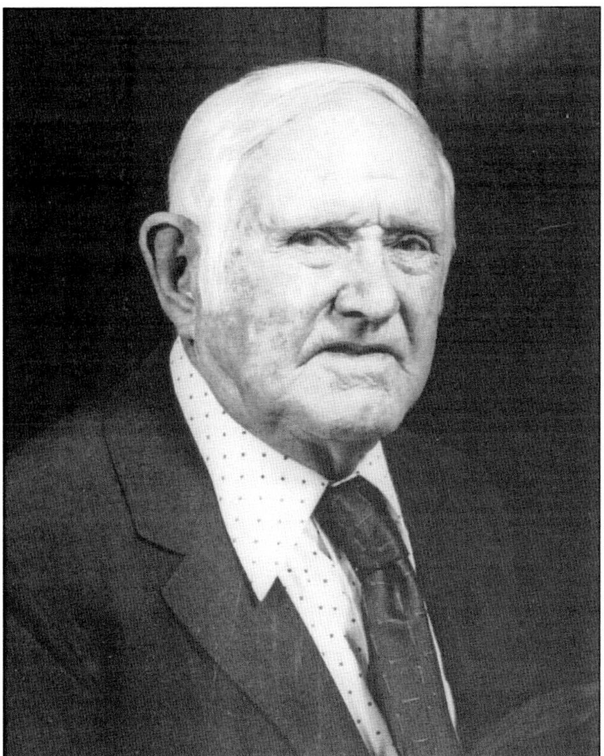

Thayer Collier served on the Littleton Elementary School board for 54 years. The school was named in his honor. He was married for 64 years and was one of the organizers of Littleton School. Until that time, the only school children in the area could attend was the old St. John School located on Southern Avenue and Avondale Boulevard. Today the old school is still there but has been transformed into apartments. Thayer was also on the Salt River Project irrigation board for many years and was a successful, hardworking farmer. (Courtesy Sally Schulkie Marcotte and the Collier family.)

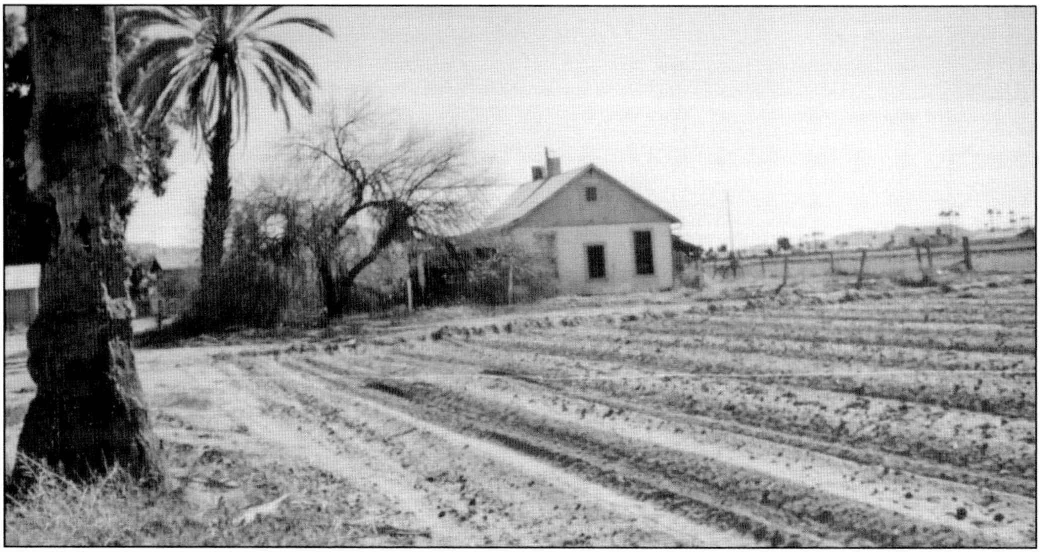

Helen H. Seargeant wrote *House by the Buckeye Road* in 1960. Helen talks about being a pioneer woman and her domestic duties. The word "duties" is used because this was a time in history when woman were required to do chores that kept a pioneer family up and running. Wood had to be chopped for the kitchen stove, chickens and other farm animals were attended to each day to supply fresh meat for the family, and the worker had to be fed. When Helen had some spare time on her hands, she built her own chicken pens and kitchen cabinets and cultivated a family vegetable garden for fresh garden vegetables, dates, nuts, and fruits. One of her favorite chores was tending her bees. Honey was eaten from the comb or used in cooking. When convenience stores were not nearby, this is what it took to survive. (Courtesy author.)

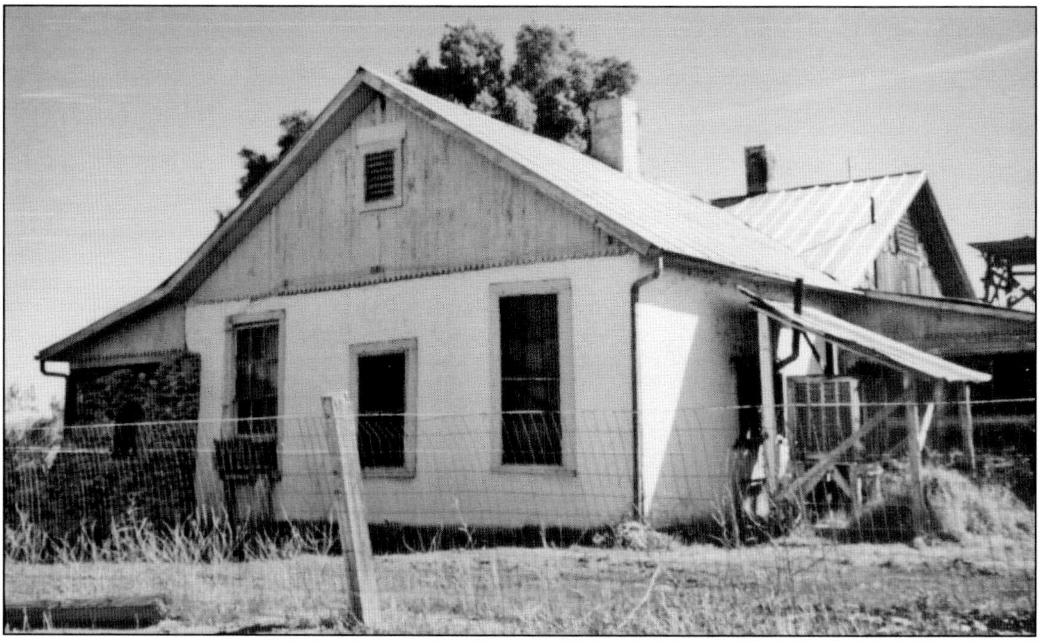

Seargeant built sections onto her home when time and money was available. Hardware stores were not abundant either, so adobe bricks had to be formed by hand from the local clay and other supplies had to be trucked in by a large wooden wagon pulled by a team of horses. (Courtesy author.)

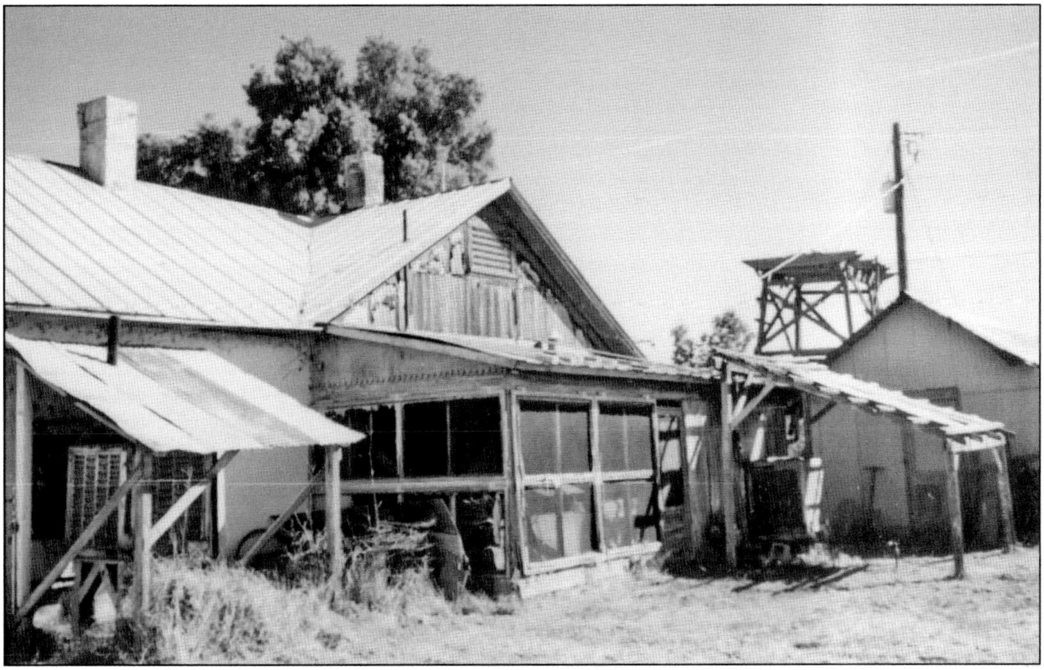

In need of repair, the "House by the Buckeye Road" still stands today. Remnants of the past—such as the old water storage tower used to collect rain—are visible. Every drop of water in the desert is extremely important. In Helen Seargeant's book, she talked about the hard water of the desert valley and collecting rainwater in large tanks on the roof of her home. She and her family used the sun to heat the water in the summer. (Courtesy author.)

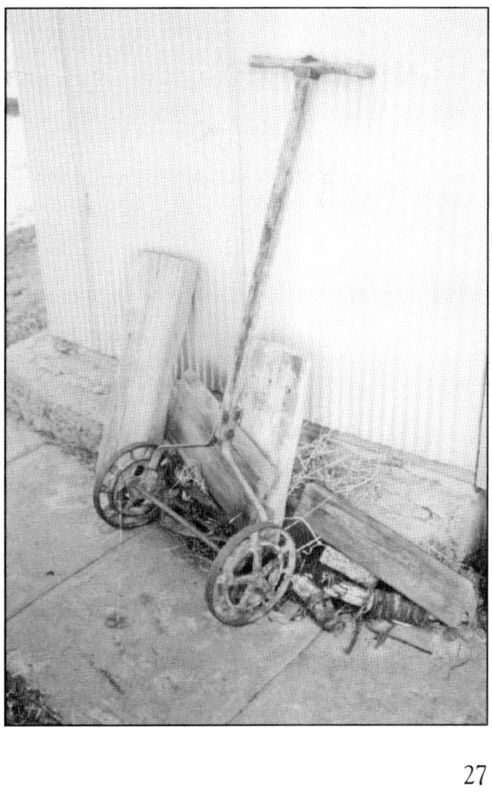

There were no engines attached to push lawn mowers in the last century. If the lawn had to be trimmed, muscle power was the only way it got done. When the job was completed, whoever had the task could jump in a nearby irrigation ditch for a cool dip or find a shady spot under a tree. (Courtesy author.)

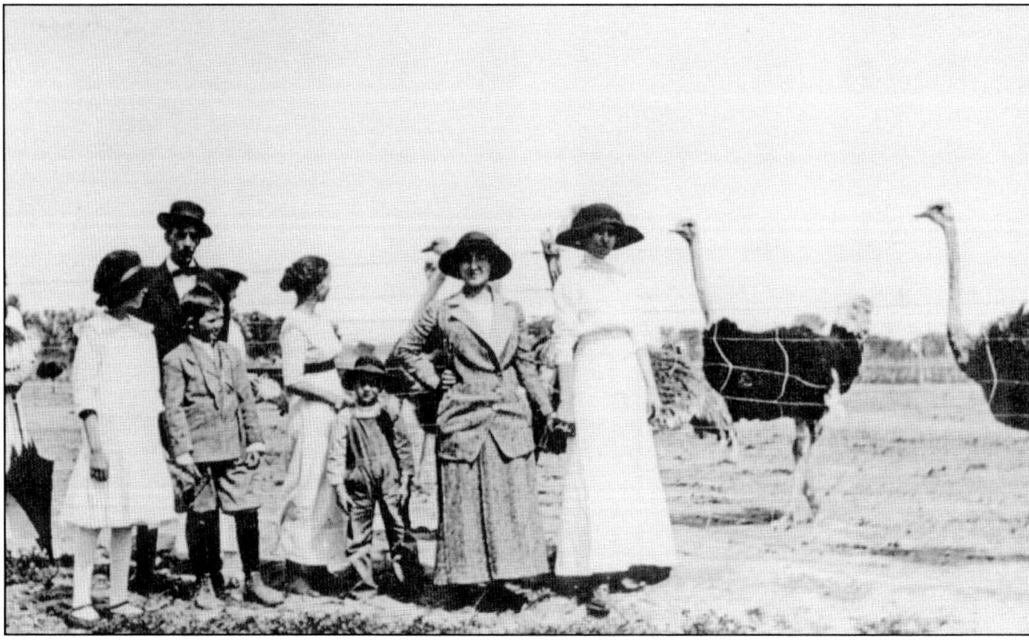

Ostriches were in high demand during the later years of the 1890s and early 1900s because of their feathers. Buyers could look their lovely best with a fancy hat and not worry about their flying frocks as they rode around in their buggies. (Courtesy Sally Schulkie Marcotte.)

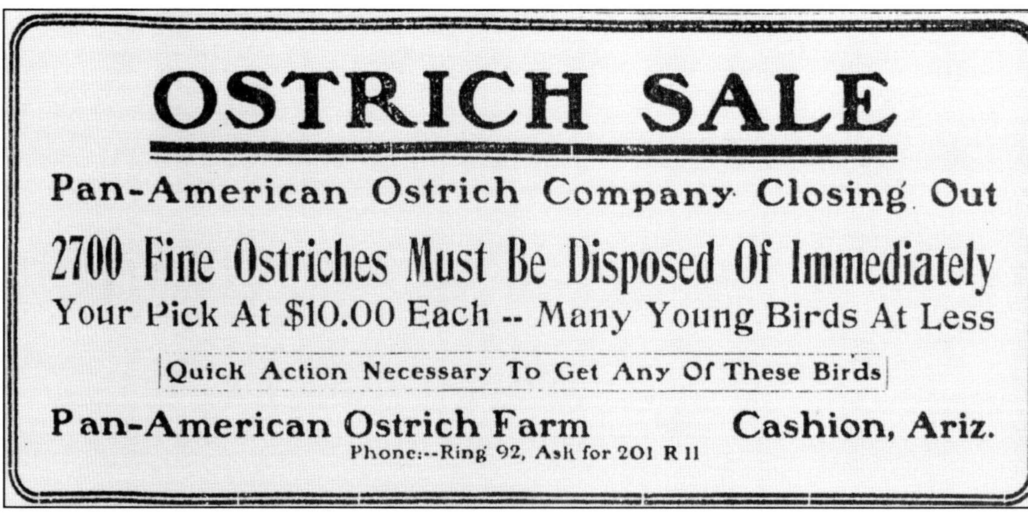

OSTRICH SALE

Pan-American Ostrich Company Closing Out

2700 Fine Ostriches Must Be Disposed Of Immediately

Your Pick At $10.00 Each -- Many Young Birds At Less

Quick Action Necessary To Get Any Of These Birds

Pan-American Ostrich Farm Cashion, Ariz.

Phone:--Ring 92, Ask for 201 R 11

Like so many fads, the ostrich hats went by the wayside when the automobile was introduced. Ladies' hats wouldn't stay put as they traveled at speeds of 20 miles an hour, and the large, cumbersome fashion statements fell out of favor. The speculators who invested in ostrich farming lost their shirts, and the big birds had to be sold. (Courtesy Wallis T. Fleming.)

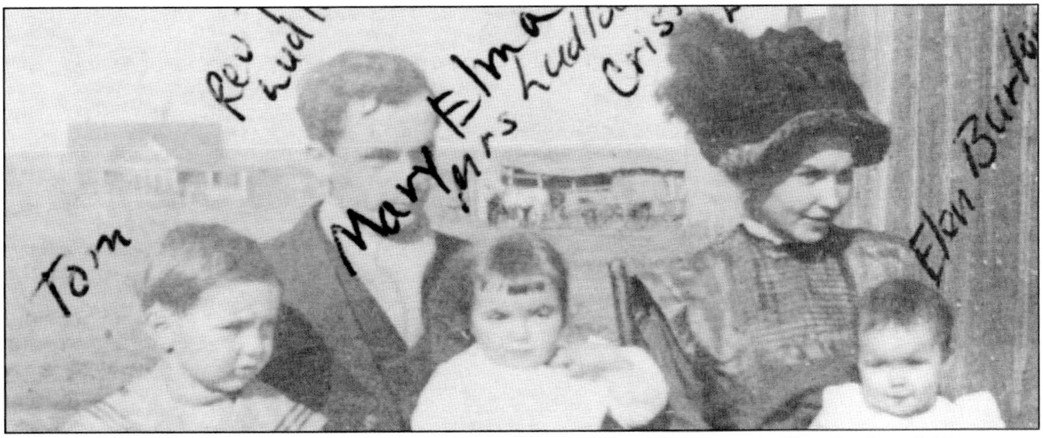

Christine Ludlow was another pioneer woman of Avondale. Christine and her husband, Vernon or "Vernie," a Methodist preacher, settled in Liberty, Arizona, in 1935. A short time later, Avondale became his calling. Vernon was asked what it would take to have him in Avondale. He said $1,000, so the community gathered together $800; he found that acceptable and made the commitment to the small town. The couple would locate on the dusty street that would eventually bear the Ludlow name. Christine Ludlow wrote a book about her life called *My Life I Give*. She touched upon Avondale toward the end of her book, which featured the migrant field workers that passed through Avondale and how difficult their lives were. (Courtesy Ludlow family.)

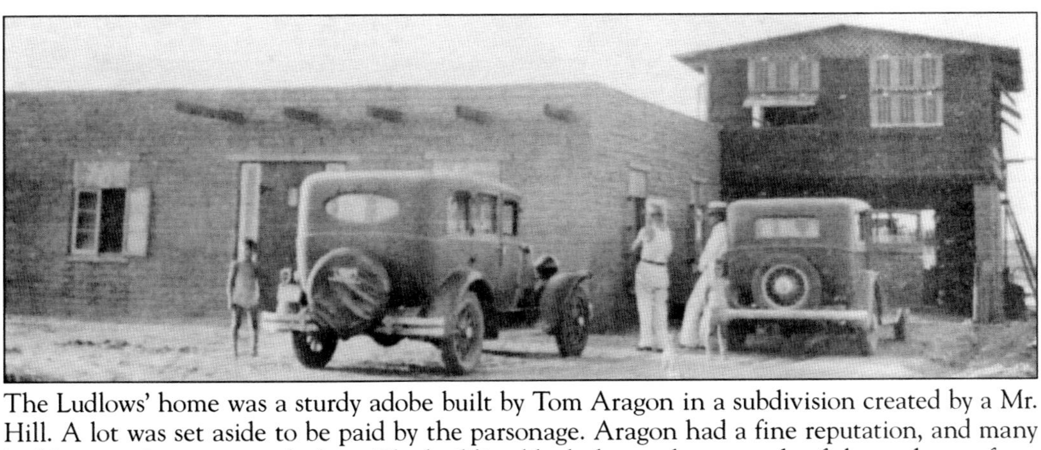

The Ludlows' home was a sturdy adobe built by Tom Aragon in a subdivision created by a Mr. Hill. A lot was set aside to be paid by the parsonage. Aragon had a fine reputation, and many buildings in the area were by him. The building blocks he used were made of clay and straw from the local surrounding desert, for there were miles of it. After stirring a dough-like consistency of mud and hay, he would slap the adobe in wooden forms laid in the sun to be dried. Aragon's recipe for mortar was simple: he added just the right amount of water and dirt to make a muddy slurry used to hold the blocks together. When he was done laying the blocks, he would then burn off the straw that stuck out so the block would be nice and smooth. (Courtesy Ludlow family.)

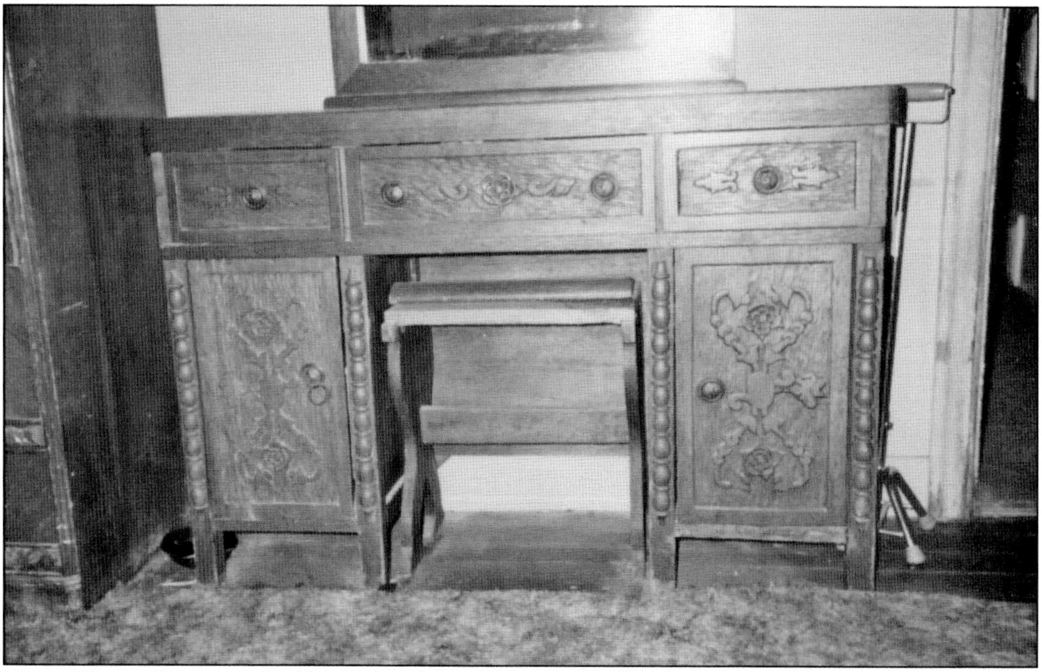

Mary Elma, Christine Ludlow's daughter, became a schoolteacher and taught at Avondale Elementary. For years, she was beloved and often visited by her students and community. Often Mary Elma would help feed and nurse the poor and unfortunate children and their families of the school. Besides being of service to her community, she loved creating furniture from her own designs for her family's home. (Courtesy author.)

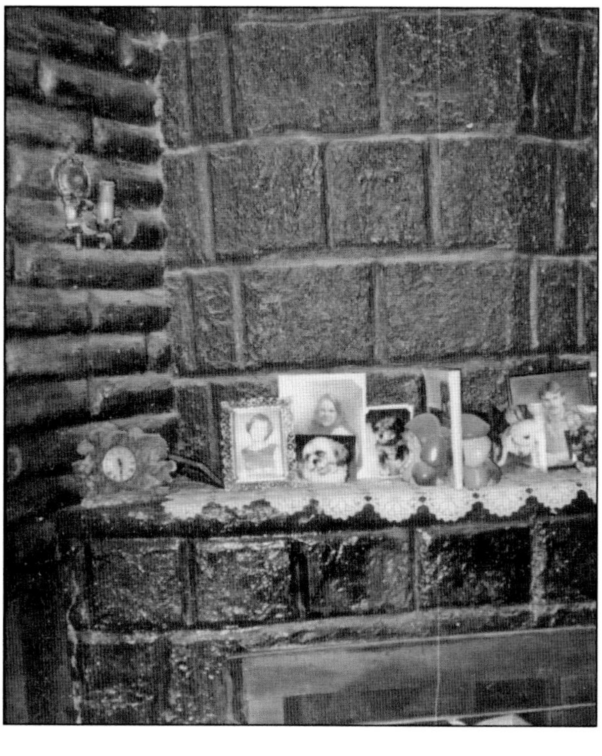

Christine wanted the walls of her adobe abode to appear similar to logs and the fireplace to be adorned with a homemade mantel. This was to remind her of her Eastern roots. Christine applied a thin coat of resin, then resicote (skim-milk hardeners that made the adobe hard like rock), after which she applied liquid glass (another hardener), and finally burnt umber was added to reinforcing oil. (Courtesy author.)

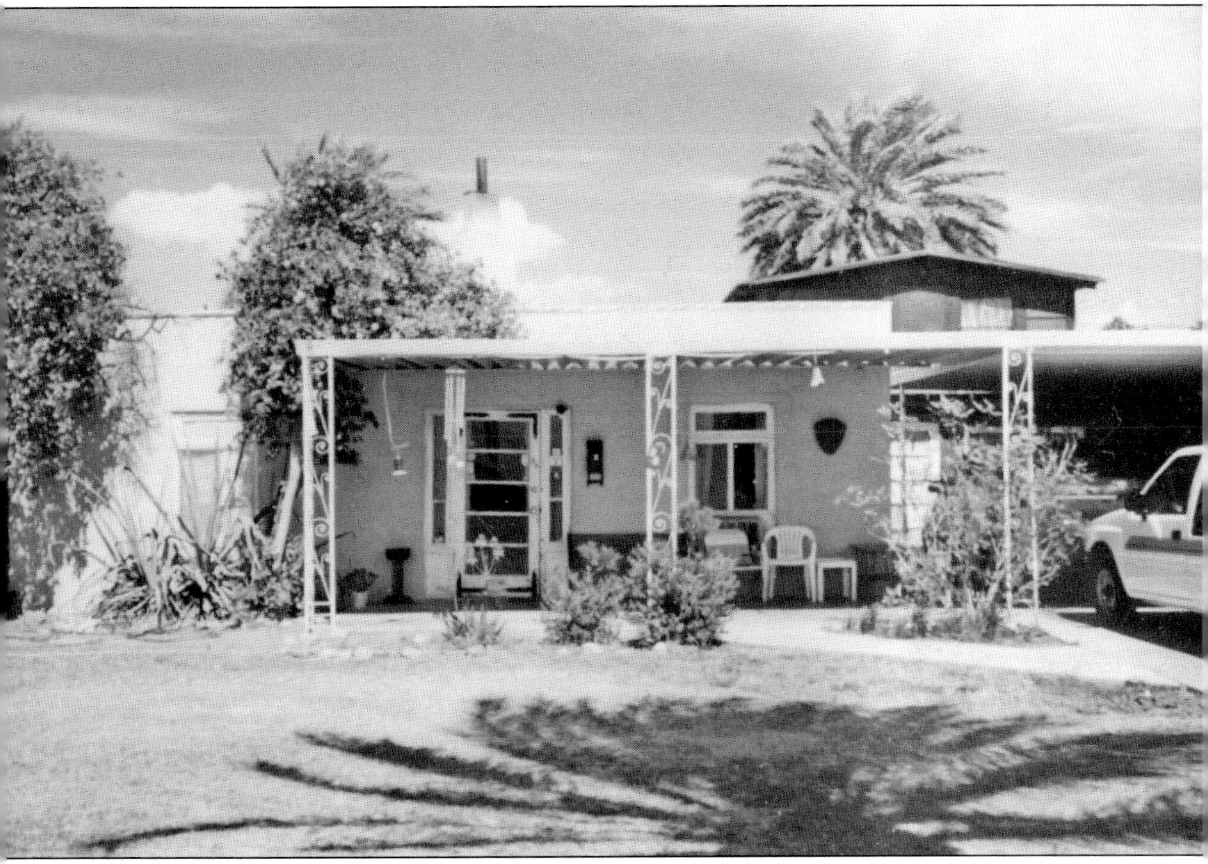

The adobe house appears much different today than the original adobe house that was built without metal awnings. A screened sleeping porch was erected above the garage. Many homes had these, or the residents just slept outside on pallets trying to get a few winks until a pesky mosquito would awaken them. (Courtesy author.)

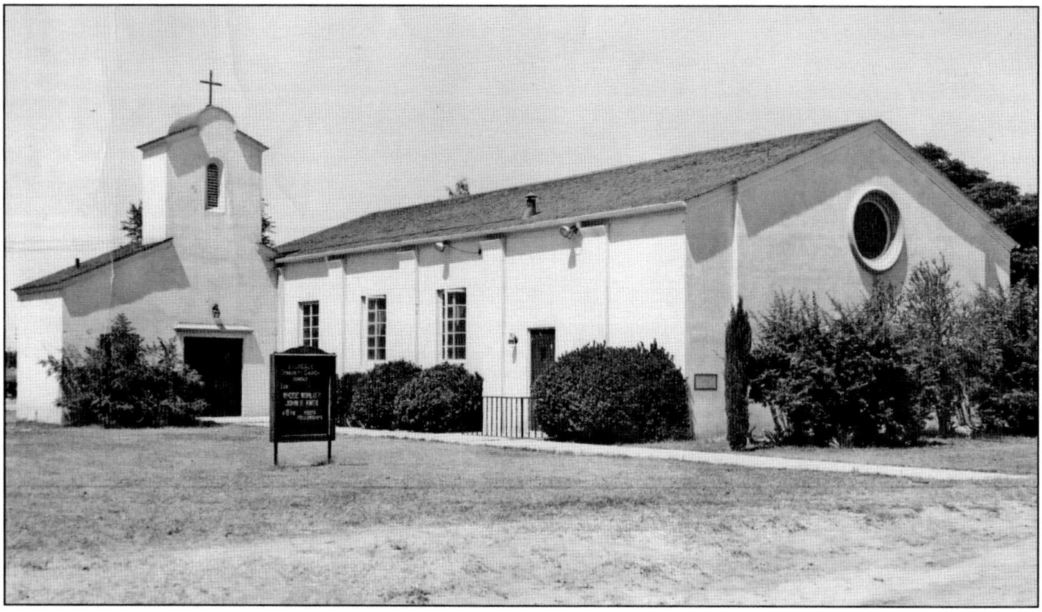

In 1939, a building fund was approved to build the Avondale Community Church, truly a cooperative effort by all. Vernon Ludlow was the first minister of the newly constructed house of worship, which operated under the auspices of the Methodist Church. (Courtesy author.)

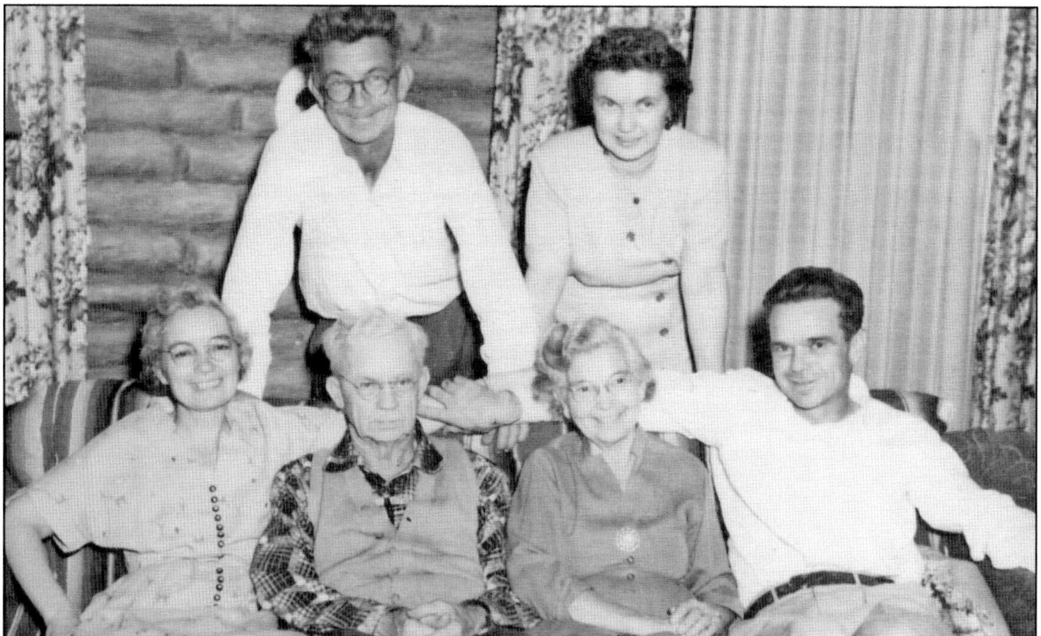

In 1939, Christine and Vernie Ludlow, Mary Elma's father, decided to organize a church in Avondale. It was to be called the Avondale Community Church. It was not until 1942 that the building was started. The Ludlows' daughter, Mary Elma, brought much joy to the Avondale children and was often their favorite teacher. Even after her golden years, grown pupils came by for chats and reminisced about the old days. It takes a special teacher to have a connection to children, but Mary Elma did. (Courtesy Jean Mathis, Mary Elma's daughter.)

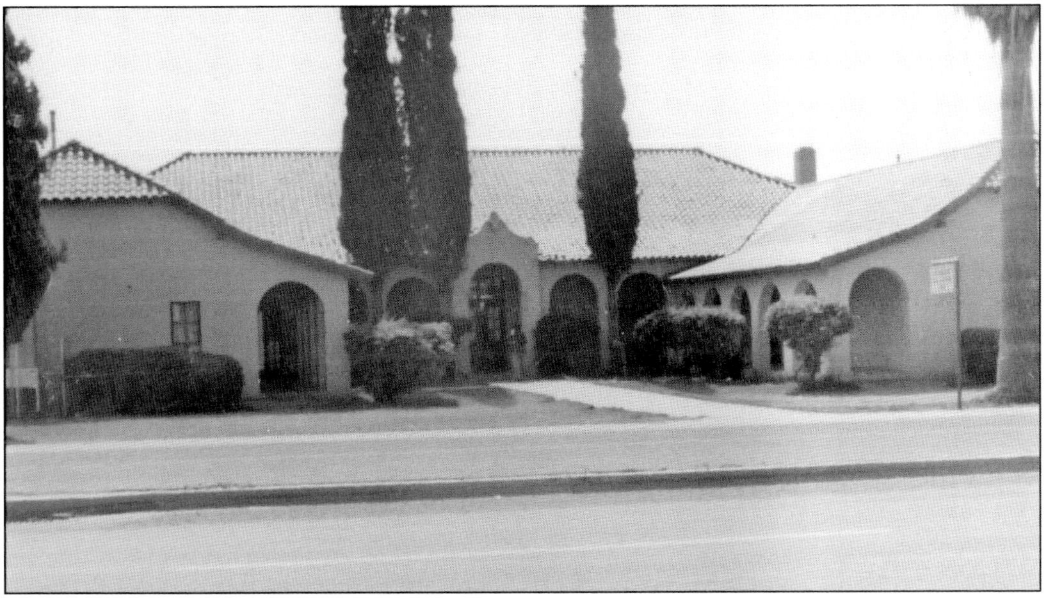

Avondale Elementary School's original building was built by the WPA, a government program to employ men during the Great Depression of the 1930s. Avondale's faculty, students, and citizens have shown great pride in the past. The respect is obvious as the original building still stands today. Other buildings have had to be added to the original structure for growth. The student population is being taught modern methods today, but it is refreshing to know the school's beginning is still intact. Some of its famous students were Lattie Coor, past president of Arizona State University, and Michael Anderson, an astronaut with NASA. (Courtesy author.)

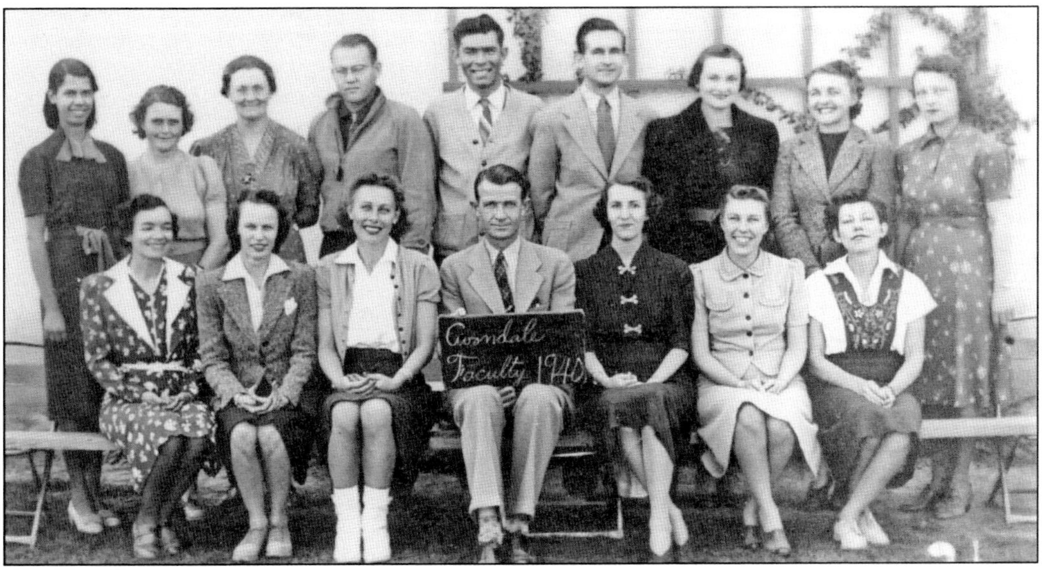

Shown here is the Avondale Elementary facility in 1940. After the Depression and Dust Bowl in the Midwest, people came to Arizona by the hordes. Most were on their way to California for the promise of land. Many ran out of money and luck, could not go any farther, and decided to lay down roots wherever they could pick cotton or work in the fields. The families had many children that needed an education. Sometimes classes were so large rooms were set up in the auditorium. (Courtesy Avondale City Library.)

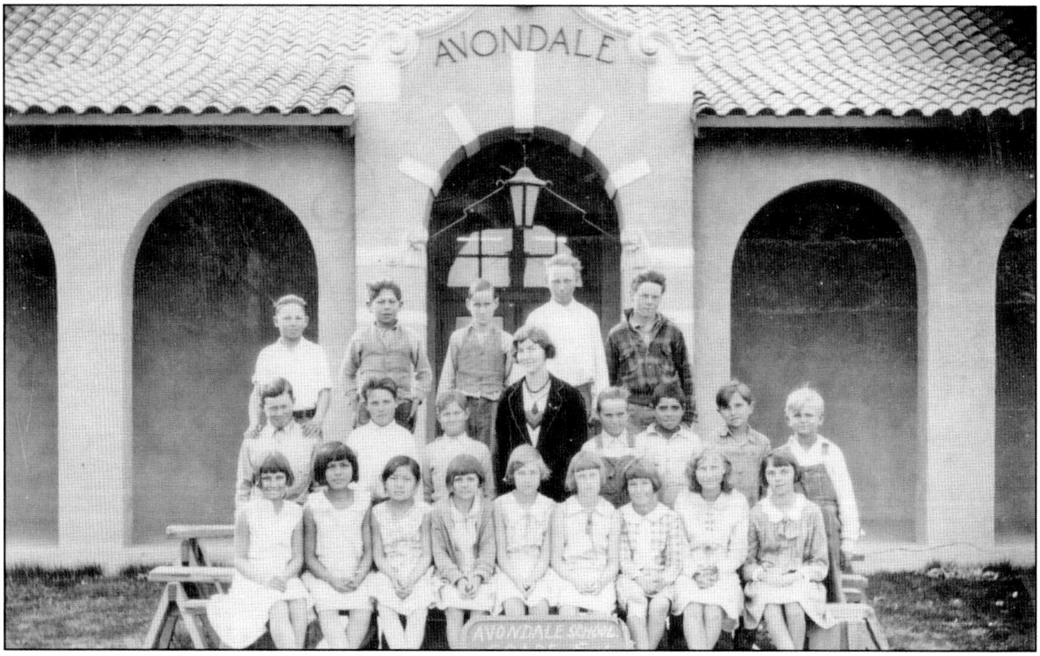

In 1931, Avondale Elementary School grades five and six were combined into one classroom. The school originated in 1925 and was christened Coldwater Elementary. Because of the declining enrollment of students, the school had to be disbanded for a short time between 1901 and 1907. It was reactivated by Maricopa County in 1908. In 1927, the WPA built the recognizable older buildings that are on campus today. (Courtesy Avondale City Library.)

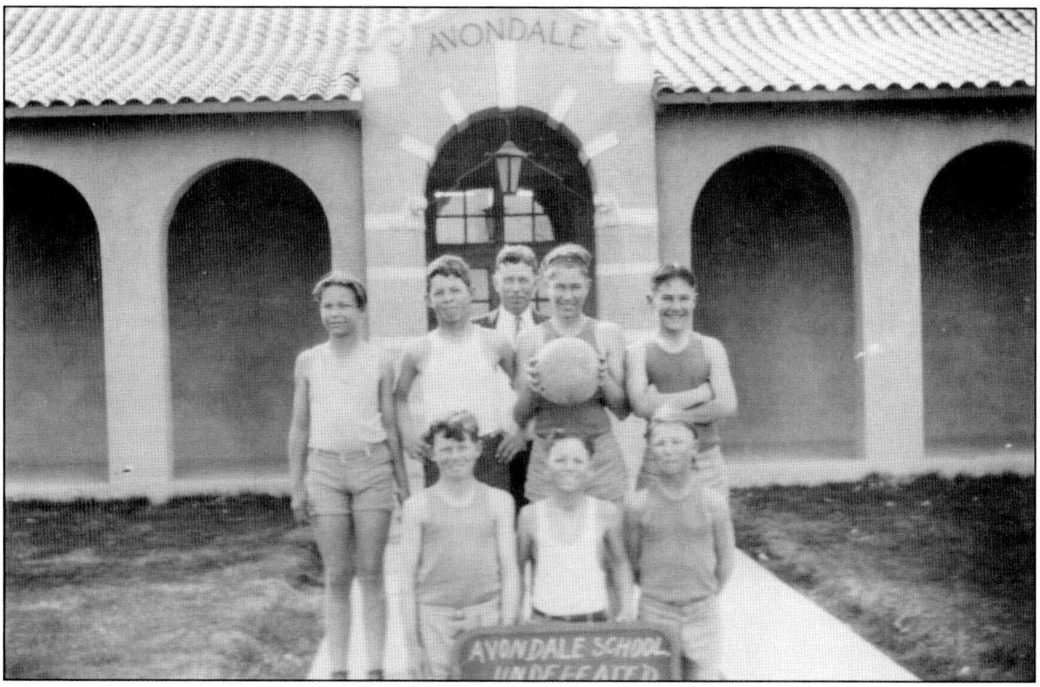

Avondale Elementary's basketball team was the undefeated champions in 1931. (Courtesy Avondale City Library.)

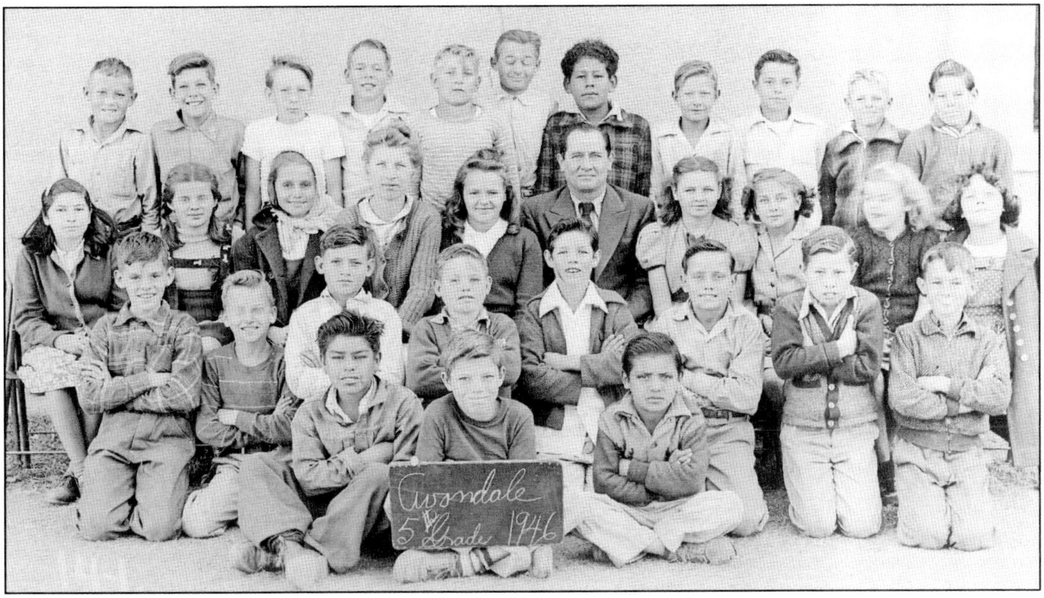

The Second World War was over, and servicemen and woman were returning home to start families. In 1946, the baby boomer generation was entering the educational system. Classrooms would burst at the seams with children, and it was always hard to keep up with the growth. (Courtesy Avondale City Library.)

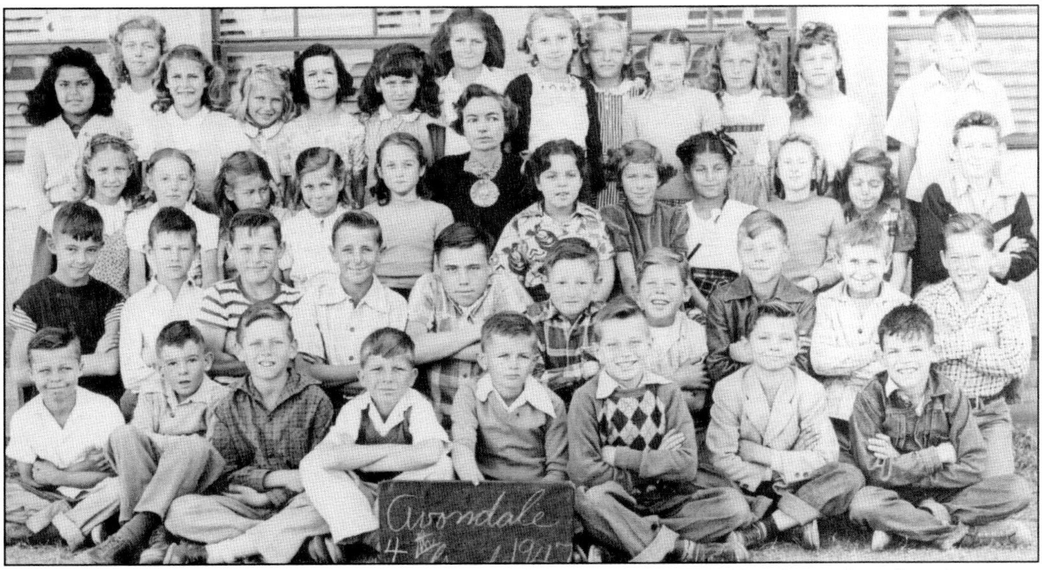

Mary Elma Ludlow began teaching at Avondale Elementary in 1937. She always kept her classroom interesting, and children wanted to learn. She was known for her generosity and caring spirit as a teacher. If there was a child who needed clothing or food, she would do her best to see that the task was taken care of. It was not unusual to have students drop by her home, especially in her twilight years. In 1947, children were packed in classrooms and there were always concern as to where to put them. Avondale Elementary found a way. (Courtesy Avondale City Library.)

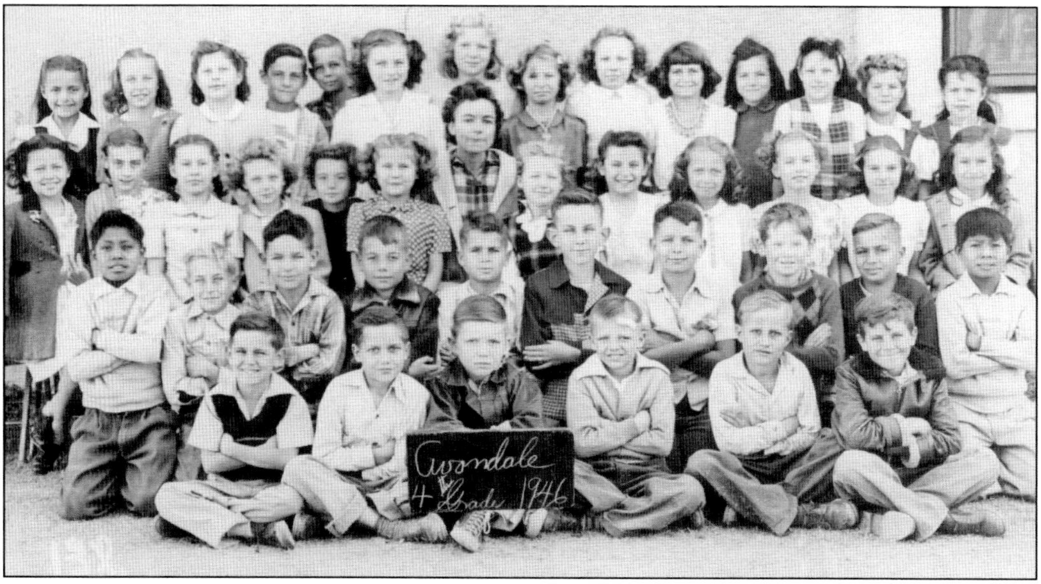

Mary Elma Ludlow's fourth-grade Avondale classroom in 1946 is crowded with baby boomers. More than 100 students were registered in her fourth-grade classroom, but the most that attended at one time were 98 students. (Courtesy Avondale City Library.)

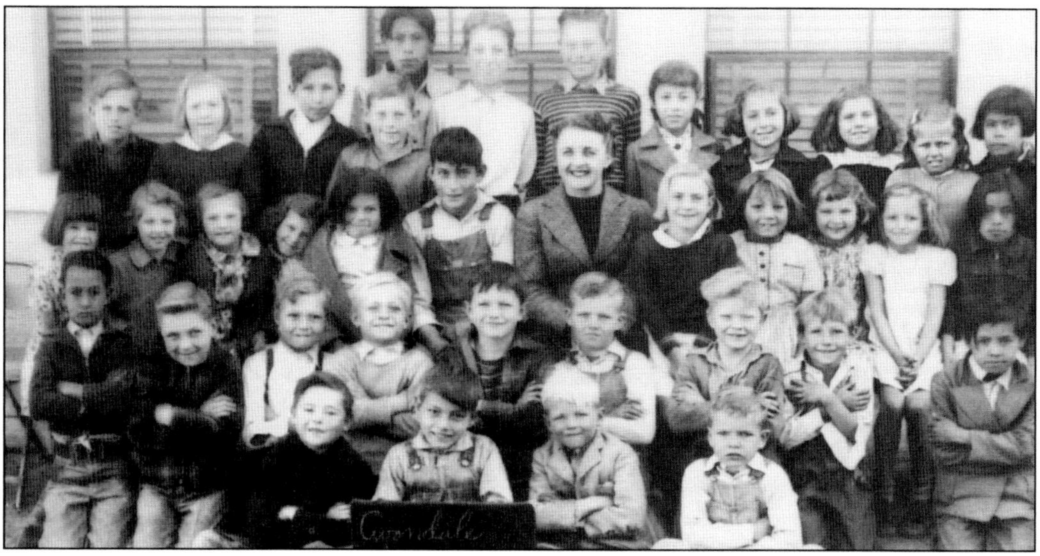

A second-grade Avondale Elementary classroom had its beginnings in 1927. (Courtesy Avondale City Library.)

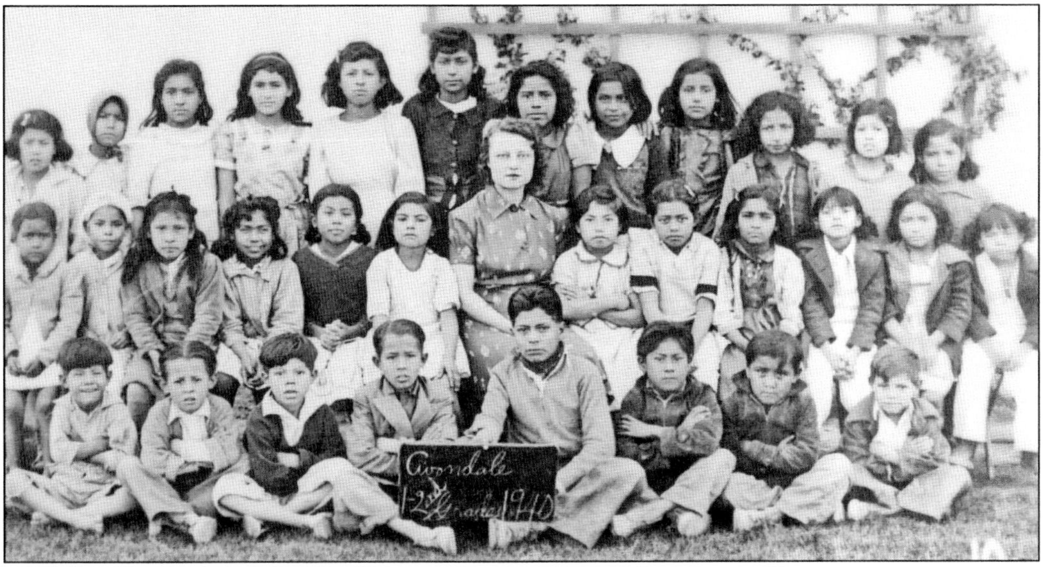

In earlier times, Avondale Elementary School thought it best to set apart Hispanic children because there was a language barrier and there were no preschool or special programs to teach children English. (Courtesy Avondale City Library.)

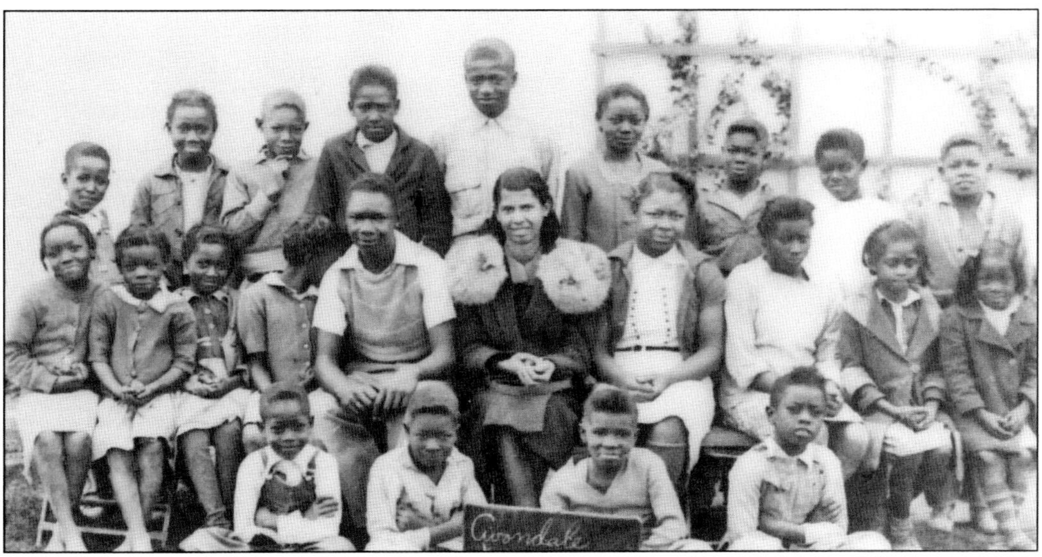

Avondale Elementary was segregated in 1940. (Courtesy Avondale City Library.)

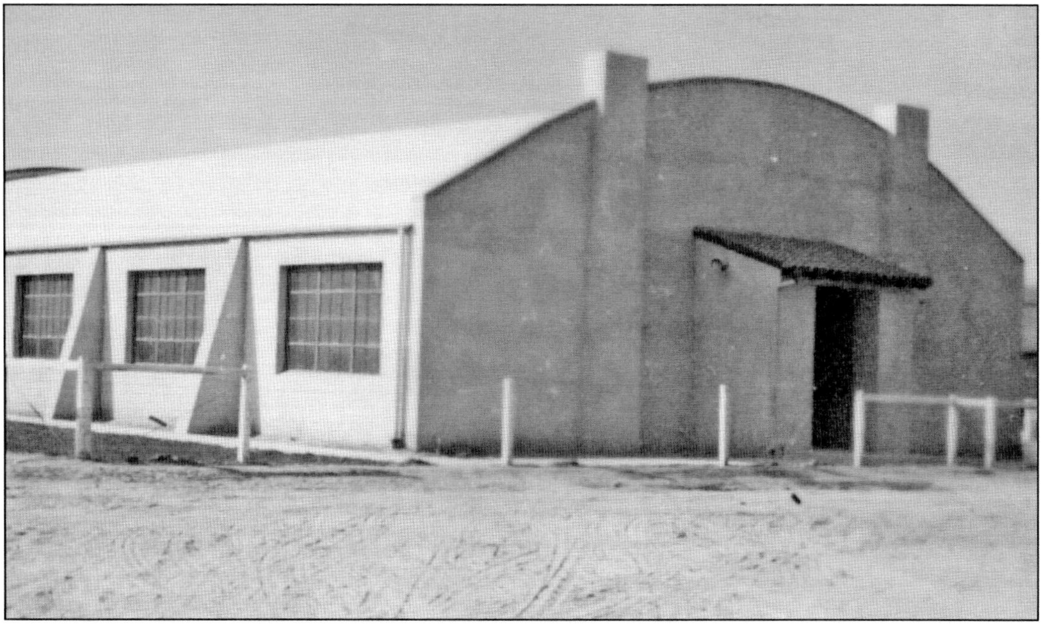

A then newly constructed gym and auditorium at Avondale Elementary School remains today and faces Central Avenue in Old Town Avondale. It was an add-on after the original classrooms were built and often used as extra classrooms as the Dust Bowl survivors and baby boomers arrived. According to Christine Ludlow's book, her daughter Mary Elma had 108 fourth graders enrolled in her classroom, but the most present on any one day was a mere 98. (Courtesy Avondale City Library.)

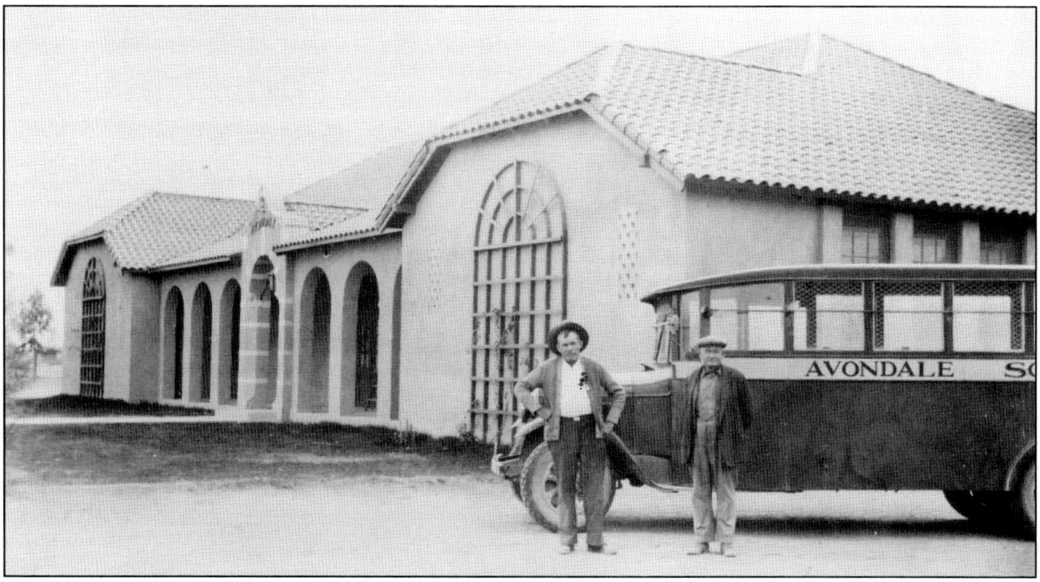

The one school bus had wire over the windows. There was no heating or cooling, and the ride was unforgettable. The roads were not paved, so the dust flew through the open windows as the bus traveled along desert sand with an occasional rut here and there. On rainy days, the school bus would skid from side to side, trying to grip the road. (Courtesy Avondale City Library.)

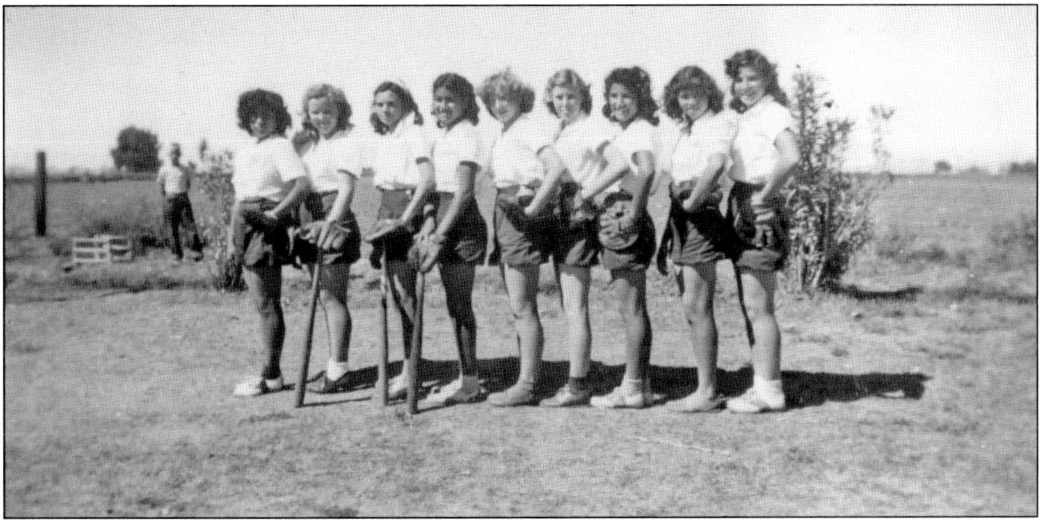

The Tom Scamp girls' softball team in 1947–1948 was a great way to spend the hours after school at Cashion Elementary. The school's official name was always Littleton, but the locals called it Cashion for the nearest community. (Courtesy Littleton Elementary district office.)

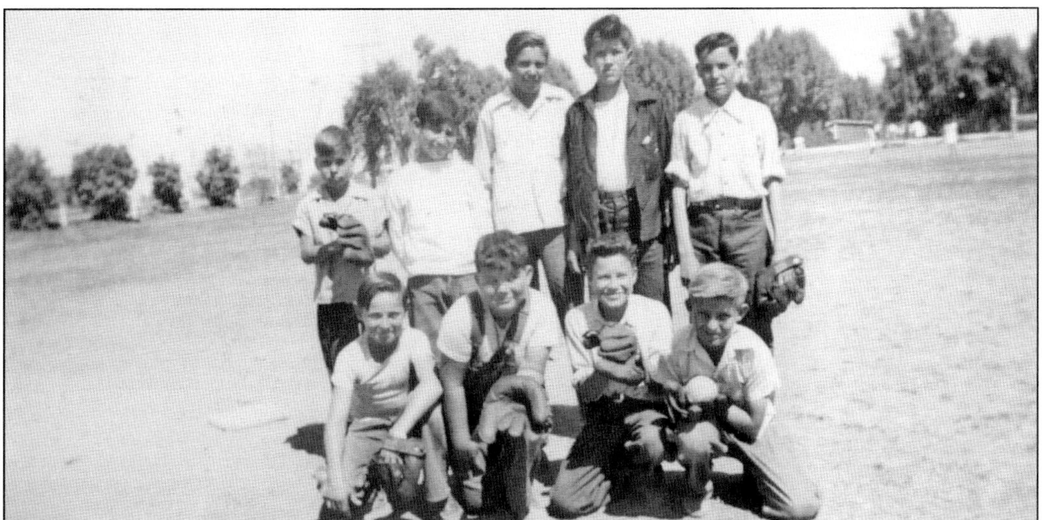

The boys' softball team of 1947–1948 played hard at Cashion Elementary School. The location was and still is at MC 85 and Avondale Boulevard. When the following picture was taken, Avondale Boulevard was called Buckeye Road, which was the way to the city with the same name—Buckeye, Arizona. Lateral 25 (laterals were named after irrigation ditches constructed one mile apart in the system) became 115th Avenue and later Avondale Boulevard. (Courtesy Littleton Elementary district office.)

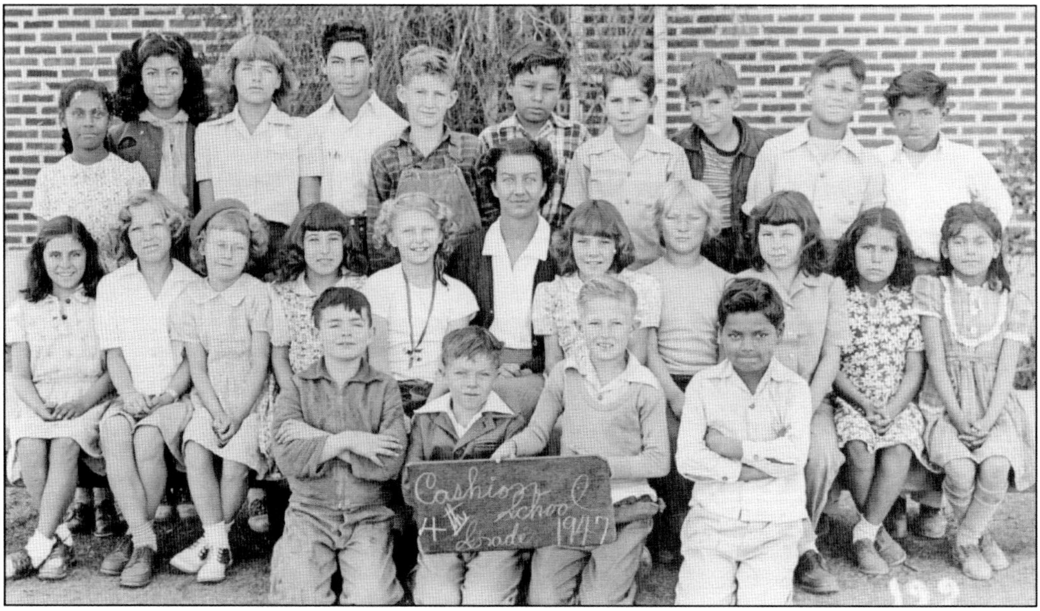

The fourth-grade class at Cashion Elementary School in 1947 is pictured here. The school was actually named Littleton after a dentist who first organized the small community hoping to create business for himself. His speculation was a bit too early, but soon after he sold out and moved to Bisbee, the area began to grow. Because the location was close to Jim Cashion's ranch, the unofficial name Cashion School was used by the locals. (Courtesy Littleton Elementary district office.)

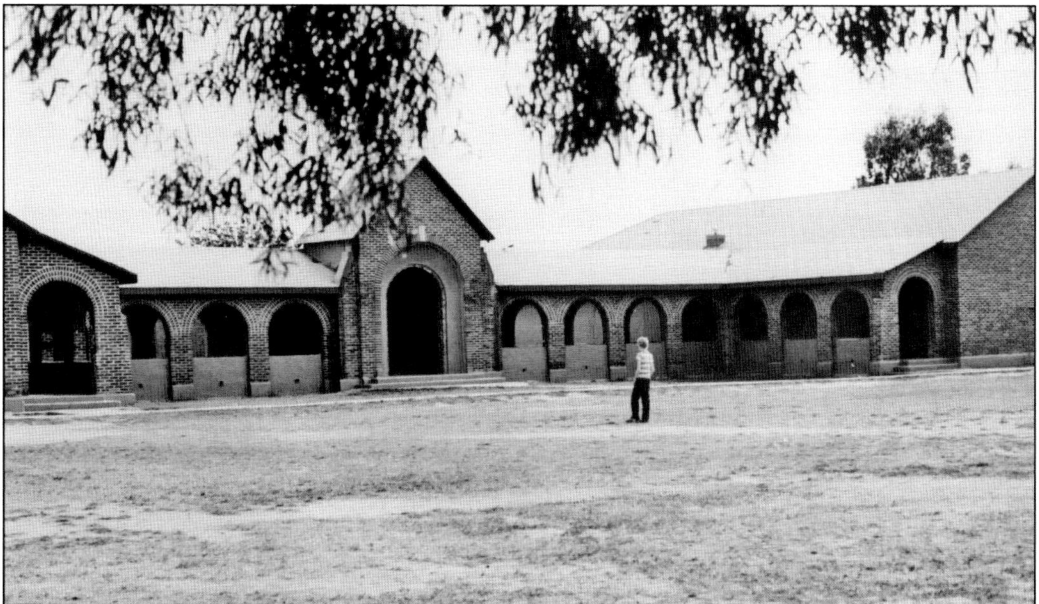

The old Littleton Elementary School was demolished in the late 1980s. The original school was built by concerned citizens in the area who wanted a school that could accommodate the growing child population. The only schools in the area were on the west side of the Agua River or the outdated St. John School, located two and a half miles south of the town of Cashion. (Courtesy Sally Schulkie Marcotte.)

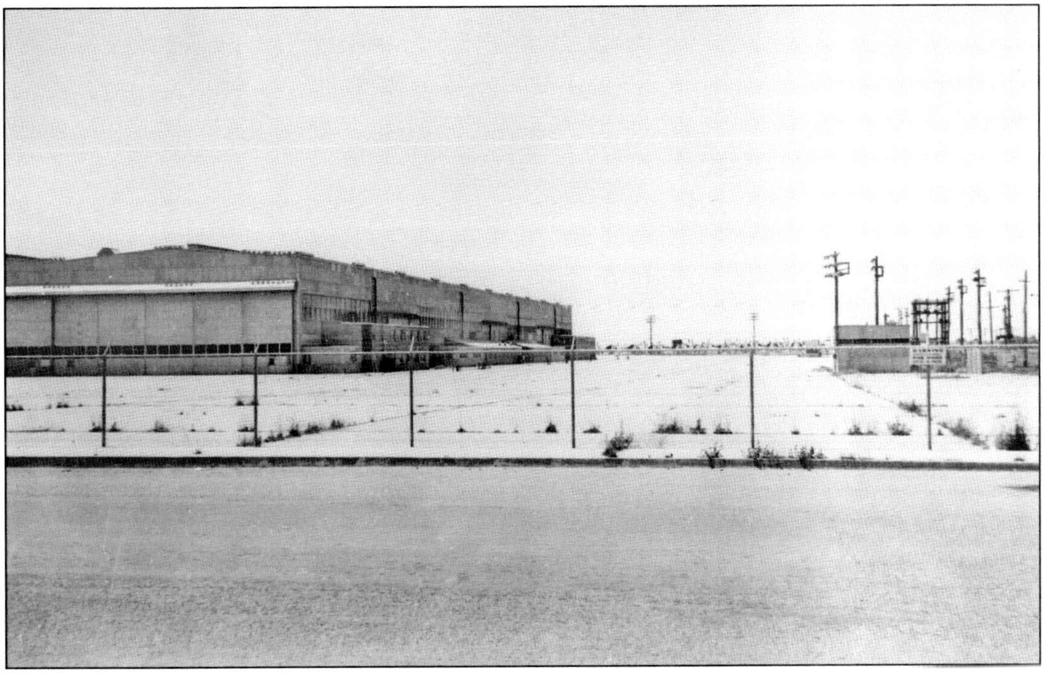

The navy base on Yuma Road features old fighter planes of World War II looming in the background of this photograph. The navy base was constructed to rebuild U.S. Air Force planes to navy standards. When the Naval Air Facility was downsized and was no longer needed, the planes were auctioned off and the City of Phoenix bought the base for $1. The city used it for cargo and storage. Today the old hangers are leased to a company that restores and refurbishes large commercial planes and small private planes. (Courtesy *West Valley View.*)

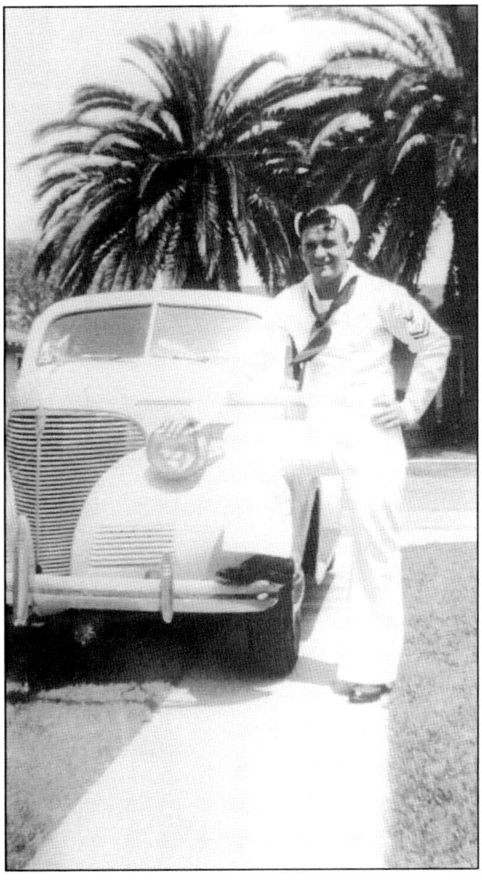

Bob Schulkie enlisted in the navy during World War II and became a pilot. He flew planes that were to be reequipped from around the country to the Naval Air Facility. He met his future bride, Margaret Callier, in Avondale, Arizona, and after the war, he resumed his life as a farmer and family man. (Courtesy Sally Schulkie Marcotte.)

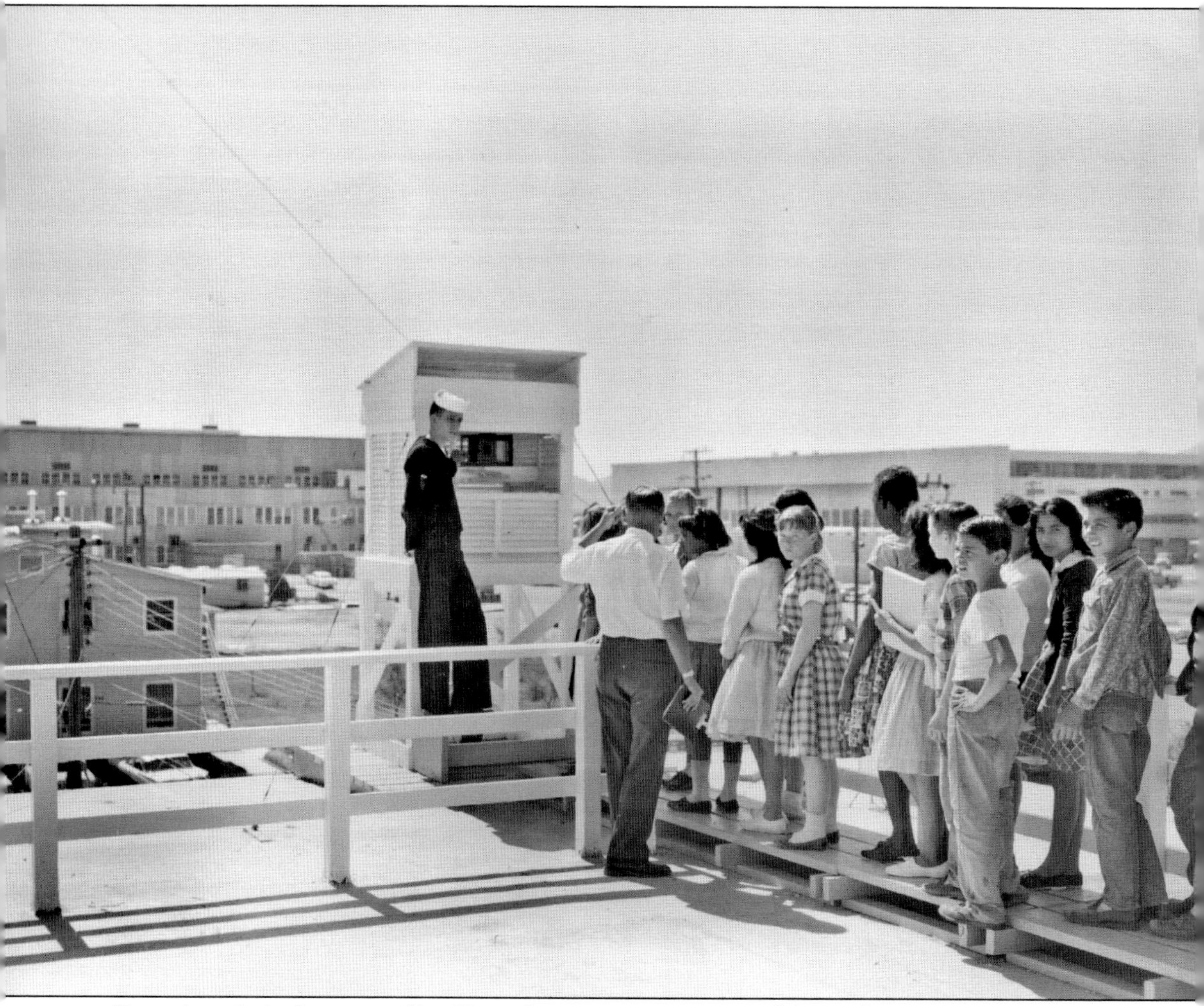

Even though the base was officially in the county, many Avondale residents were either employed there or had some other kind of involvement with the navy base. The base was near Goodyear and Avondale and provided many informative opportunities for Avondale Elementary School children to visit often on field trips and learn how the naval base operated. (Courtesy City of Avondale.)

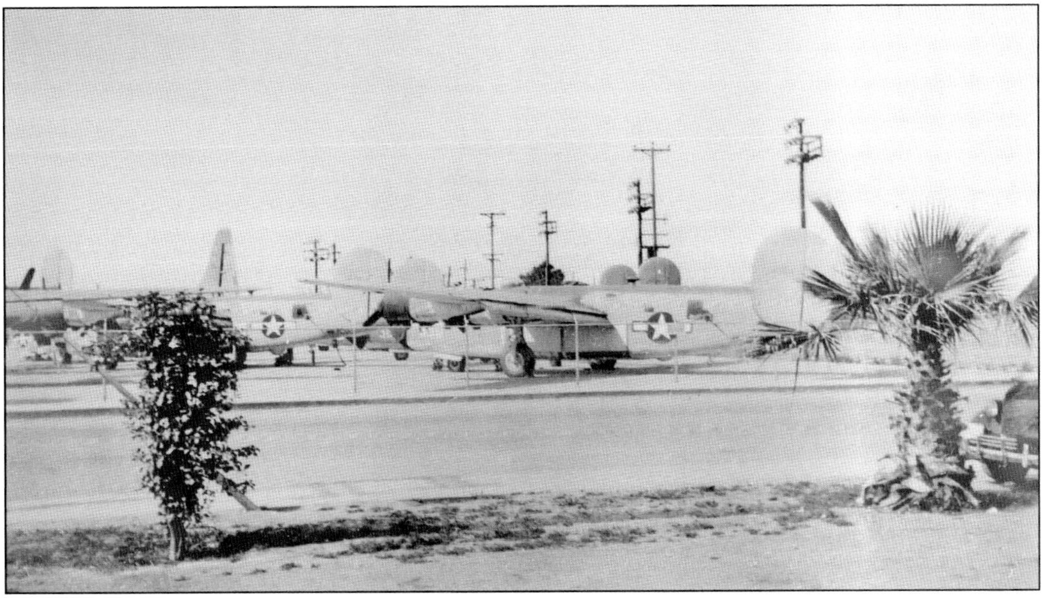

PB4Y airplanes were flown to the navy base to be modified to navy standards; and later they were stored in great numbers there after World War II. The dry weather was great for citrus, palm trees, and airplane storage. (Courtesy *West Valley View* and the Lauer family.)

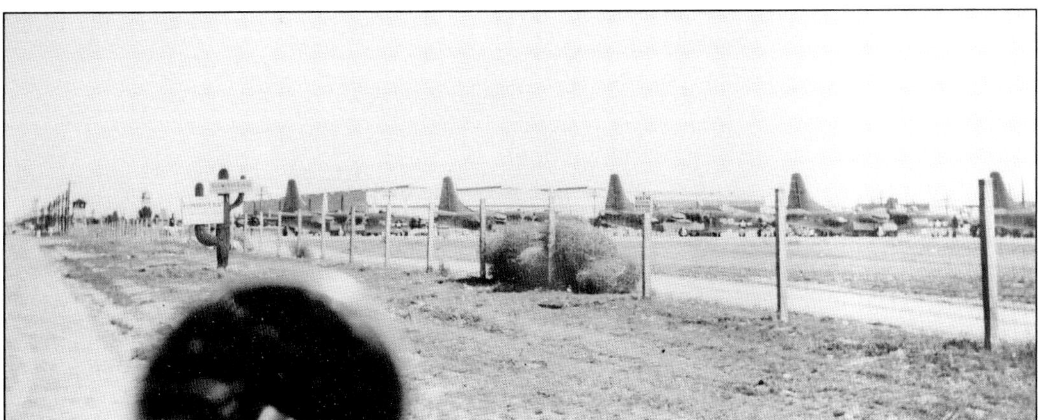

The tumbleweed says it all. The plane boneyard had large tracts of land with mothballed fighter planes. As a kid, Bonnie Mostert and friends jumped the fence and played in the cockpits of the old fighter planes. She has tales of mothballed planes fresh from World War II with bullet holes and some of the equipment intact, wondering what stories the planes could tell. (Courtesy *West Valley View* and the Lauer family.)

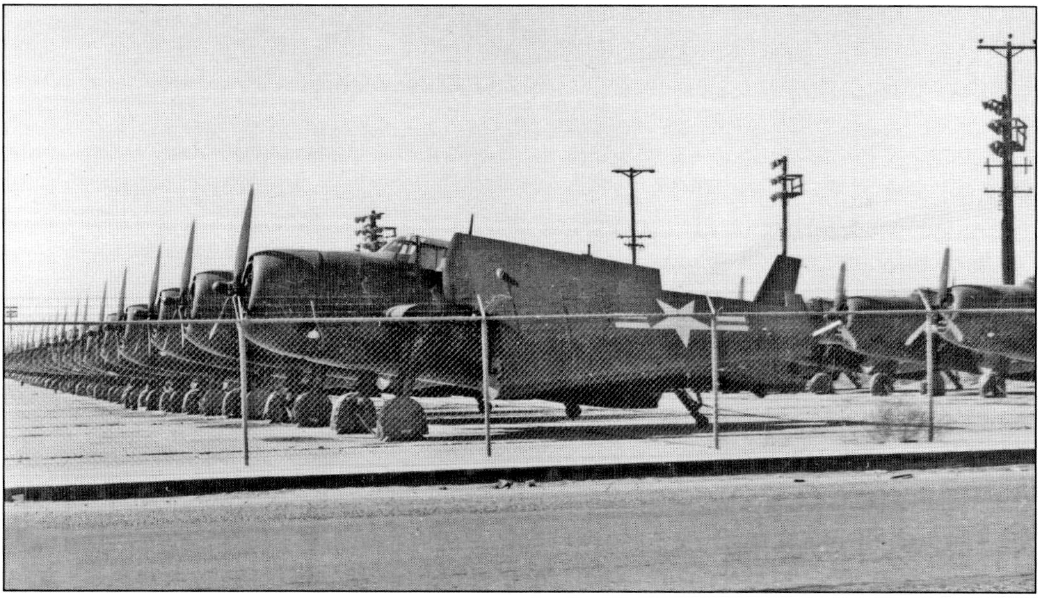

TBM Torpedo surplus planes were flown in from Long Beach, California. These types of planes were once used to carry crew for three former presidents. President Bush Sr. was shot down in this type of plane during the Second World War. The TBMs were the same planes that were lost in the Bermuda Triangle during the Second World War. The airplane's wings would fold to make room for other planes onboard a cramped aircraft carrier, and they were agile enough to take off and land on the short runway on a bouncy sea. Row after row of neatly placed fighter planes were parked on the tarmac. In 1943, the planes were sold or melted to recycle the aluminum and other metals. (Courtesy *West Valley View* and the Lauer family.)

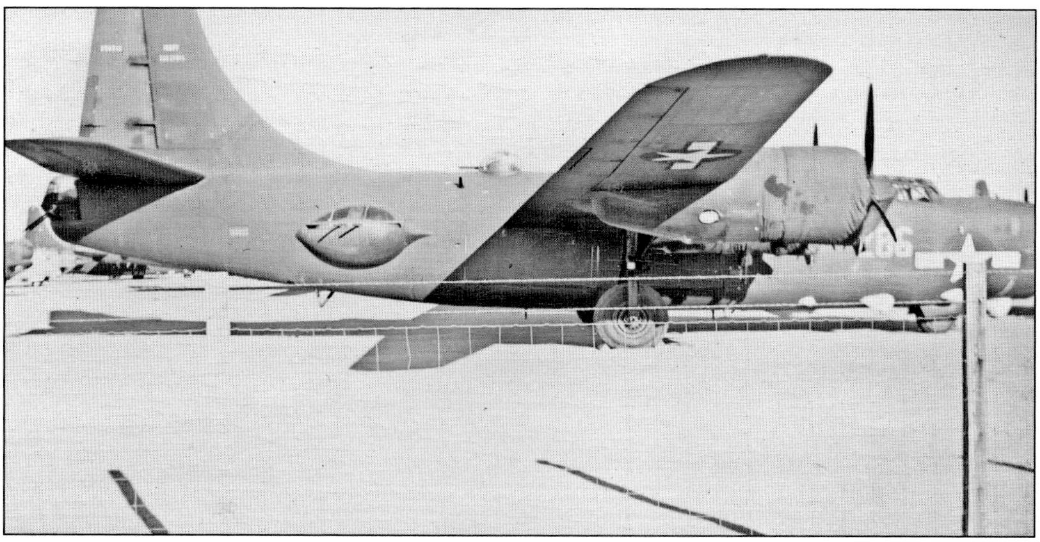

The privateer cousin to the PB4Y was used briefly by the navy in World War II. It too was mothballed by the military. As the base was closing and was sold to the City of Phoenix, the planes were removed by sale or were incinerated and melted down to aluminum slag on property located at the west end of the runway. The working aluminum smelter still operates today in the same location. At night, one can spot puffs of smoke coming from the business at the end of the old runway. (Courtesy *West Valley View* and the Lauer family.)

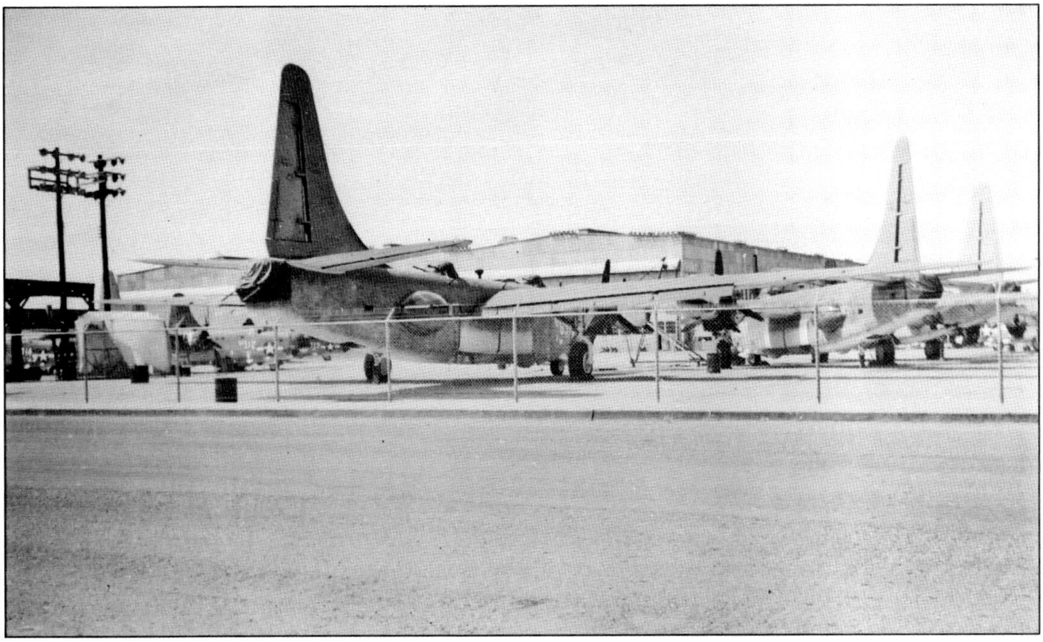

At one point in time, the mothballed PB4Y planes were a new phenomenon. This photograph shows the north side of the hangers. The larger hanger was used to construct bags for blimps after the Second World War for the Goodyear Corporation. They used them for parades and other functions. (Courtesy *West Valley View* and the Lauer family.)

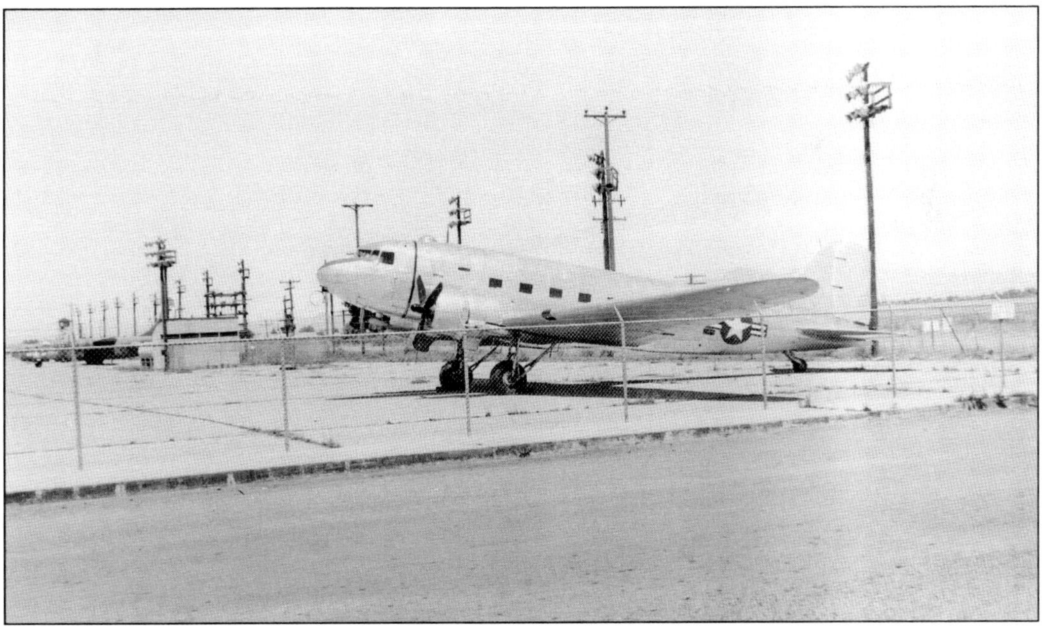

Navy R4D transport planes were used by American Airlines, United Airlines, and others. They were the workhorse of the airlines industry. They carried 23 passengers and were the mainstay of all passenger planes before and after the Second World War. (Courtesy *West Valley View* and the Lauer family.)

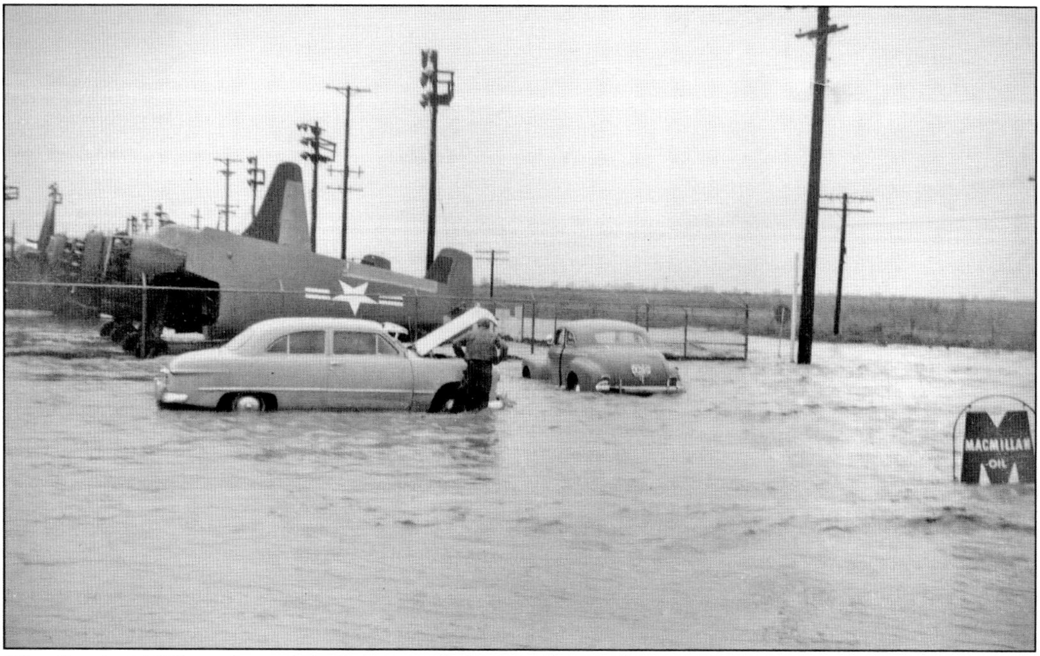

The flood of 1950 in Avondale devastated the navy base, the Goodyear facilities, and the civilian population. Yuma Road on the northwest corner of Litchfield Road and Western Avenue was hit hard. Believe it or not, some of the water came from the Agua Fria River a mile away. (Courtesy *West Valley View* and the Lauer family.)

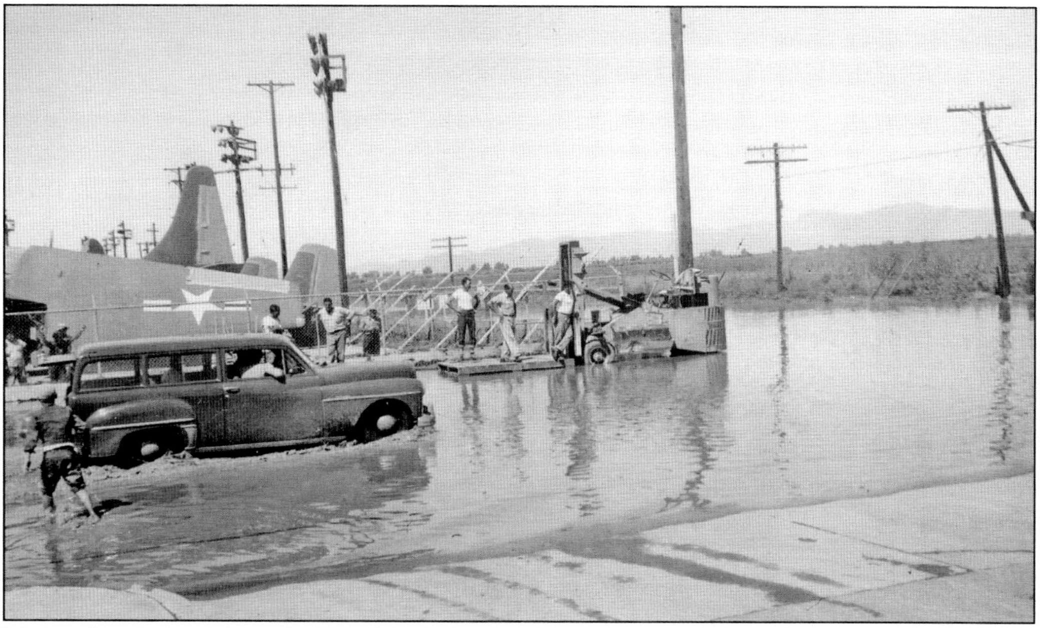

Men and equipment from the navy base were used to help dam water in the 1950 flood. All means were deployed to save the planes and base, not to mention homes and businesses that were water-soaked. All that water took many by surprise; after all, they lived in the desert. There were no shopping centers on the northwest corner of Litchfield Road and Western Avenue, just cotton fields and lots of open sky. (Courtesy *West Valley View* and the Lauer family.)

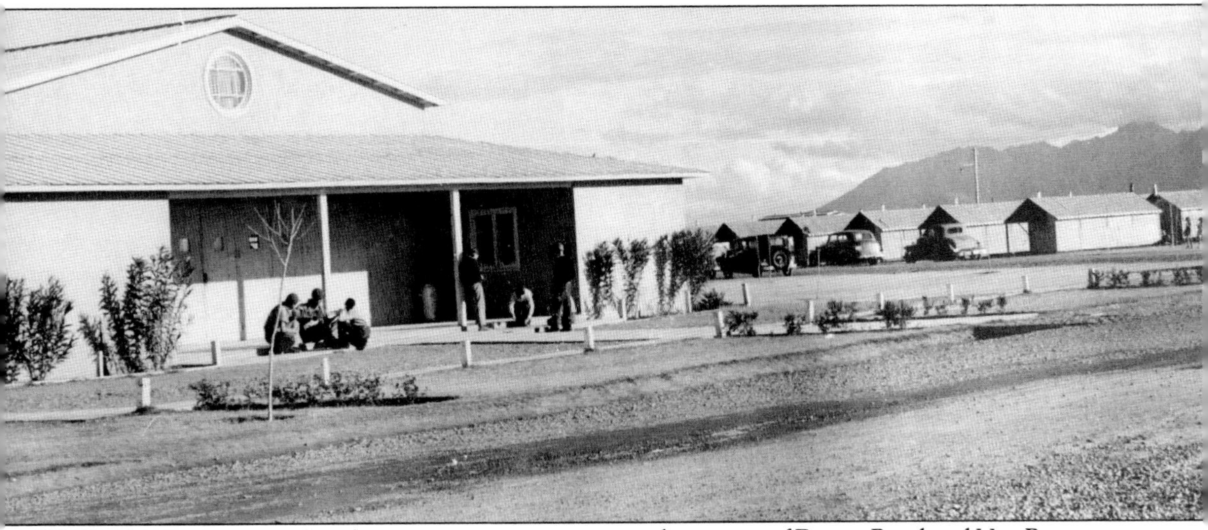

Where Walgreens is today, there was a migrant camp on the corner of Dysart Road and Van Buren Street. The large main building was the mess hall. Migrants streamed in from the dust bowls in the Midwest during the Great Depression of the 1930s. Hopeful people heard about the promised land in the West, so off they traversed with all their worldly possessions either on their persons or attached to the automobiles they were traveling in. Often cars would break down and couldn't travel any longer. Displaced, struggling people camped under trees and bridges and down washes with small tattered canvas coverings for shelters. The conditions were bleak and unhealthy, so the government and the WPA erected a community camp of small metal houses to provide shelter for as many homeless as possible. One probably cannot imagine how uncomfortable they were in the summer and winter, but a roof over one's head was more important than weather conditions. (Courtesy Sally Schulkie Marcotte.)

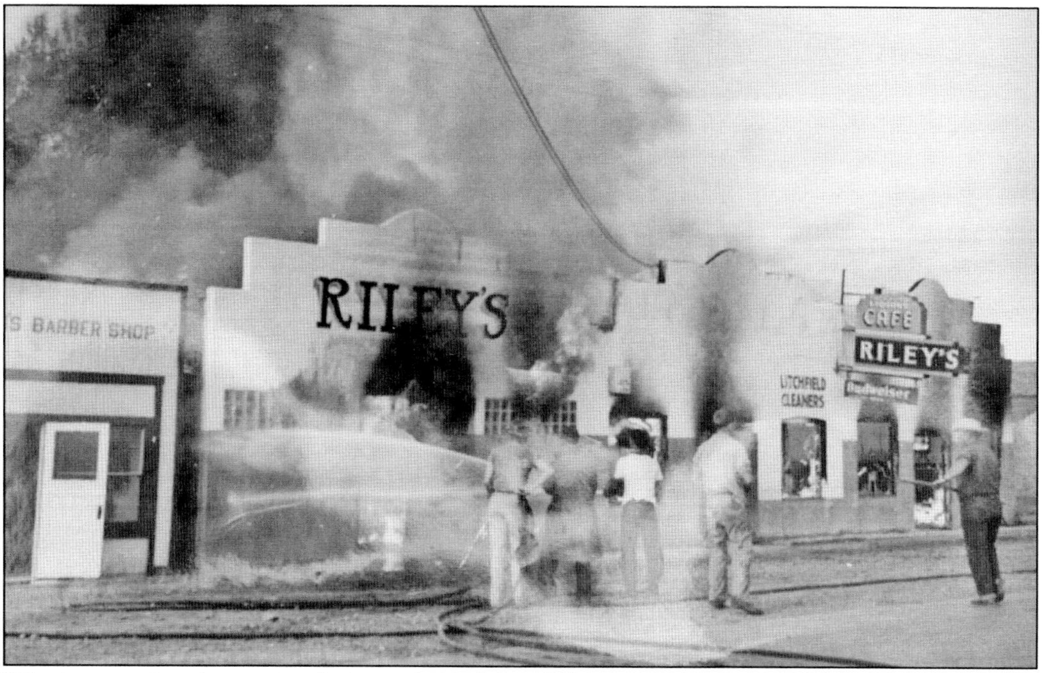

Riley's was a local watering hole in Avondale. Old-timers have tales of the Hurst mortuary across the road from Riley's. The mortician had a recently deceased body that needed immediate attention, but he first decided to take a little refreshment across the street. The following day, a local doctor walked past Hurst and complained to authorities of a foul odor coming from the building. Needless to say, the mortician was charged with drunken negligence and the body was promptly removed and put to rest. (Courtesy City of Avondale.)

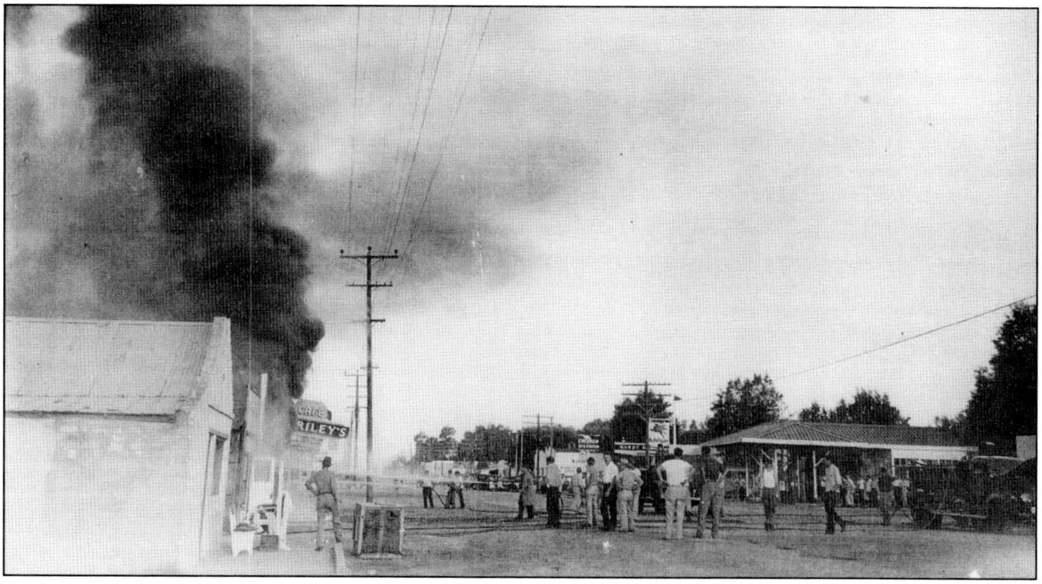

The great Riley's fire of the 1940s was dangerous, and many local citizens pitched in to fight it. Fires are always dangerous, but buildings of that era had little building codes if any, and often the fire would spread quickly throughout the city. Brave Avondale men pulled up their sleeves to fight the fire together. (Courtesy City of Avondale.)

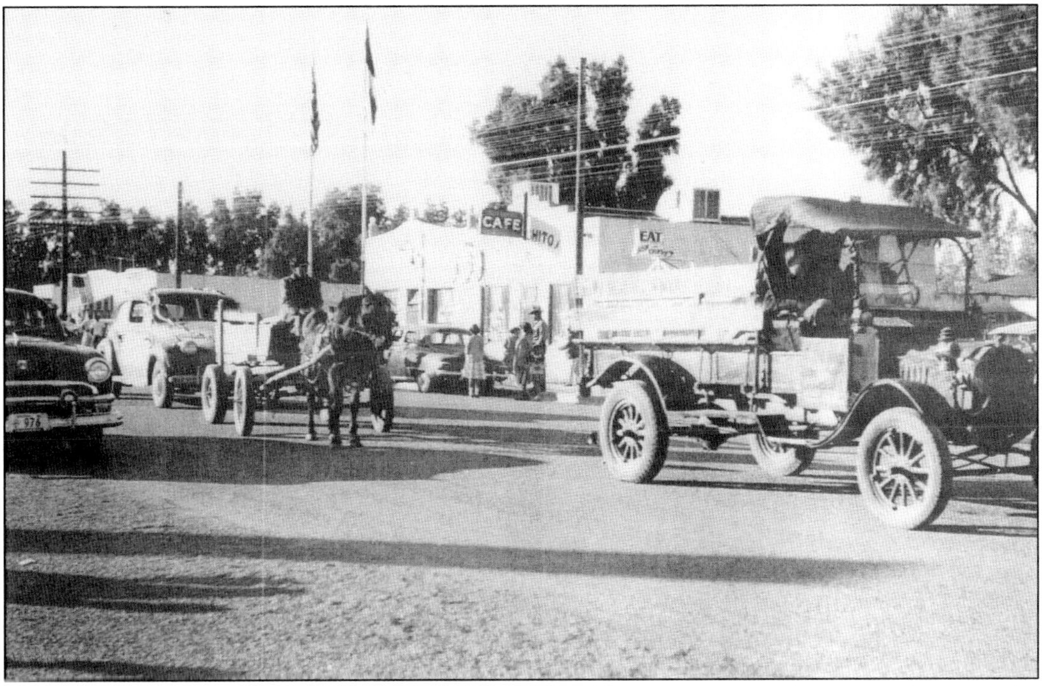

A parade down Western Avenue during Billy Moore Days was always fun to watch under the large trees that lined the road. The City of Avondale has taken on a tree replanting project to reflect Avondale's past. Many beautiful trees adorn Western today and add to the ambiance of an intact small town. (Courtesy City of Avondale.)

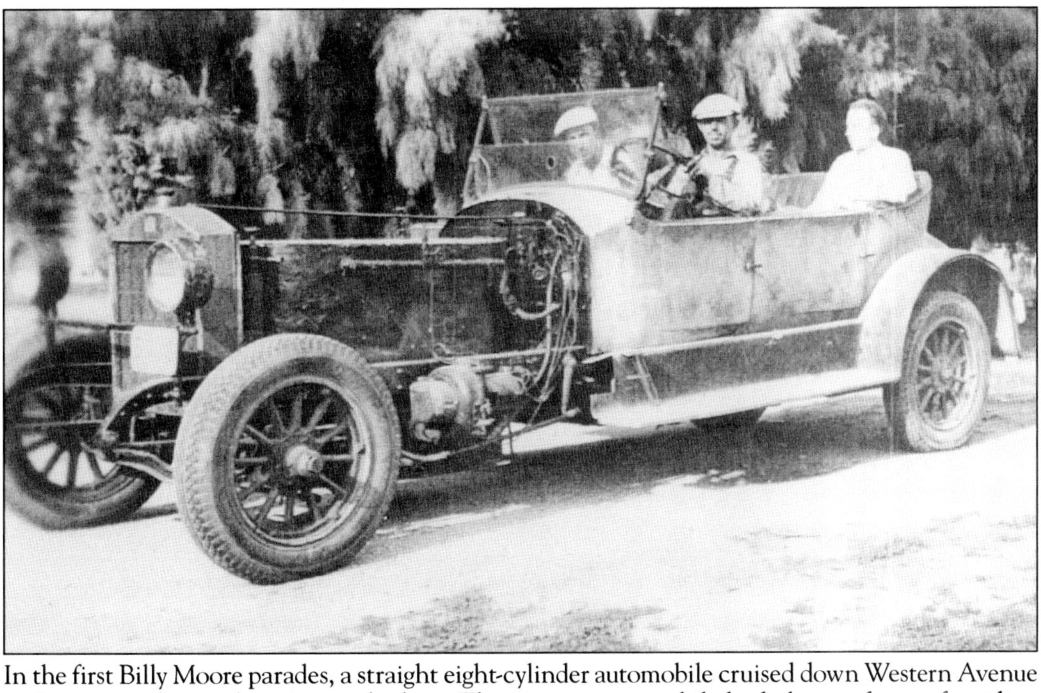

In the first Billy Moore parades, a straight eight-cylinder automobile cruised down Western Avenue with joyous riders and envious onlookers. The vintage automobile had plenty of room for riding and lots of power to get down the road. (Courtesy City of Avondale.)

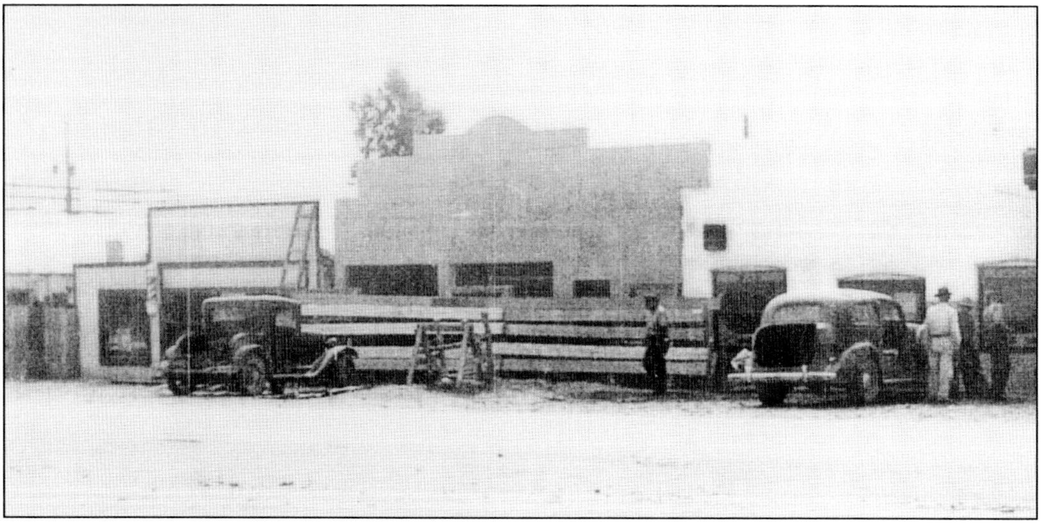

Old-timers are not sure what year Riley's Bar was built, but they often reminisce about it. The construction was not built to today's standards, but in the past there wasn't a building code. Later the bar would burn to the ground, but not before giving Avondale patrons a place to do a little imbibing. (Courtesy City of Avondale.)

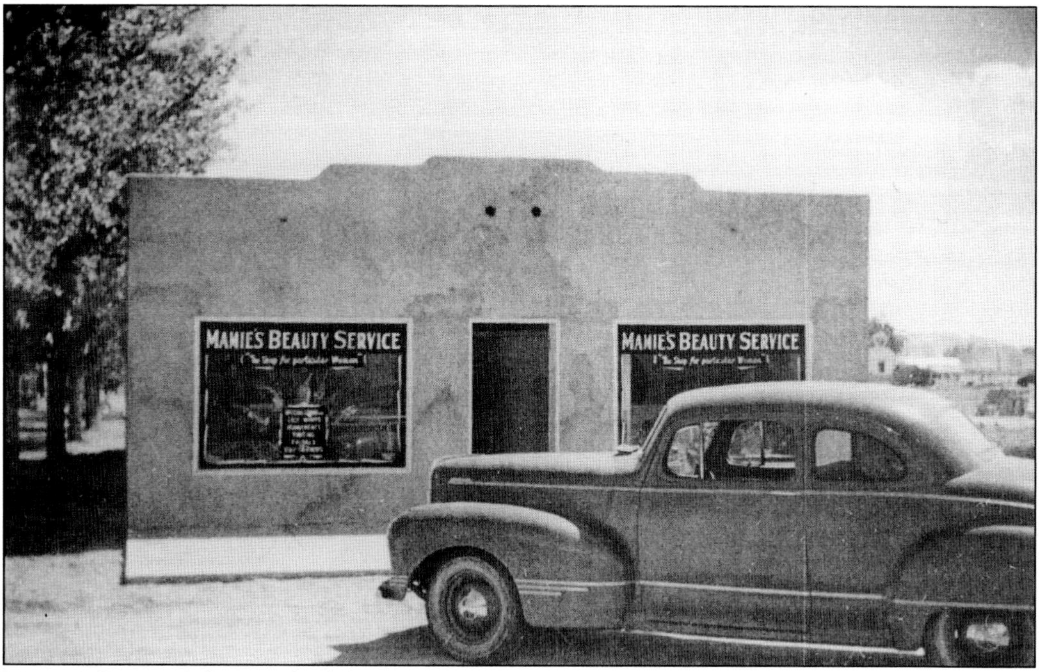

Mamie's Beauty Salon was built by Tom Aragon for the Combs family, and many a coiffure was done at Mamie's for proms and special celebrations. John Combs was the first elected mayor of Avondale. Combs sold the beauty shop in 1954 to Tony Schneider, who turned it into a drive-in liquor store. Tony was married to Lila Aragon Schneider, so Tom Aragon's building later came full circle to his daughter's new family. Adobe bricks were created by Aragon with his bare hands from the desert earth and used in the construction of the building. The Schneiders had a hand in the store until recently, when it was sold, but new owners have kept the drive-in liquor store as it was. (Courtesy City of Avondale.)

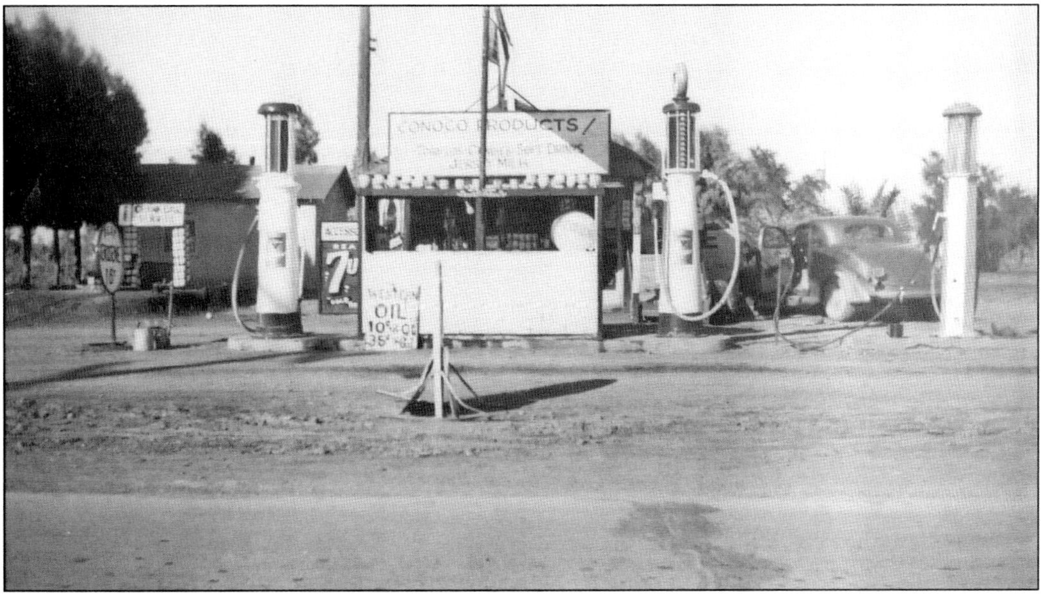

In an interview, Joe and Juanita Hill talked about Joe's first gas station on Western Avenue and how his father pioneered Coldwater. A large portion of Avondale was brush and cactus cleared by Joe Hill Sr. Joe Sr. planted an orchard and grew produce for the surrounding area, and Roosevelt Irrigation District (RID) still uses the ditches today. Joe Sr. saw people settling in his small town of Coldwater and had the foresight to clear enough land to sell lots for $50 each, for which he carried the papers. Joe Sr. had a vision and several mules that provided the horsepower to tame the dusty desert. In 1938, Joe Jr. wanted to use horsepower of another kind and set up a gas station that would sell gas, not hay. (Courtesy City of Avondale.)

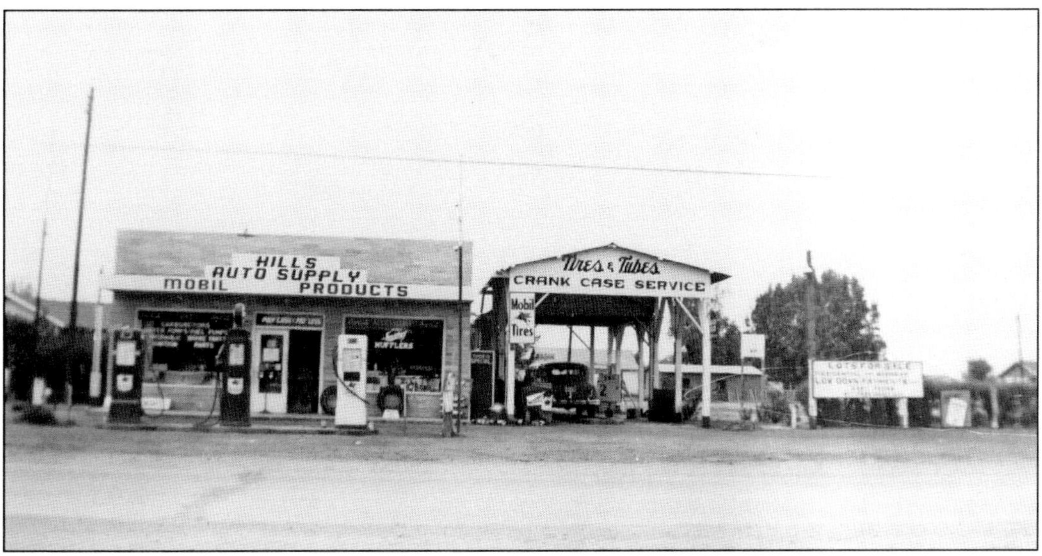

As time passed, Joe Hill would carry Mobil oil products and Conoco goods. He updated his business by providing a bay to do mechanical work and selling auto supplies. Today the Hill property is still standing, though many businesses have given the old place a try. (Courtesy City of Avondale.)

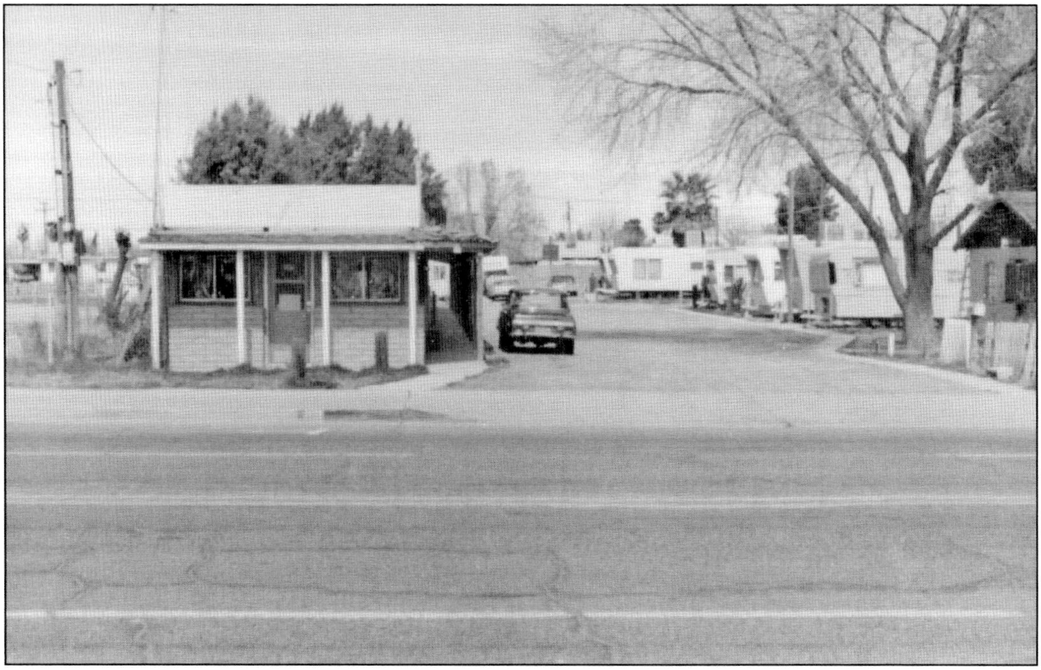

The motor court on Western Avenue was converted to apartments that currently house tenants. (Courtesy City of Avondale.)

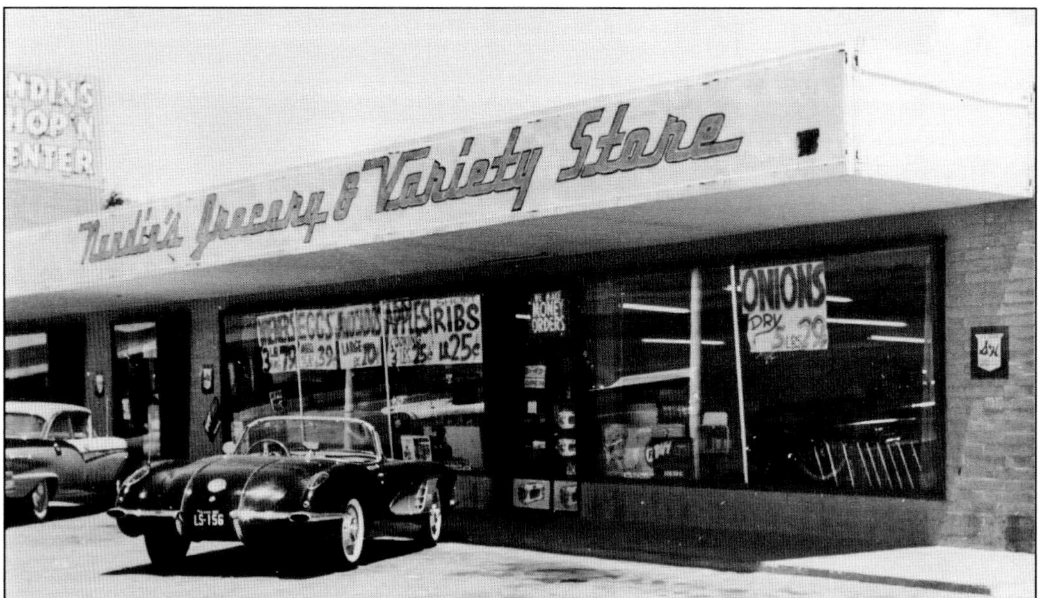

Nandin's Grocery store faced Buckeye Road, also known as Main Street. Today the old sign still exists, but it is hardly legible as it hangs quietly over MC 85 just east of Central Avenue. The Nandin family was highly thought of in the community and often gave credit to struggling families. The Nandins no longer have a store, but the family still resides in the Avondale area. (Courtesy Gilbert Nandin family.)

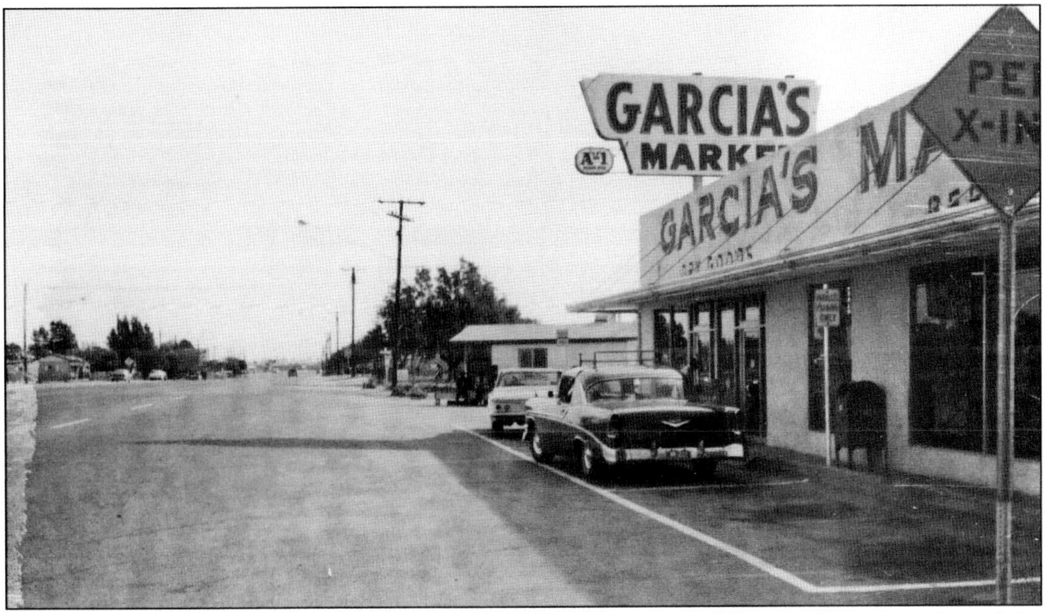

Garcia's Market sat just east of the Nandin's store on Main and Fourth Streets in Avondale. Garcia's Market was family run and beloved by the community. One could always count on Garcia's during the Great Depression to donate food for hungry families. Today the store has been bought out by the Bashes chain to become Food City. The Garcia family is still living and working in the Avondale area, and some of the family works at the old location at Food City. (Courtesy City of Avondale.)

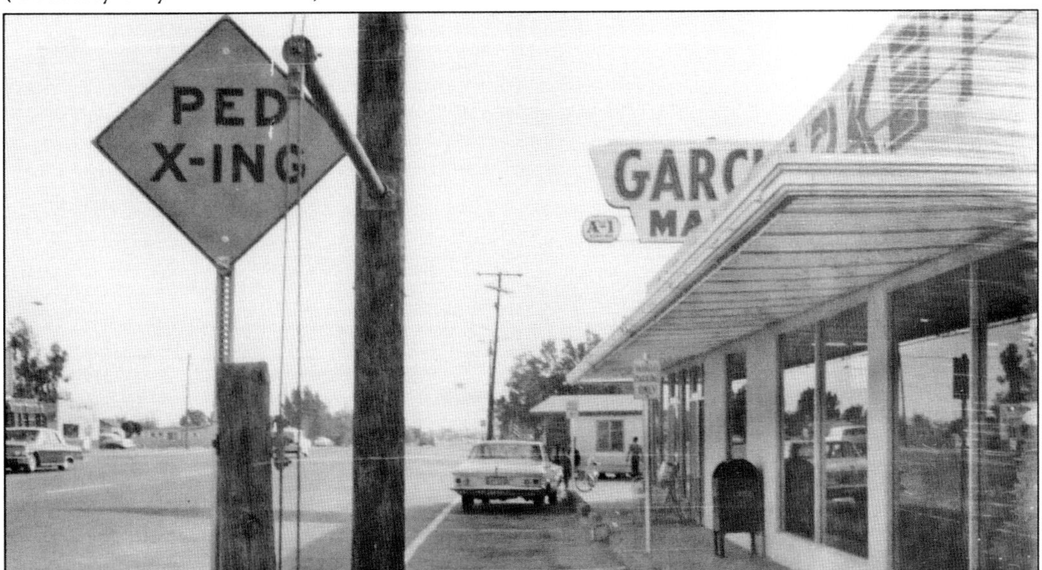

Garcia's Market was built on the south side of the road that has had many names. The name Buckeye Road is still in use; its title was due to the fact it carried travelers from Phoenix to the town of Buckeye, Arizona. The quiet country thoroughfare was then christened Main Street. The leaders of Avondale decided the heavy traffic traversing through the center of town on Western Avenue was dangerous and distracting, so traffic was diverted to Buckeye and thus the name was changed to Main. (Courtesy City of Avondale.)

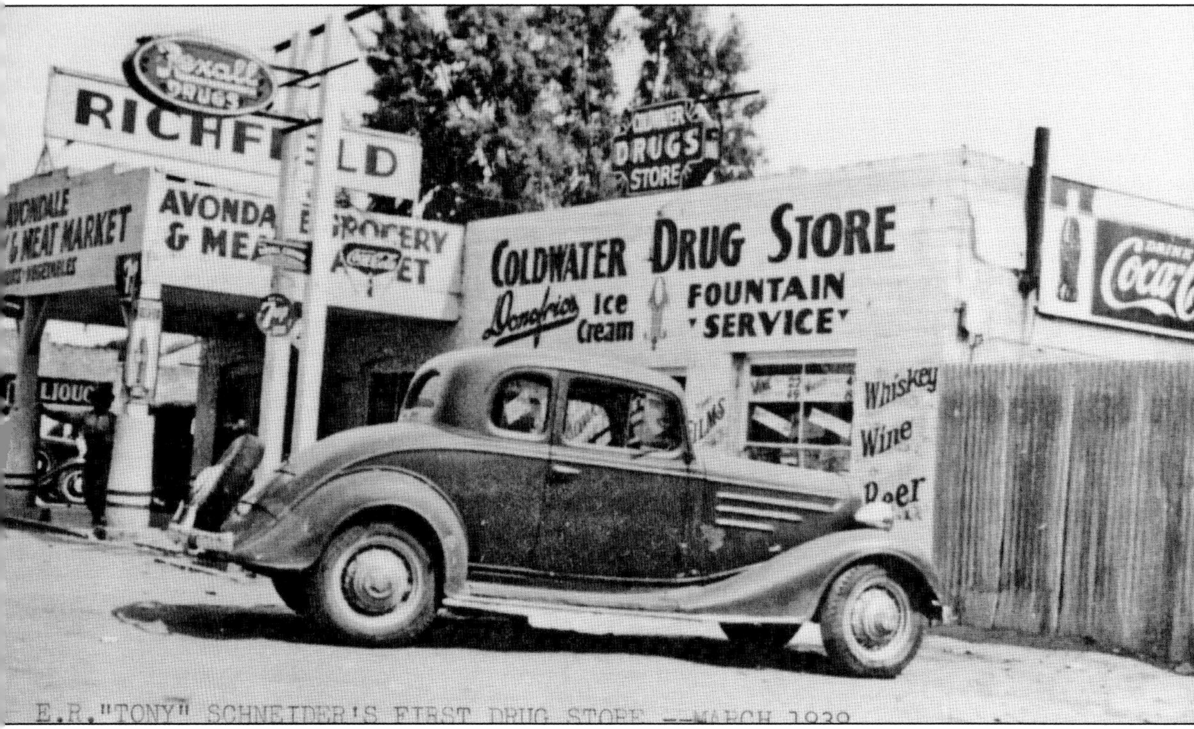

Schneider's Drug Store was important to the development of Avondale. In 1937, Sam Barker, one of the first owners, had spent a great deal of money on his father-in-law, Mr. Zander, in his bid for governor of Arizona. Mr. Zander was favored to win but was killed in an airplane accident shortly before Election Day. Barker needed quick cash, so he sold the drugstore to Mr. Granada in 1939. Mr. Granada then sold the business to Elton Roy "Tony" Schneider, who was a druggist and businessman. The drugstore burned in 1945. After a few more moves, Tony finally built his own store on the corner of Central and Western Avenues in 1964 and became one of Avondale's beloved and most prominent citizens. (Courtesy City of Avondale.)

Three

Pioneer Families

As the Great Migration passed through Avondale, folks either broke down or ran out of money. Some believe earlier residents decided they liked what they saw and stayed, but the lure of California brought in most of Avondale's early population. Some families were stranded with neither a mode of transportation nor money and became desperate. Pioneers already established gave a helping hand to others in need. Garcia's Market would provide food to emaciated children when asked with no hesitation. Churches rallied around their new neighbors and gave not only their blessings but clothing, shoes, and medical needs.

Christine Ludlow recalled in her book, *My Life I Give*, while delivering toys and food for Christmas, she and her husband came upon a wet soggy tent in the desert. They called out but received no answer. Just as they were about to leave, a faint cry for help was heard. As they investigated, they found a soaked mattress with a crippled man, a semiconscious woman, and tragically a dead newborn baby. The man had great difficulty telling that they had not eaten in days and had given up hope and were waiting to die. Stories like this one were not uncommon. People had makeshift home made of cardboard, paper, rags, and small tents thrown together for shelter.

The government energized the people by creating jobs for those willing to work. One successful program was the WPA. The WPA built the government camp on Dysart Road and Van Buren. Metal houses were constructed to provide shelter for as many dispossessed souls as possible. Those in charge of constructing the camp thought it best to have metal buildings so as not to have the poor people tear it apart for firewood and cooking. The buildings featured baths and showers with hot and cold water. A large auditorium was in the center of the complex to conduct church services and entertainment. Avondale citizens who endeared themselves to the migrants were T. C. and Luella Rhodes, Mary Brooks, Mamie Colmes, Elnora Coor, Marandra Flemming, Jessica Bittick, and many others.

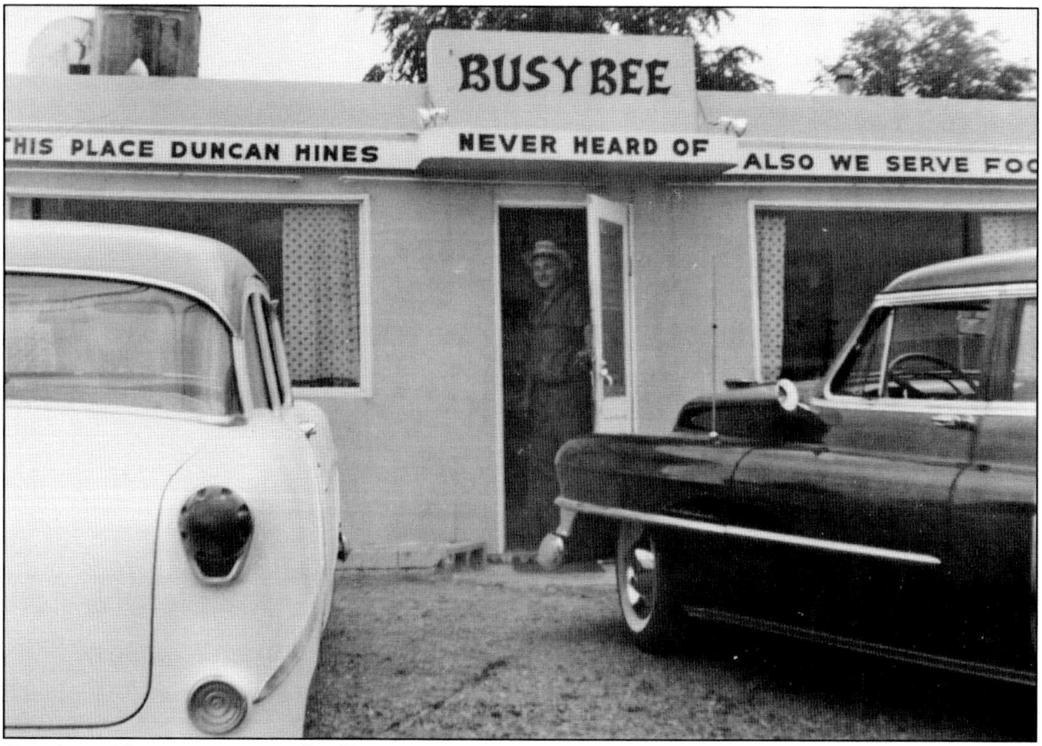

On the 15th anniversary of Billy Moore Days, Avondale, Goodyear, Litchfield Park, and the chamber of commerce purchased a headstone to mark the final resting place of William Graham Moore, who died on May 26, 1934. (Both courtesy City of Avondale.)

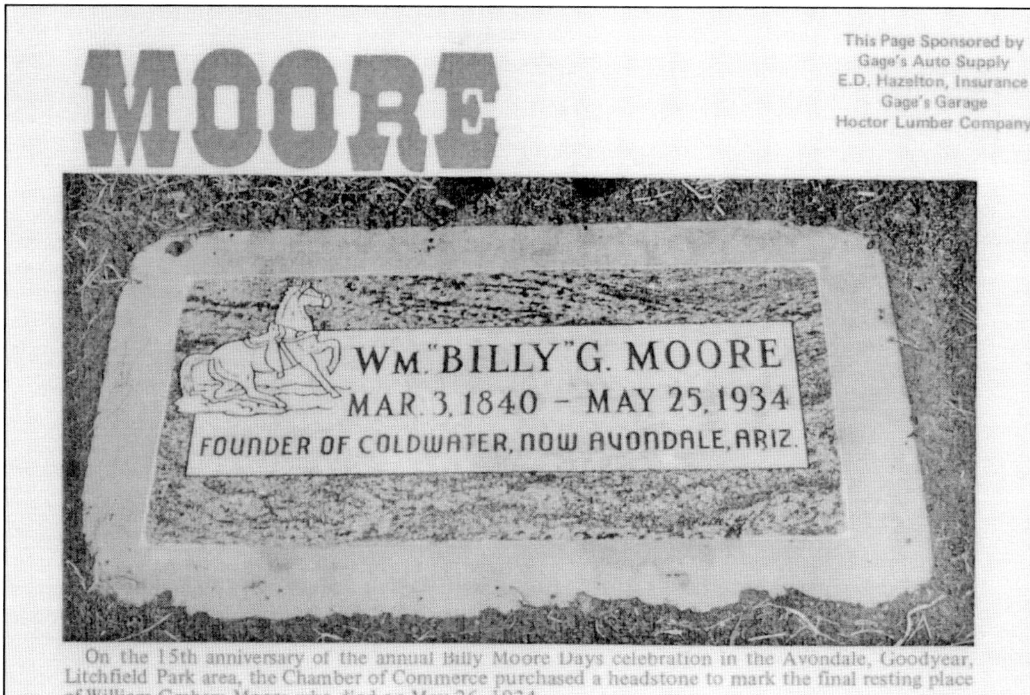

MOORE

This Page Sponsored by
Gage's Auto Supply
E.D. Hazelton, Insurance
Gage's Garage
Hoctor Lumber Company

WM."BILLY"G. MOORE
MAR. 3, 1840 – MAY 25, 1934
FOUNDER OF COLDWATER, NOW AVONDALE, ARIZ.

On the 15th anniversary of the annual Billy Moore Days celebration in the Avondale, Goodyear, Litchfield Park area, the Chamber of Commerce purchased a headstone to mark the final resting place of William Graham Moore who died on May 26, 1934.

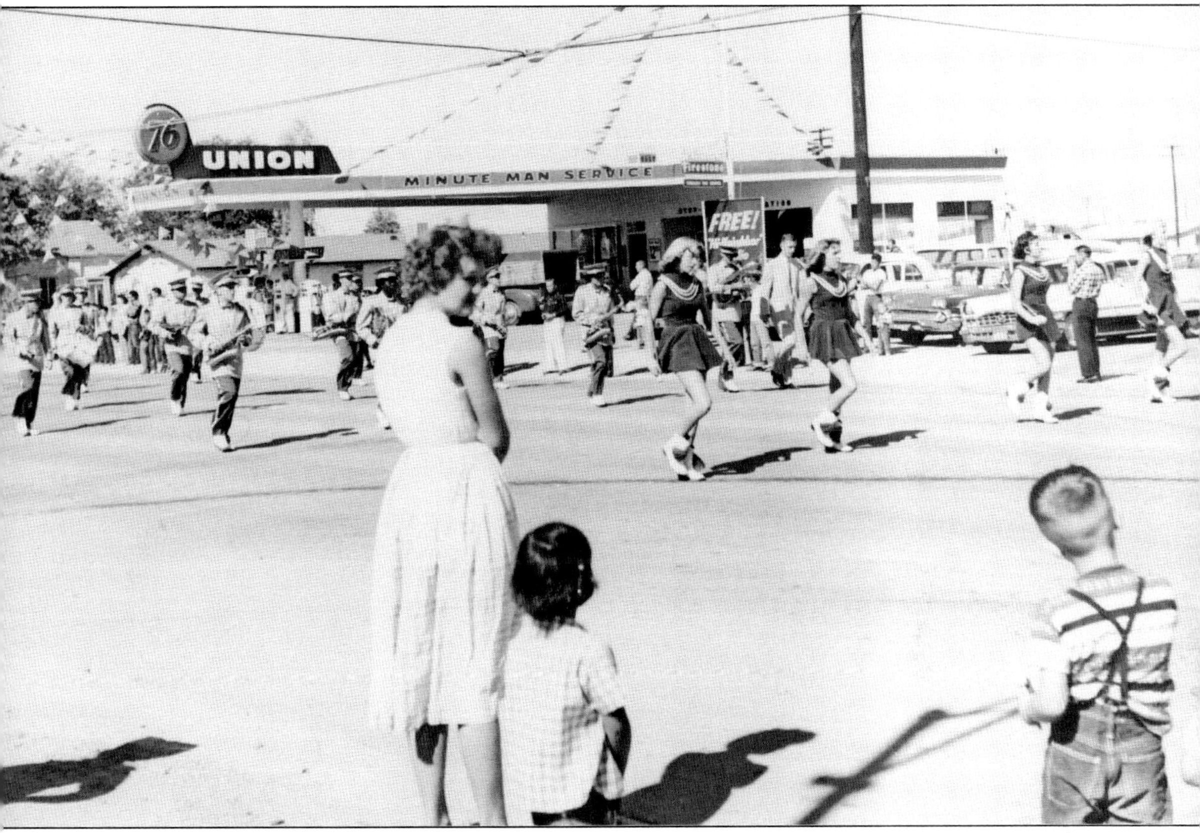

Some of the participants in the Billy Moore parade are Eileen Werner (first baton) and Patti Falls (second baton) leading the band. (Courtesy City of Avondale.)

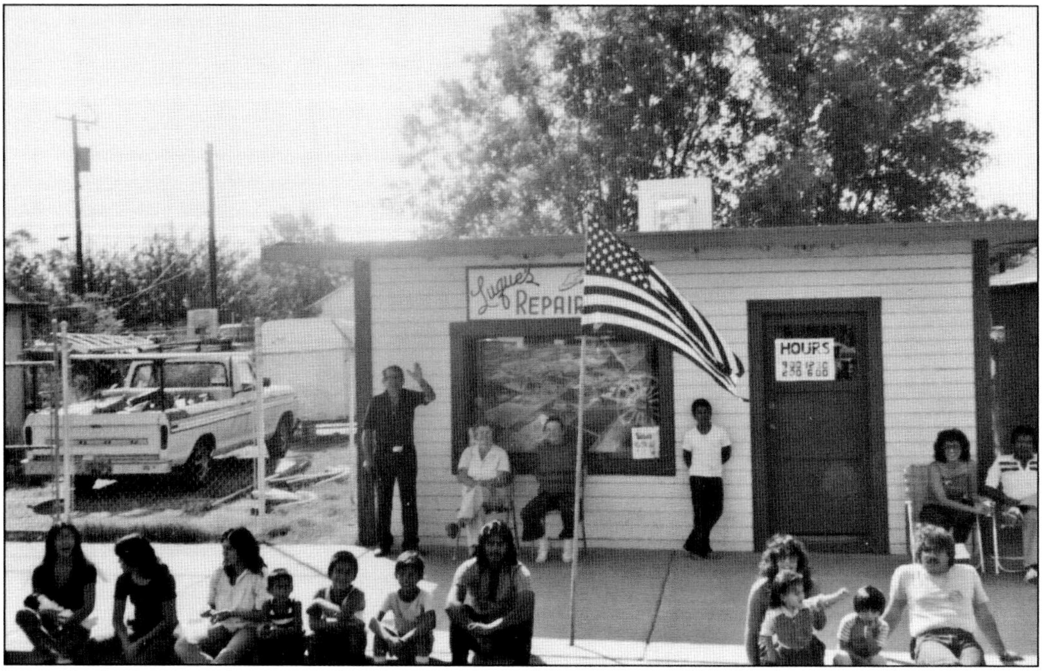

Luque's shoe repair shop was always there for a favorite pair of boots that needed new soles or a little stitch here or there. The one quirk that Luque had was that the shoes were done on his time, not the customer's; if sandals were brought to him to be repaired in the winter, he would say he would have them finished the coming spring, as it was to cold for sandals right now. But if it was an emergency repair, he would get right to it. (Courtesy City of Avondale.)

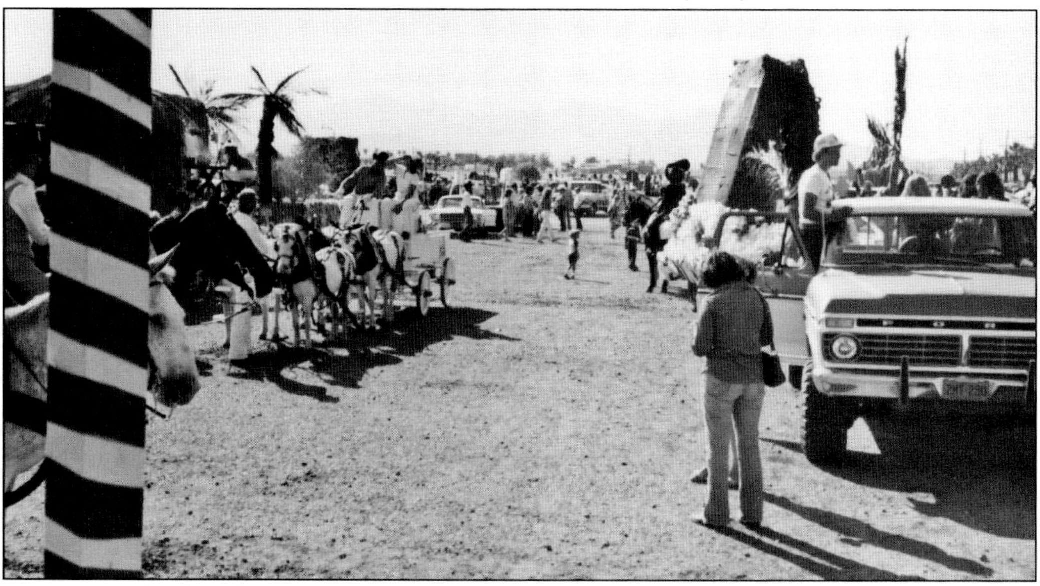

Participants for the Billy Moore parade would line up at one end of town or the other depending upon who was in charge at the time. Parade participants would scramble to their assigned spots and always looked excited and anxious as horses kicked and horns squawked. Local dignitaries would show for the big event, especially politicians or those who wanted to be politicians. (Courtesy City of Avondale.)

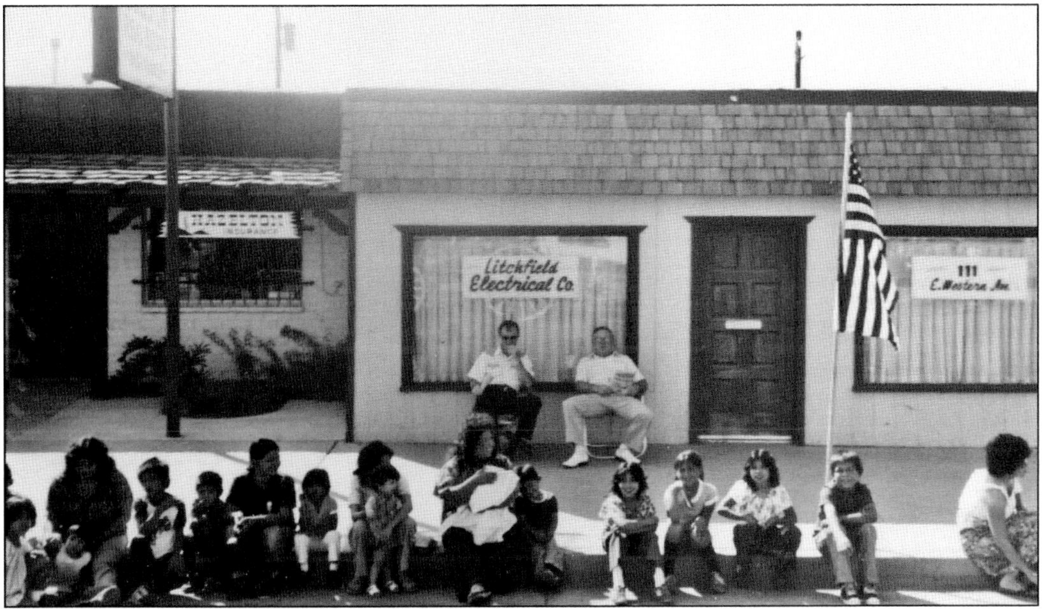

Ed Hazelton's Insurance and Real Estate Company was where locals did their business because Ed was always in good spirits, people knew he could be trusted, and he was active in the community. Ed and his wife, Paulene Hazelton, were some of those who honored Billy Moore with his headstone. Next to Ed's business was Litchfield Electrical Company. (Courtesy City of Avondale.)

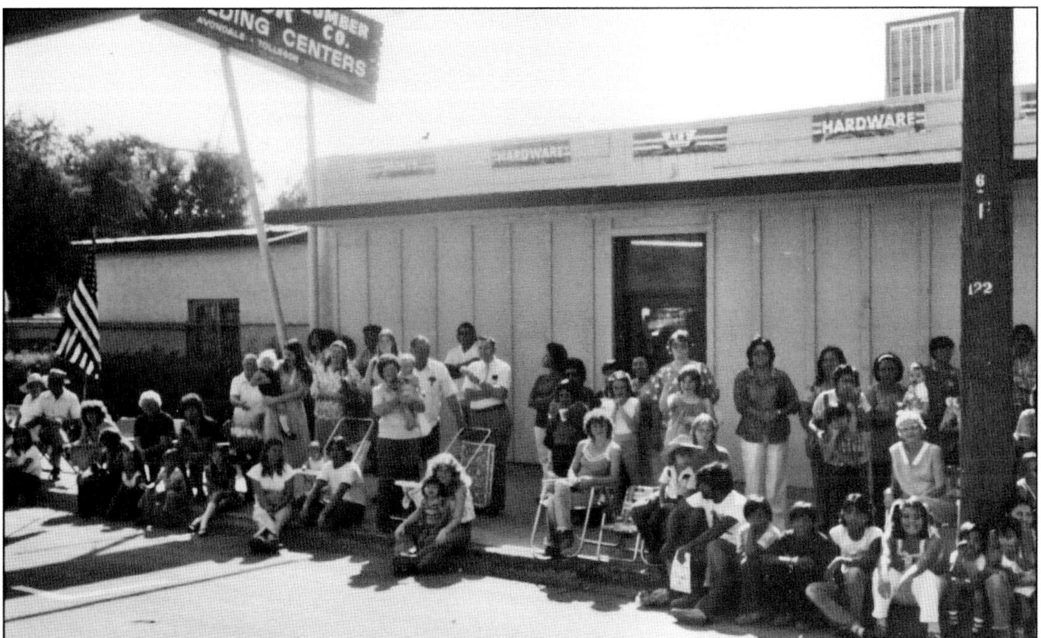

Hoctor Lumber and Hardware store had two locations, one in Tolleson and the other in Avondale. The lumberyard was well stocked, and the locals didn't have to travel into Phoenix thanks to the two locations. Goodale Hardware came later and was the other hardware store in town. They have managed to stay in business even with large corporate home centers nearby; their service, knowledge, and integrity are the reason. (Courtesy City of Avondale.)

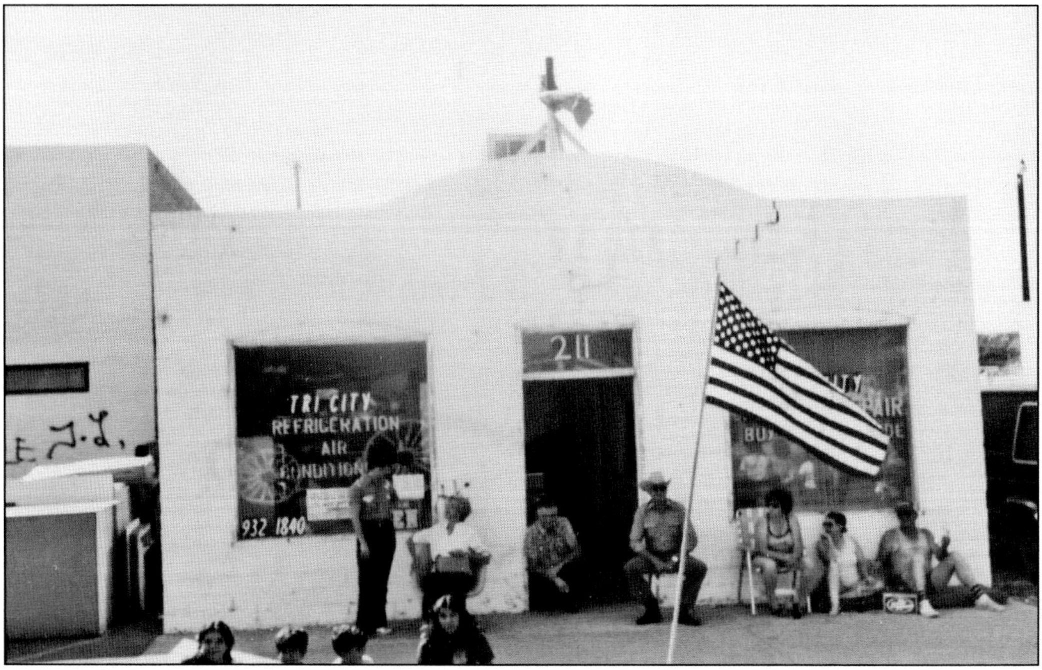

Every Billy Moore parade displays American flags. Flags would wave along the parade route. Parade themes and grand marshals headed the parade, and both were voted on, usually by the chamber of commerce. Pride in hometowns and the country were respectfully used. (Courtesy City of Avondale.)

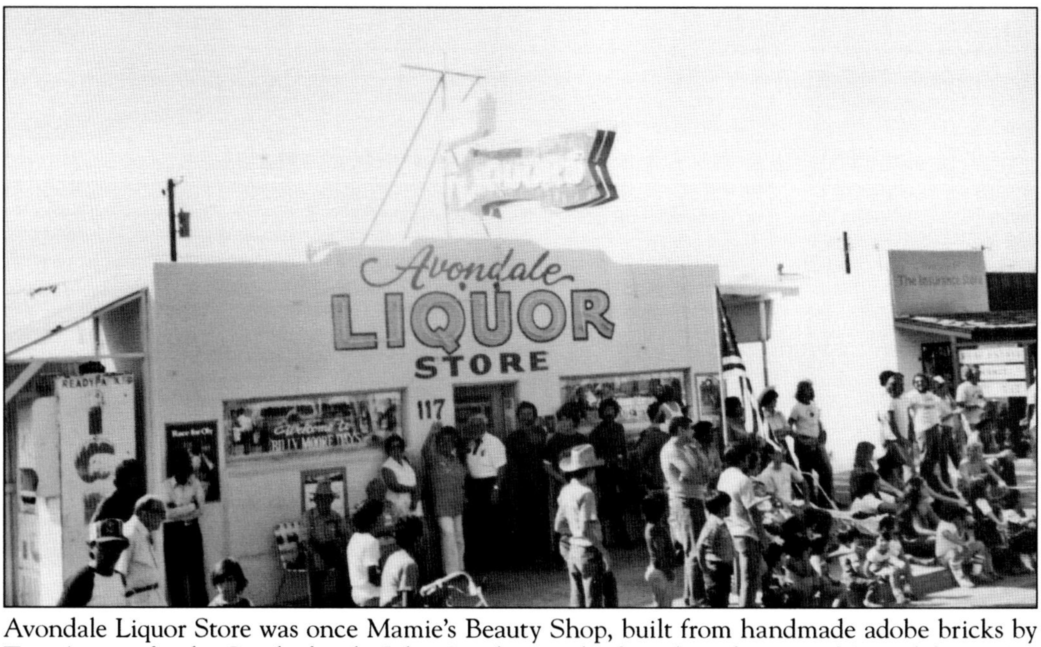

Avondale Liquor Store was once Mamie's Beauty Shop, built from handmade adobe bricks by Tom Aragon for the Combs family. John Combs was the first elected mayor of Avondale in 1947 and served many years on the Avondale Elementary School board. In 1939, the building was sold to Tony Schneider and his partners. (Courtesy City of Avondale.)

There can't be any other job nearly as much fun as being an editor. I should pay them for the pleasure. Despite occasional reporters with axes to grind, it is a craft I have always been proud of, and I would be glad to follow it forever, if I were allowed.

Maybe, at least, for another 25 years.

Westside's Newspaper History

The first newspaper of a num- er which served the Westside rea, and the ancestor of the Vestsider, was the Tolleson In- ependent. It was started in July 941, and was succeeded a few nonths later by the Westside Enterprise.

Publishers of the Westside Enterprise were Ted Allen and Leeta Cox, owners of the Valley Printers in Glendale.

In the fall of 1941 work had started on the Goodyear Aircraft plant on the corner of Litchfield Road and Old Highway 80 and the Goodyear Subdivision was plan- ed.

Soon afterward Mrs. Cox ap- roached Gene Ely to take over as editor. In August of 1942 Em- ni and Gene Ely purchased the Westside Enterprise from the Valley Printers.

He and Emmi published the weekly during the war years, after V.J. Day moved from Litch- field Park to Goodyear. In 1953 they moved the printing of the Westside Enterprise from the Valley Printers to Bill Ryan's Glendale News shop.

The News printed the news- paper for three years when it was moved again to the Phoenix Sun plant. It was during 1955 that Ray Woodside, now owner of the East Asia Publishing Co., a firm that has its own five- story building in Tokyo, was editor of the Westside Enter- prise.

In the summers of 1956 and 1958 Ed Ford acted as editor of the weekly. In the meantime the Enterprise was printed in the Sunnyslope Journal and the Pe- oria Times plants.

grant made to Moore.

The Elys sold the Westside Enterprise to Victor J. Morgan, later owner of the Scottsdale Pro- gress. Morgan at that time own- ed the Glendale News, and Ely was named publisher of the West- side paper and later the Glendale paper.

A little over a year after the Elys sold to Morgan in March of 1959, Morgan sold his Glendale interests to Warren and Lucille Morrell of Tyler, Tex. The Elys remained as editors of the West- side Enterprise. Mr. and Mrs. Morrell sold the combined Glen- dale News and Enterprise to Burt Freireich, Sun City publisher, in the fall of 1961.

In March of 1962 Jack Wills replaced Gene Ely as editor of the Westsider, and shortly after- ward Mrs. Bobbi Hassard took over the helm of the Westside weekly. A succession of editors was named in 1964 when the former Mrs. Morrell, Lucille Bufford, took back the combined Glendale News and Westside Enterprise property from Frei- reich.

For a brief period in 1964 Mr. and Mrs. Robert Packwood were owners of the combined newspapers. In August of 1964 Mrs. Bufford sold her interests in the two papers to Derrick Publishing Co. of Oil City, Penn. Mrs. Hassard and Pat Roberts acted as editors of the Westside Enterprise until it was merged in February of 1965 with the Westside Citizen, a rival weekly edited by Jim and Betty Werner.

The resultant newspaper was called The Westsider, and was edited by Gene Ely.

In June of this year a group composed of Roberts, Mrs. Has- sard and the Elys purchased the Westsider from the Oil City in- terests.

Two other weeklies were merged with the Westside Enter- prise before the Morrells took over. In 1956 the Elys merged a free-distribution newspaper call- ed The Westside Weekly with the Enterprise, and when Morgan purchased the Westside Enter- prise, he merged the West Valley News, edited by Bill Armstrong, into the Westside Enterprise.

First Papers Record Early Westside

The first six issues of the West- sider's predecessor were called the Tolleson Independent. After those first half dozen issues, the name was changed to the West- side Enterprise, a name which was continued until February of 1965.

Those first issues of the Tolle- son Independent are interesting as a commentary on the West- side as it was before World War II.

The lead story in volume one, number one, was the Tolleson town budget. H. C. Arnold, town clerk, noted that total expendi- tures for the coming year would be $7,405, and $1,417 would have to be raised by taxation.

Also in Tolleson the Miller and Johns shed was opening for the shipment of cantaloupes, the first to be shipped from the Valley. The Robertson, the Washburn

Continued on page 2B

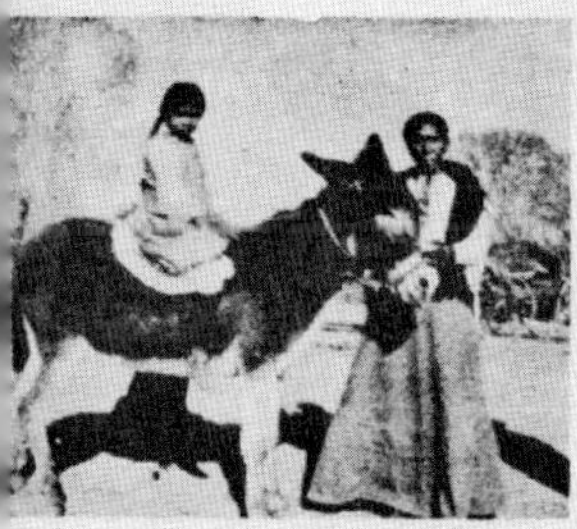

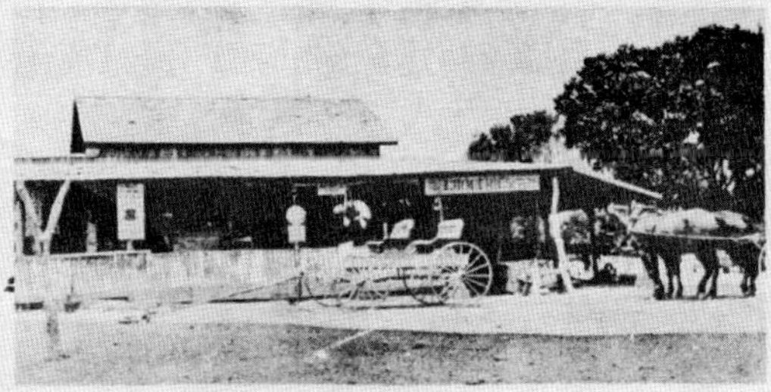

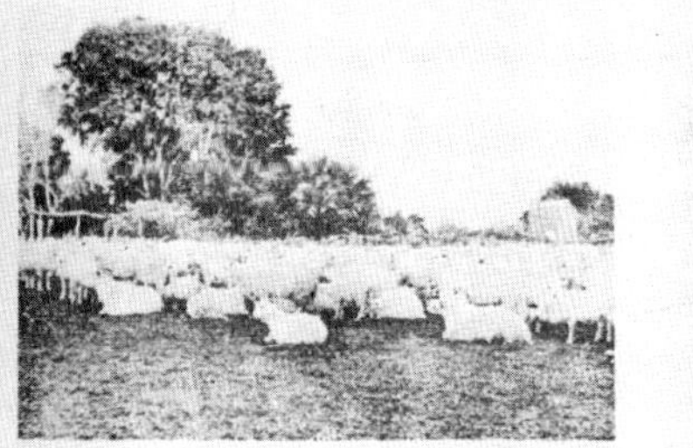

EARLY COLDWATER – Three pictures of early Coldwater Crossing are shown. At left is a picture of Aunt Cynthia, wife of Uncle Billy Moore, and their adopted daugh- ter. The girl was later killed by a burro, whether it was the one she is riding is not known. The picture was taken by Mrs. Cliff Armstrong, then Mrs. Lida Hedger, Westside pioneer now living in Tolleson. The second picture is of Uncle Billy Moore's store. It was made in 1907 by Albert J. Ross. The central sign says, "Post Office", and the one at left lists men's wear. The picture at right shows goats belonging to Billy, and were taken at the same time as the store picture by Ross. Huge cotton- woods grow along the Agua Fria River in rear. Billy had 1,400 head of goats at one time, Ross said.

The old *Westsider* newspaper ran a long-forgotten article that recalled Uncle Billy Moore's life with a picture of "Aunt Cynthia," as the locals called her, and her adopted daughter. The stage stop in its later years ran flocks of goats, farmed feed for the horses, and grew produce for the community. (Courtesy City of Avondale.)

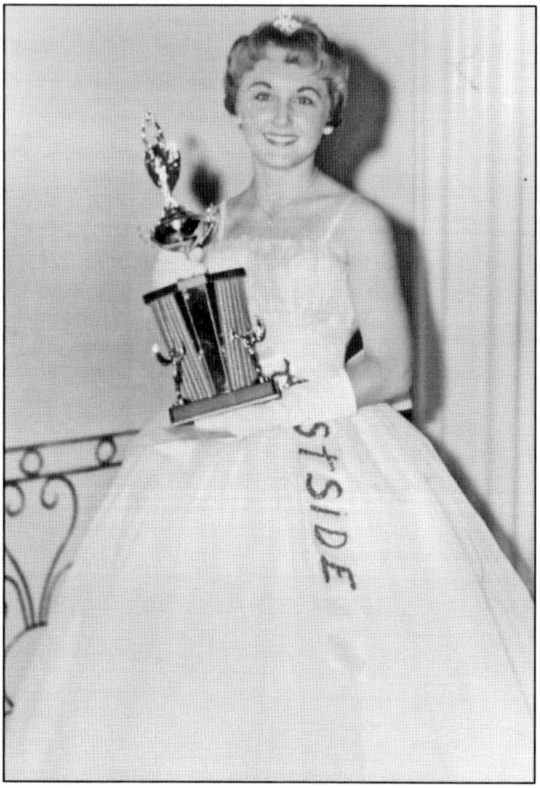

Beauty queens have been and still are part of small-town parades. Tradition is a good thing, but some want to know what they look like today. What did the queens and kings accomplish with their lives? A beautiful and talented Westside Queen was Beverly Watson. (Courtesy City of Avondale.)

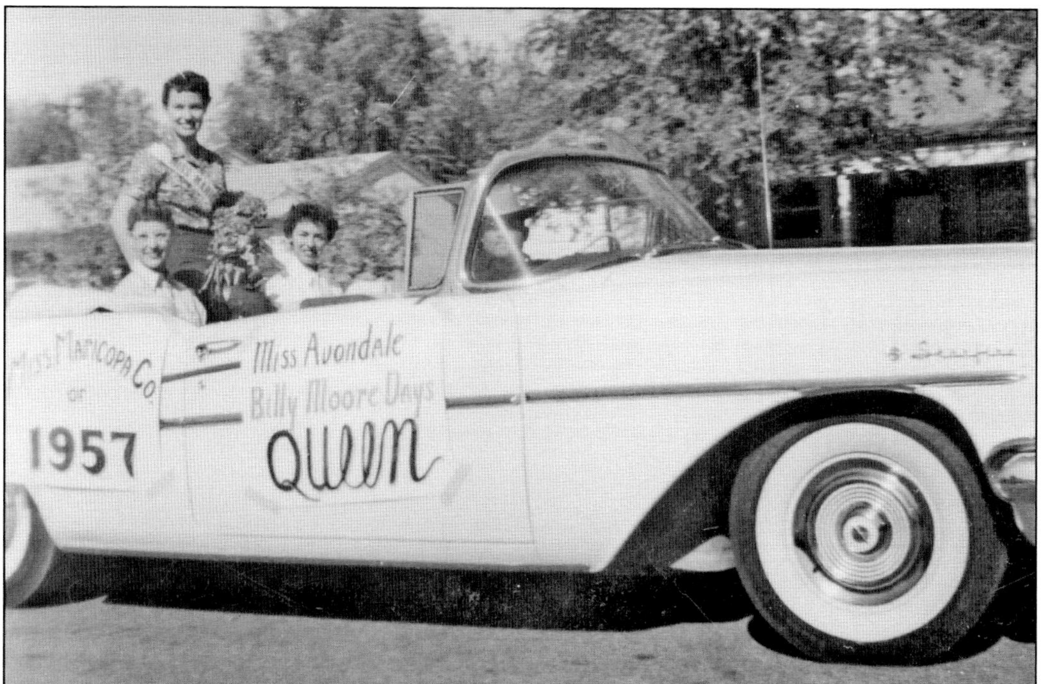

Billy Moore Days featured prominent figures of Avondale. In 1957, Miss Avondale won the Miss Maricopa County beauty pageant. (Courtesy City of Avondale.)

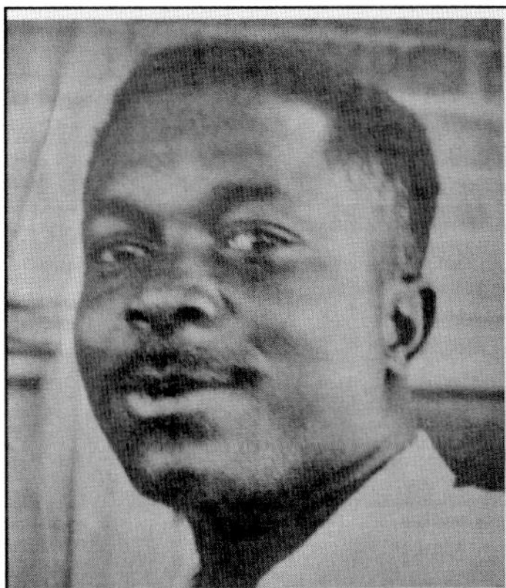

WILLIE YOUNG was awarded Avondale's top service presentation, the 1969 Outstanding Community Service Award by the council. Young, 32, a dropout of the 1950's, is a counselor with the Migrant Opportunity Program. He was cited for coordinating community activities. "Willie Young," Joe Acevedo, Avondale City Manager said, "has been a liaison between the city and the people south of Highway 80. He has brought their problems to us, and our problems to them. As a result there is better communication between us both."

Willie Young Receives Community Service Award

Last week Willie Young, 32, received the highest award given by the council and mayor of Avondale, the 1969 Outstanding Community Service Award.

A counselor with the Migrant Opportunity Program, Mr. Young was given the prize for his work in coordinating activities for the less-privileged residents of the Westside.

Mayor Vic Allen praised Young for working for better understanding between Avondale officials and the residents of the city south of U.S. Highway 80.

"Young is one of the most active citizens of our community today," Mayor Allen said, "Call on him to help, and he is ready and willing."

Although Young dropped out of Tolleson Union High School as a teen-ager, he has continued to improve himself.

"My aunt promised to give $5 a week to stay in school. When the money was not produced, I figured school was a waste and dropped out," he said.

After working in the fields, pitching melons, chopping cotton, stacking lettuce crates, Young made up his mind to go back to school, this time in a poverty program. Then the Westside man entered a Manpower Training Class and received his General Education Equivalency Diploma. Three years later Young joined MOP, serving Avondale, Cashion and Santa Maria areas.

"With all the training I had in the poverty programs," he said, "I could not help but develop an interest to better the community, want to train people to help themselves and become involved in community activities."

"It rubs off on you," he stated. "You believe what you practice. I am a very strong believer in community development. And I'm going to try to convince my children to stay in school and go to college."

Young helped start a [illegible] in which anyone living within a mile radius of Avondale is eligible to become a member for $5.25, to be paid within two years. He is a member of the Avondale Citizens Committee to Improve Our Neighborhood, which works to upgrade the community.

The Avondale Voters League, which he helped organize in 1967 is designed to encourage southside Avondale people to become involved in city and school affairs.

LIVE WITH IT

Learn to adjust — it's useless to stew about things you can't change or influence.

Willie Young has been a neighborhood activist for many years. In the above newspaper article, Willie talked about working in the small towns of Cashion and Santa Maria, which no longer exist. Santa Maria, located at Sixty-Seventh Avenue and Lower Buckeye Road, was annexed into the City of Phoenix. Cashion was positioned between 107th Avenue and 115th Avenue and was annexed by the City of Avondale. The author, Jerry Squire, met Willie while Squire was writing a book for the City of Avondale during their 50th anniversary. Willie is still an activist for his community, and his neighbors love and respect him to this day. (Courtesy City of Avondale.)

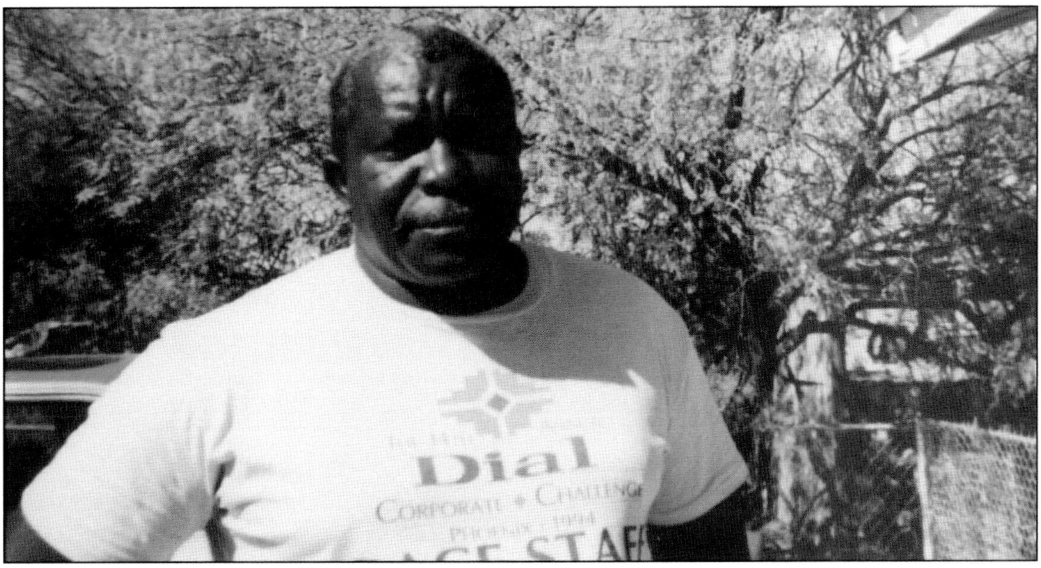

Willie Young grew up on the south side of Coldwater in the 1930s and 1940s. He was interviewed by the author for Avondale's 50th anniversary book. As a child, he wasn't allowed to cross the railroad tracks, and it was unheard of to have a black child in the city after the sun went down. He also told Squires that some businesses wouldn't let people of color do business there. After the 1960s, some attitudes changed. Willie was one of those great people who stood up for his neighborhood and wanted to see changes. It was people like Willie that led the way to change. (Courtesy author.)

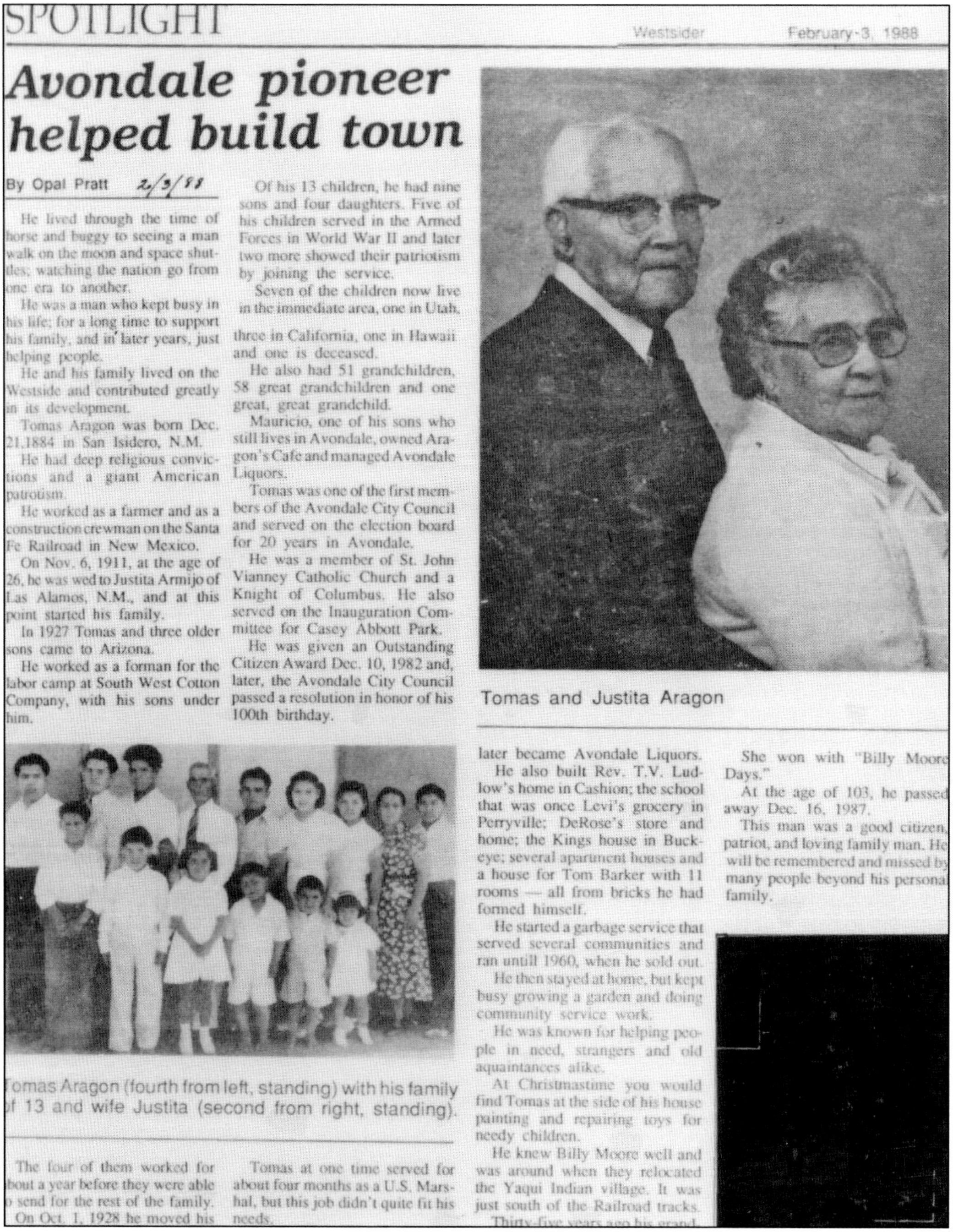

SPOTLIGHT   Westsider   February 3, 1988

Avondale pioneer helped build town

By Opal Pratt 2/3/88

He lived through the time of horse and buggy to seeing a man walk on the moon and space shuttles; watching the nation go from one era to another.

He was a man who kept busy in his life; for a long time to support his family, and in later years, just helping people.

He and his family lived on the Westside and contributed greatly in its development.

Tomas Aragon was born Dec. 21,1884 in San Isidero, N.M.

He had deep religious convictions and a giant American patrotism.

He worked as a farmer and as a construction crewman on the Santa Fe Railroad in New Mexico.

On Nov. 6, 1911, at the age of 26, he was wed to Justita Armijo of Las Alamos, N.M., and at this point started his family.

In 1927 Tomas and three older sons came to Arizona.

He worked as a forman for the labor camp at South West Cotton Company, with his sons under him.

Of his 13 children, he had nine sons and four daughters. Five of his children served in the Armed Forces in World War II and later two more showed their patriotism by joining the service.

Seven of the children now live in the immediate area, one in Utah, three in California, one in Hawaii and one is deceased.

He also had 51 grandchildren, 58 great grandchildren and one great, great grandchild.

Mauricio, one of his sons who still lives in Avondale, owned Aragon's Cafe and managed Avondale Liquors.

Tomas was one of the first members of the Avondale City Council and served on the election board for 20 years in Avondale.

He was a member of St. John Vianney Catholic Church and a Knight of Columbus. He also served on the Inauguration Committee for Casey Abbott Park.

He was given an Outstanding Citizen Award Dec. 10, 1982 and, later, the Avondale City Council passed a resolution in honor of his 100th birthday.

Tomas and Justita Aragon

Tomas Aragon (fourth from left, standing) with his family of 13 and wife Justita (second from right, standing).

The four of them worked for about a year before they were able to send for the rest of the family.

On Oct. 1, 1928 he moved his

Tomas at one time served for about four months as a U.S. Marshal, but this job didn't quite fit his needs.

later became Avondale Liquors.

He also built Rev. T.V. Ludlow's home in Cashion; the school that was once Levi's grocery in Perryville; DeRose's store and home; the Kings house in Buckeye; several apartment houses and a house for Tom Barker with 11 rooms — all from bricks he had formed himself.

He started a garbage service that served several communities and ran untill 1960, when he sold out.

He then stayed at home, but kept busy growing a garden and doing community service work.

He was known for helping people in need, strangers and old aquaintances alike.

At Christmastime you would find Tomas at the side of his house painting and repairing toys for needy children.

He knew Billy Moore well and was around when they relocated the Yaqui Indian village. It was just south of the Railroad tracks.

Thirty-five years ago his grand-

She won with "Billy Moore Days."

At the age of 103, he passed away Dec. 16, 1987.

This man was a good citizen, patriot, and loving family man. He will be remembered and missed by many people beyond his personal family.

From Avondale's beginnings, the Aragon families were always pillars of the community. Tomas Aragon built many businesses and homes using adobe he crafted from desert soil. Tom dug by hand the clay and mixed it with straw to a certain consistency that only he knew from his years of experience. Tom then shoveled the wet clay in wooden forms to dry in the sun. The dried blocks were dumped onto a bare patch of land to season and were ready to use when needed. Tom never ran out of dirt for his adobe, for Avondale had plenty of clay and sunshine. (Courtesy City of Avondale.)

Chuck Lakin is quite the poet as well as a cowboy and businessman. His famous poem—titled "Flies"—talks about the pesky critters and how they wreaked havoc on farmers and their livestock but that the worst kind of fly of all is time and how it flies. This picture was taken during the 50th anniversary of Avondale where Chuck, the guest speaker, shared his poems with the crowd. (Courtesy City of Avondale.)

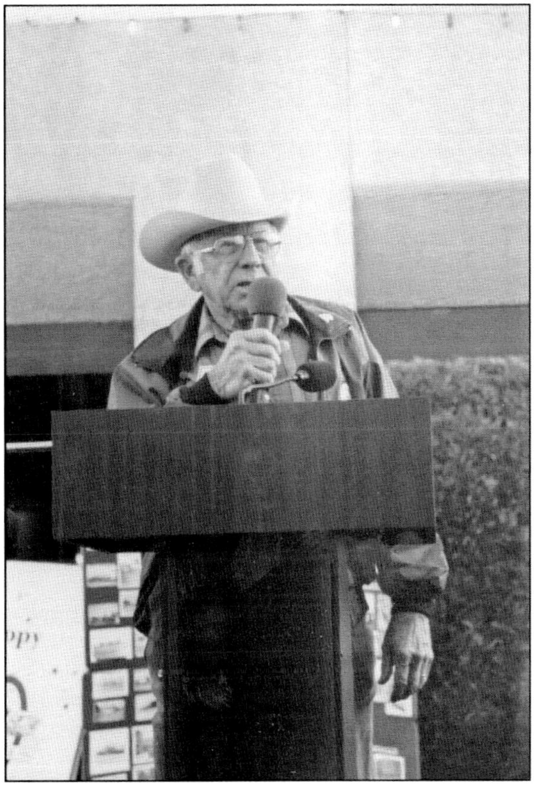

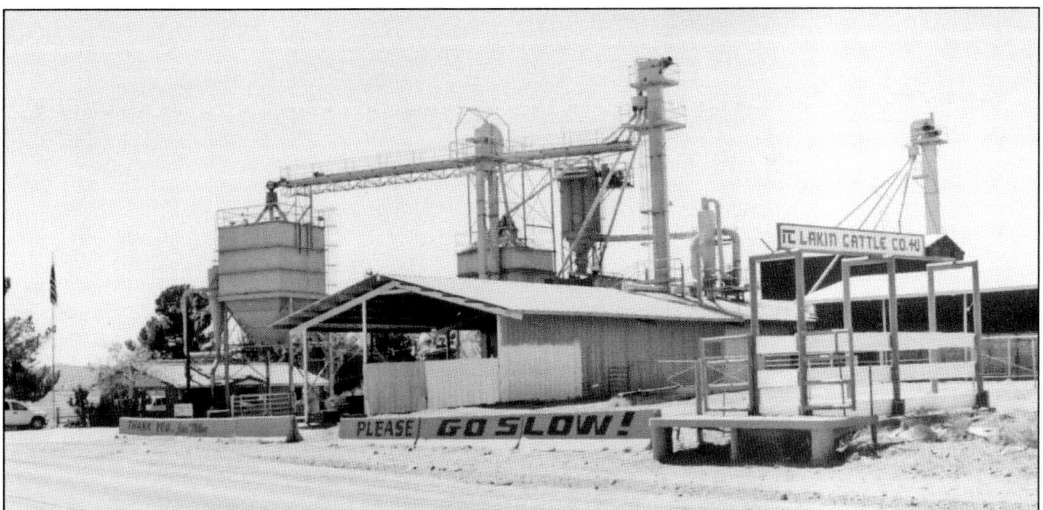

Chuck Lakin came to Arizona aboard the Atchison, Topeka, and Santa Fe in 1921. Chuck attended Phoenix Union High School and the University of Arizona. In 1943, Lakin entered the U.S. Army and got his commission at Fort Riley, Kansas, in the U.S. Cavalry. After the war, Lakin came back to Arizona and to his father's ranch in 1946. He and Eddie Miller had the alkali, "salty" land cleared of desert vegetation and with determination and hard work planted Bermuda grass over and over. Over time, the Bermuda grass absorbed the salt and made the land valuable and productive. Chuck conquered the "Great Alkali Wars" 40 acres at a time. (Courtesy author.)

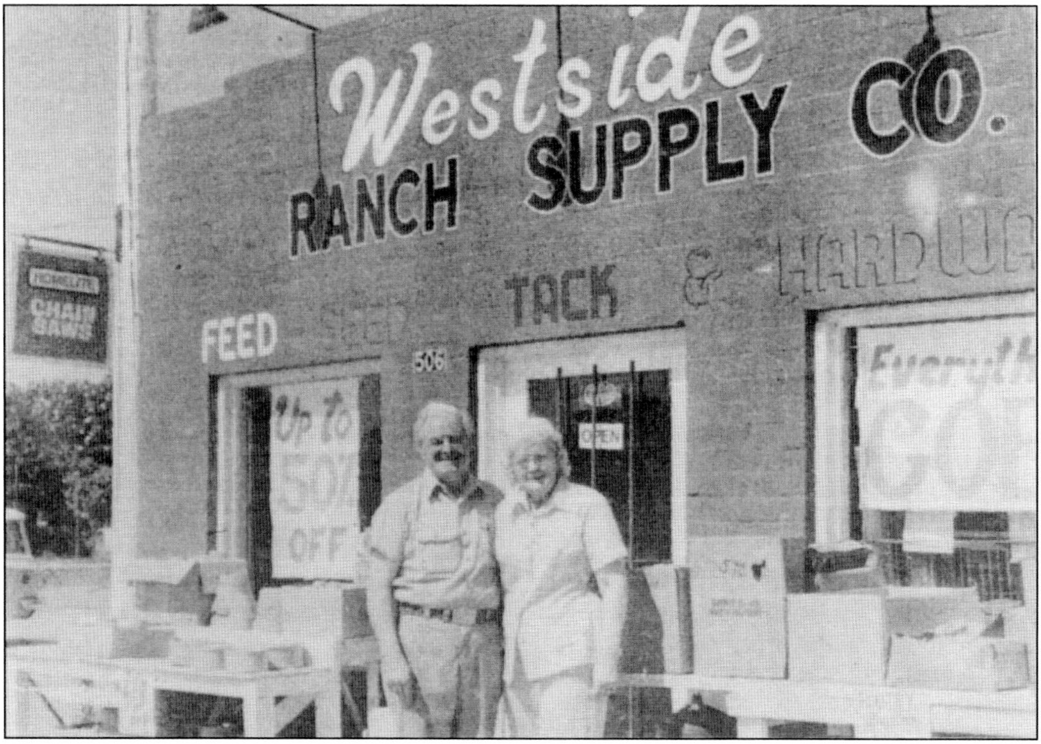

The Brinkers were active citizens in Avondale organizations and activities. The citizens appreciated them so much that a street was named in their honor. (Courtesy City of Avondale.)

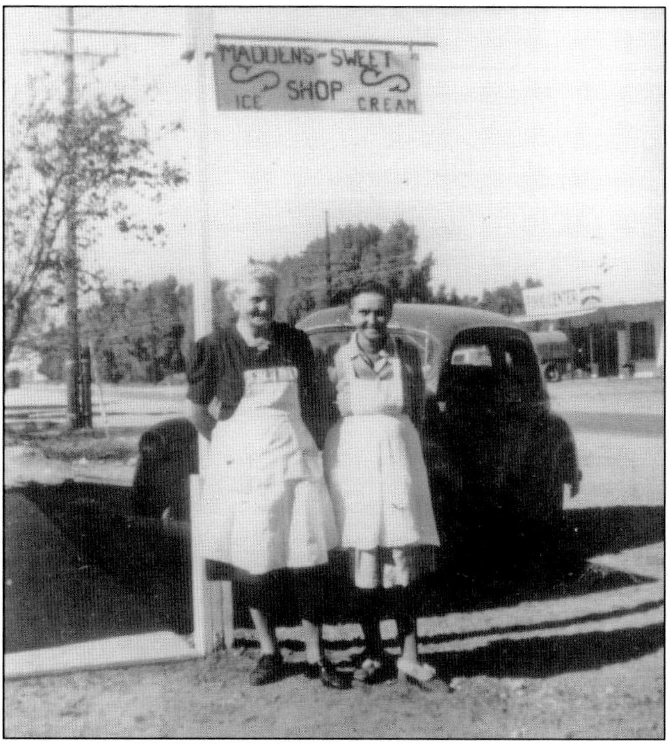

Madden's Sweet Shop was run by Effie Victoria Madden; she sold ice cream, candy, and other sweet goodies. According to the Madden family, the business operated in the late 1930s or early 1940s. The shop wasn't on Madden but at Western Avenue and Second Street across from Jeff's Food Fair. The Maddens came from Arkansas to Cashion in the 1930s, then on to Avondale proper. "Grandpa" Madden worked with the local WPA. He had a street named in his honor when Avondale was young and newly formed. (Courtesy City of Avondale.)

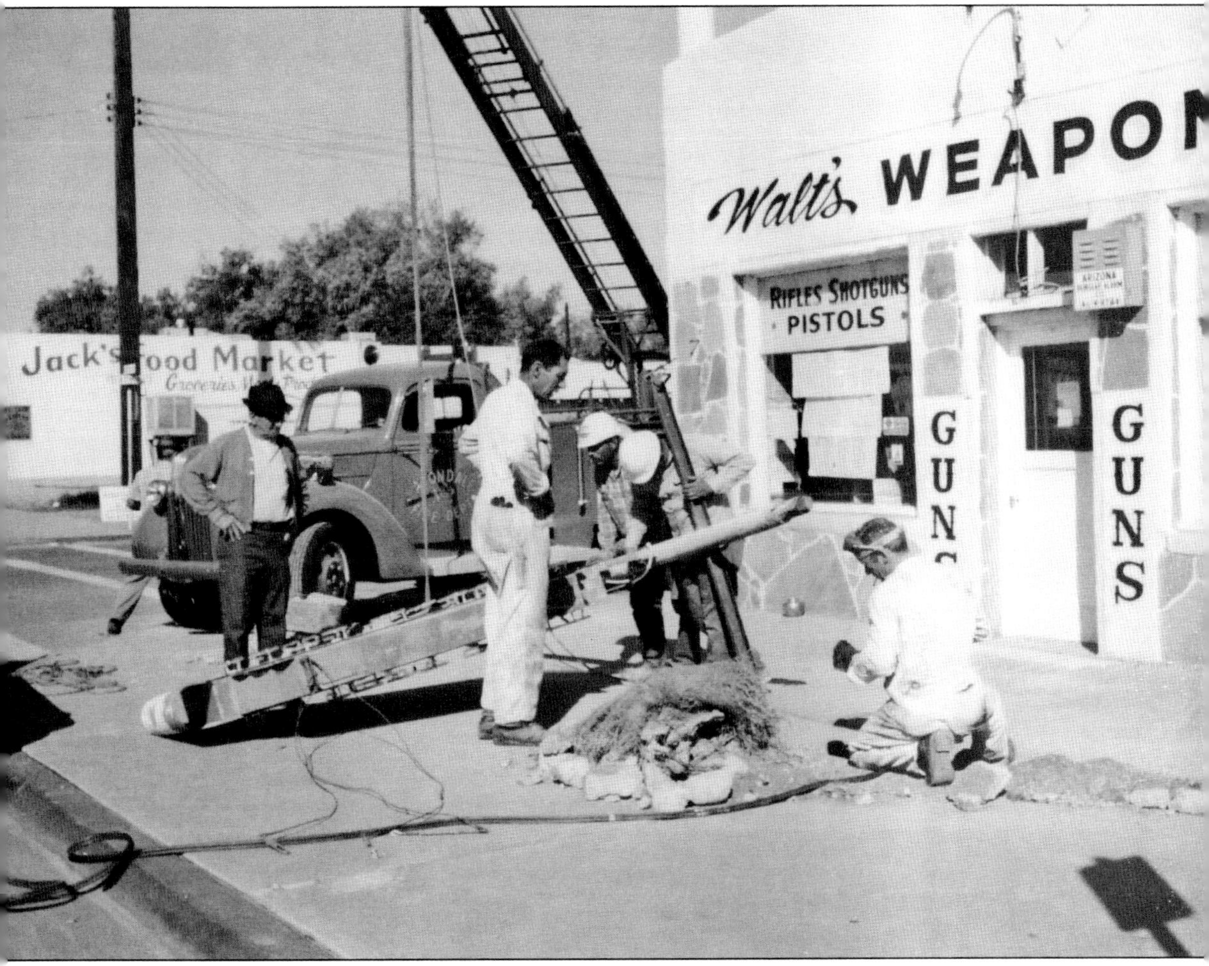

Walt's Weapons was owned by Walter Lonergan, who was married to Connie. Walt was on the board of directors for the chamber of commerce and a member of the Black Vest Gang, a community-minded organization. As a member of the gang, he and others were instrumental in obtaining a headstone for Billy Moore. Walt also provided the blank shells and black powder during the Billy Moore festivities. (Courtesy City of Avondale.)

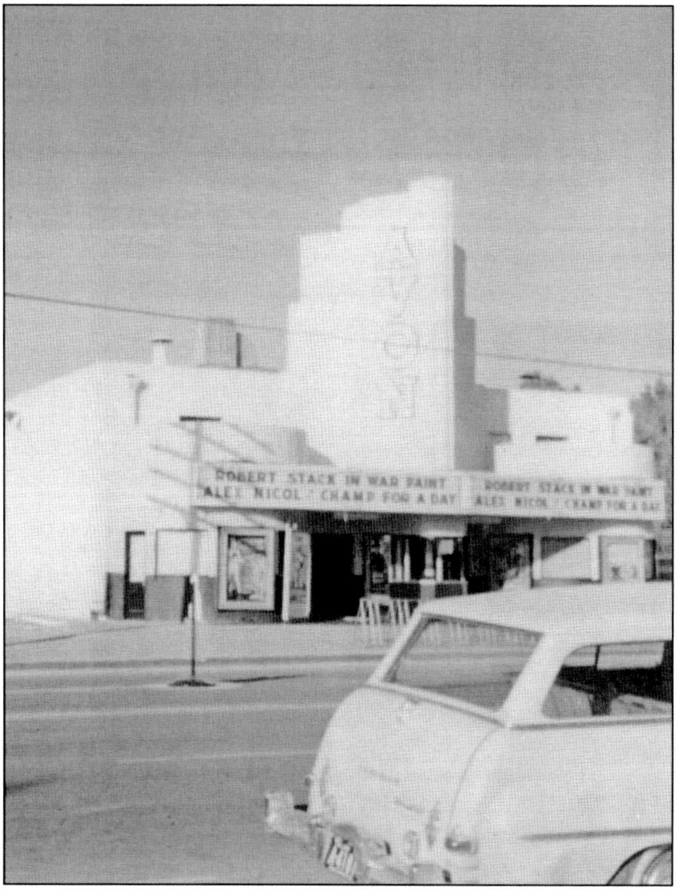

The old Avondale Theater had various uses over the years. Of course, the first was as a theater, but at the moment, it is a reception hall used for weddings and other gatherings. In the past, the movie theater would provide hours of entertainment. There were no televisions or video games, so evenings and Saturdays were often spent watching the big screen. The Schneider family later leased the theater to Moe's and later Jeff's Food Fair. The marquee features Robert Stack starring in *War Paint* and Alex Nicol starring in *Champ for a Day*. (Courtesy City of Avondale.)

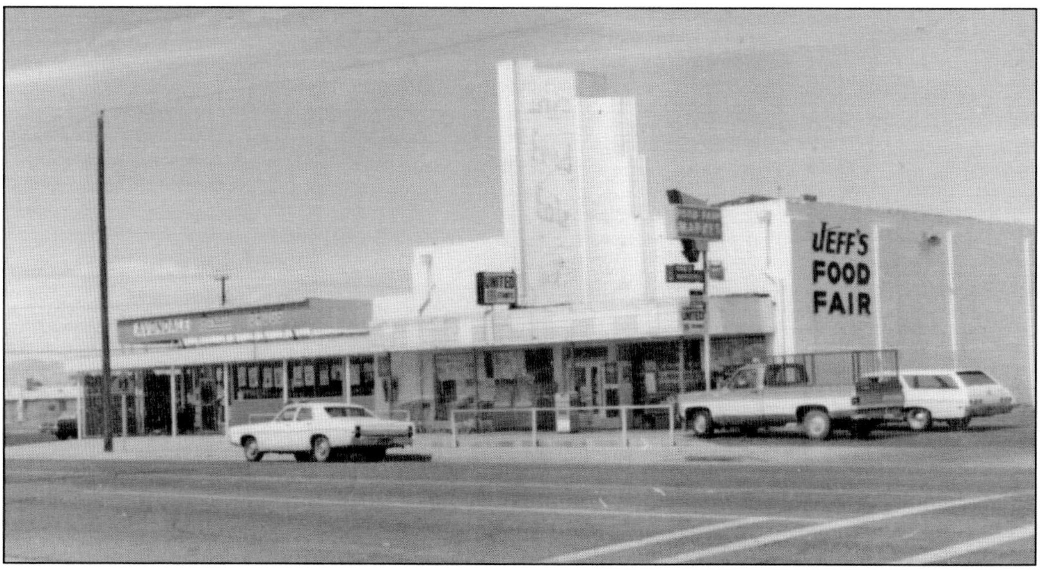

This is how the old movie theater looked in later years. After it was Jeff's Food Fair, the Kings used it for a department store. From there, an alternative school leased the building. It subsequently became the VFW Hall and today is a reception hall. (Courtesy City of Avondale.)

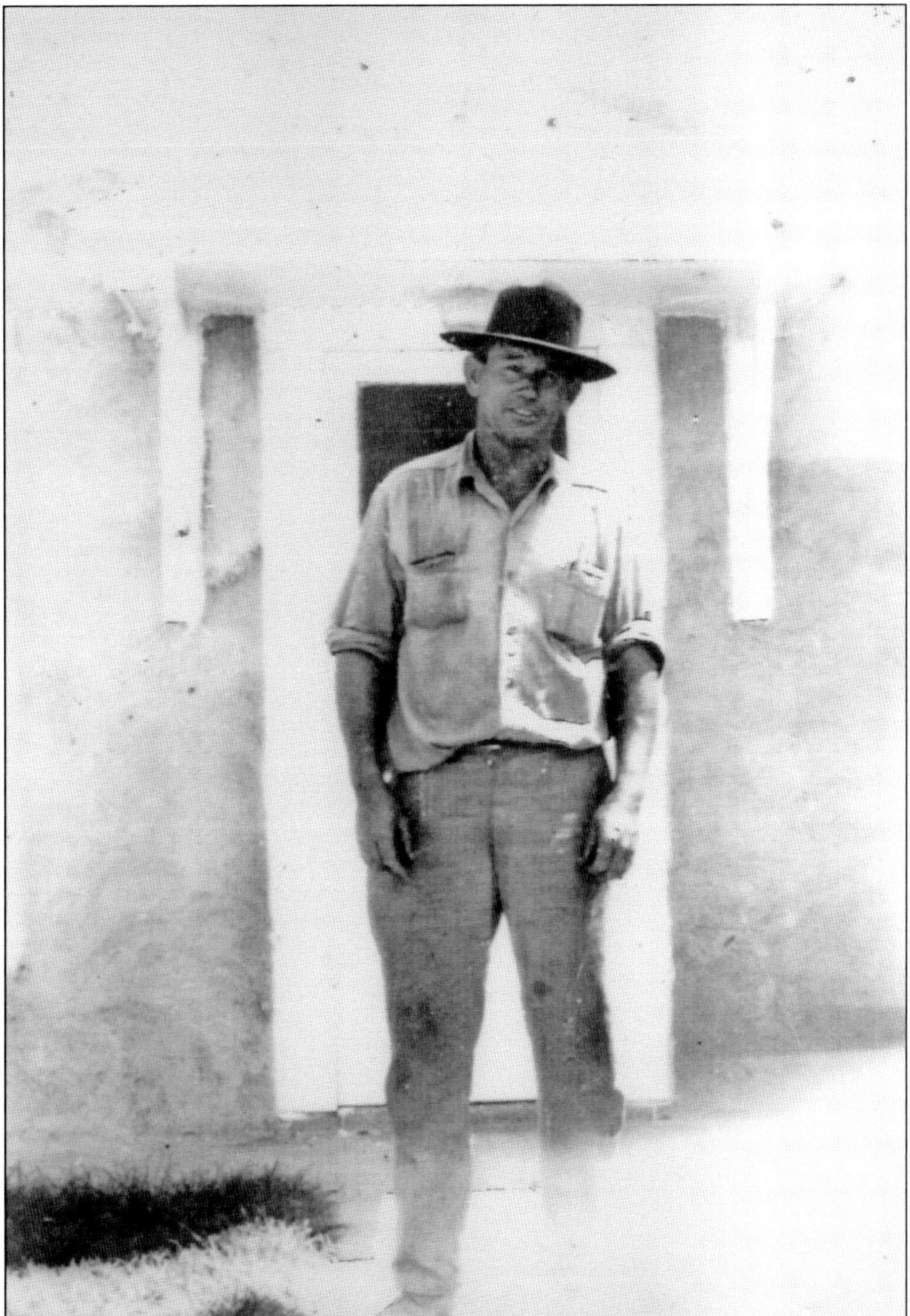

John Summers was born in 1924 in Texas and died October 19, 2007. He spent his early years following the crops with his parents, who settled in Avondale in the 1940s. He served in the army in World War II and met his wife, Louise, in Arkansas. They had two children—Courtney "Corky" and Pat. Pat would tell stories of how his father loved to buy and trade things, and it wasn't uncommon to come home after school and find out that their hi-fi had been traded for a stereo or that there was a new television in the house taken in trade. (Courtesy City of Avondale.)

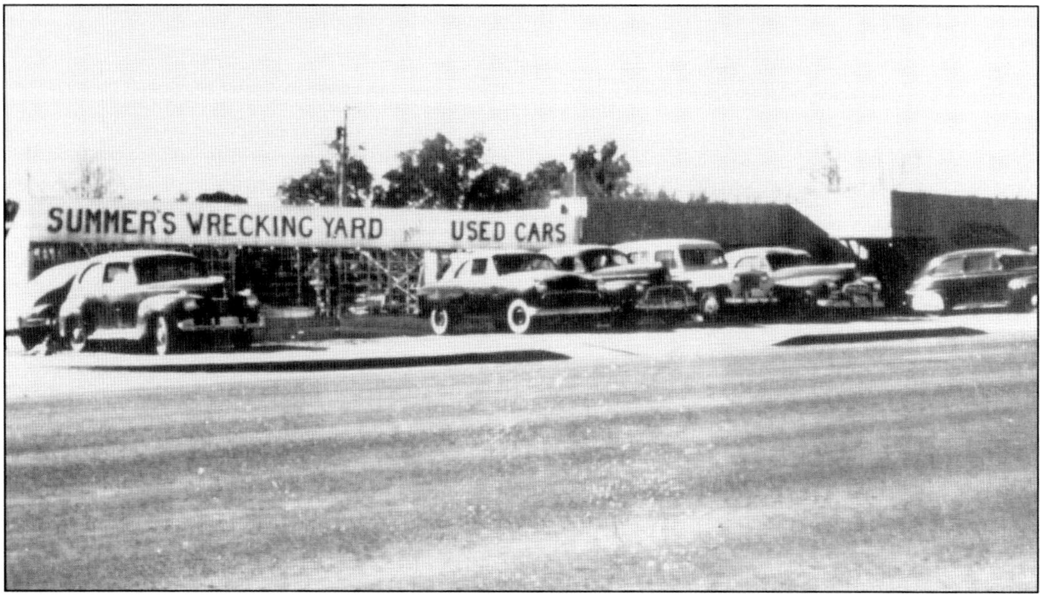

Johnny Summers' Wrecking Yard was all Avondale's adolescent boys could dream about. They wondered, "When can I get my license, and do I have enough money saved up to buy my first car?" John's junk yard was where most of the teenagers purchased their dream cars. Of course, they needed parts and his wrecking yard was a first-class place to purchase them. Johnny's was known throughout the West Valley. He did right by his customers, young or old. (Courtesy City of Avondale.)

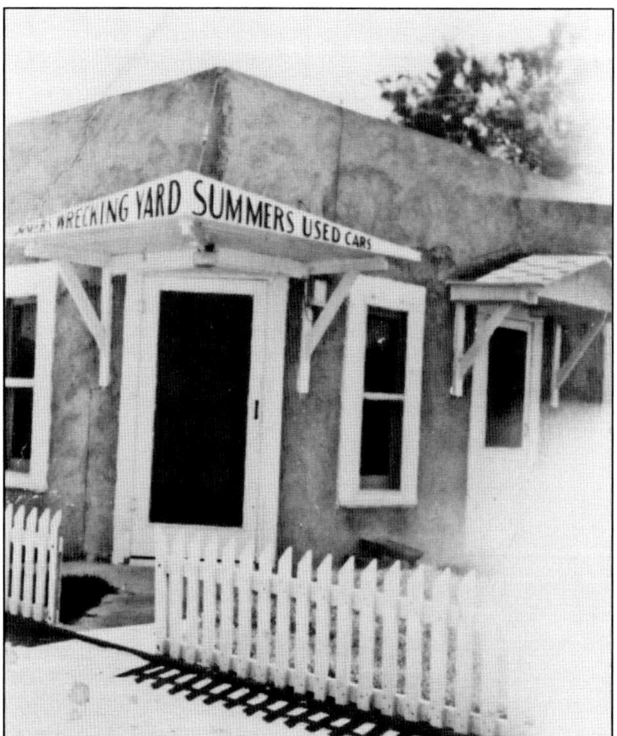

The first Summers' Wrecking Yard was on Western Avenue where the new library is being constructed. It was owned and operated by John's father, Courtney Summers. Johnny later took the business over and moved it to Dysart Road next to his friend E. G. Gage's garage. (Courtesy City of Avondale.)

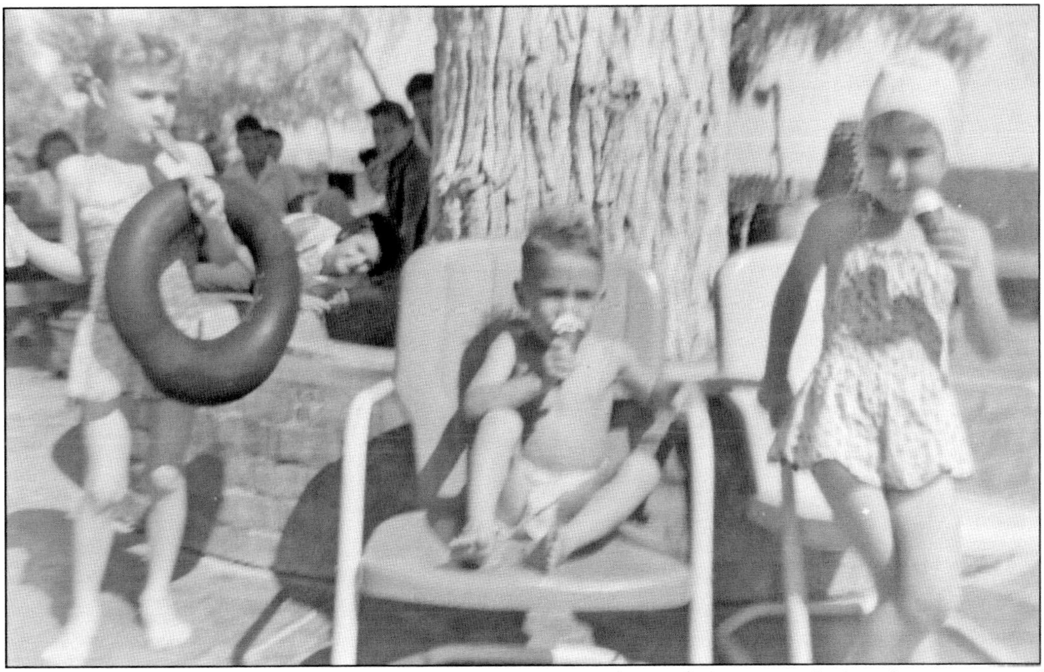

In 1956, the Schulkie and Vanosdell children spent many leisurely hours poolside. The Green Leaf swimming pool was the place to be when summertime arrived. Kids from all over the valley would come to swim in the icy cold water. It was pumped straight from the ground into a cement-lined pool. Large trees and green lawns provided perfect places to picnic. After a cool swim, nothing tasted better than an ice cream or some candy. (Courtesy Sally Schulkie Marcotte.)

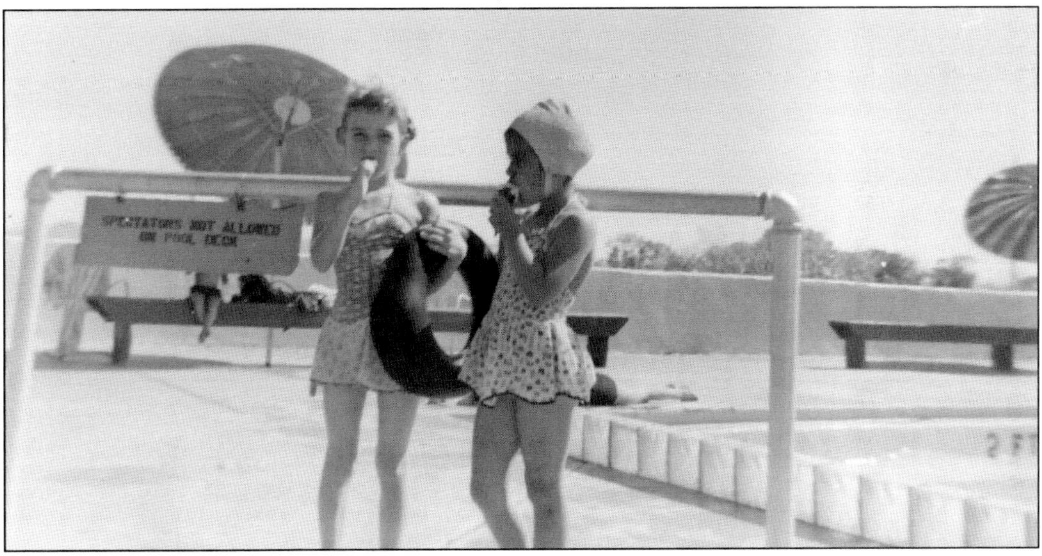

Glass blocks lined one end of the cement swimming pool at Green Leaf in Avondale. There were metal umbrellas that could be adjusted for a little more shade, and many girls and women wore swimming caps. The caps snapped under the chin and they never kept your hair dry, but that was the style of the day. This was back when mothers always said not to go swimming right after eating; there was to be a 30-minute waiting period. The girls are Susan Schulkie and Pam Vanosdell. (Courtesy Sally Schulkie Marcotte.)

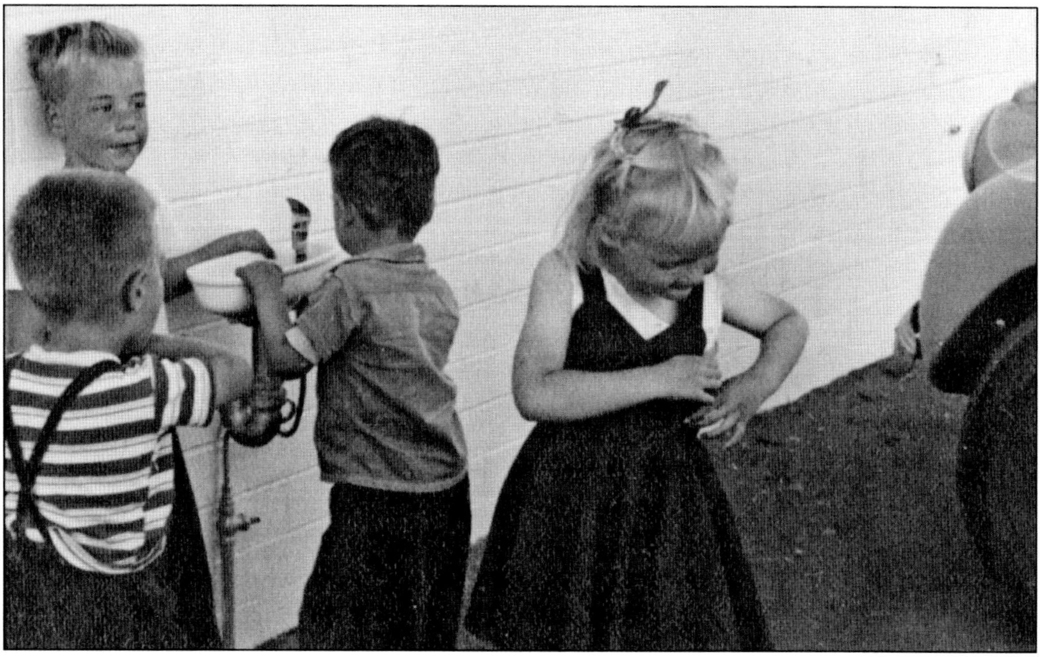

Adjustments, adjustments—a girl has to always look her best. This picture was taken at an Avondale drinking fountain at the side of an Avondale ice cream shop. There wasn't a better treat on a blazing hot summer day. Most people had no refrigeration. A fan propped up in a window with a gunny sack dripping water from the back was the appliance used. (Courtesy author.)

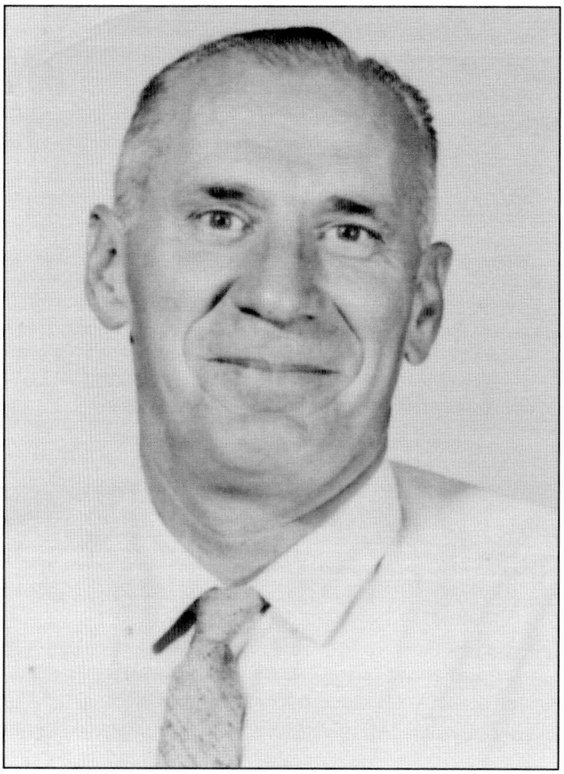

Eldred Underdown was the superintendent of Littleton Elementary School District in the 1940s and 1950s. He had many hats; not only was he the superintendent, but he also served as the principal and school bus driver. (Courtesy Littleton School District.)

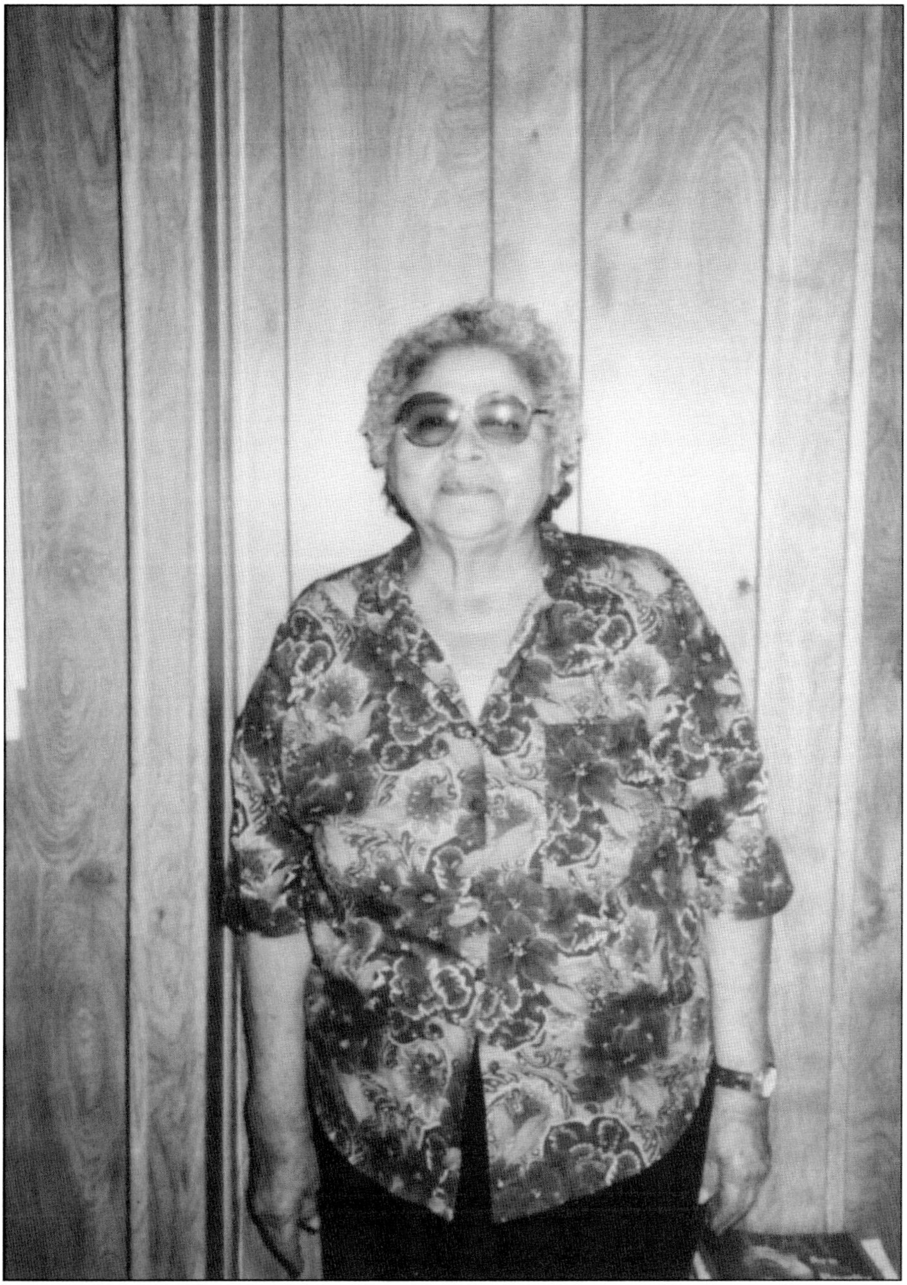

Oralia Lopez was born in Chandler, Arizona, in 1924. She is the mother of Marie Rogers Lopez, the current mayor of Avondale. Oralia was raised in Camp 52, which was west of Litchfield and just south of Indian School Road. She spoke of mules and oxen used to plow the fields and how early in the morning, the men would get everything ready to go out in the fields to work. She remembered washing clothes in large tubs and warming the water with a mesquite fire since the desert was all around and wood was easy to find. The camps had wooden structures with no insulation, so cardboard and paper were put on the inside walls to keep out the winds and weather. Oralia's daughter has become the second female mayor of Avondale. Oralia has passed on, but she and other pioneers have left their footprints in the past. (Courtesy author.)

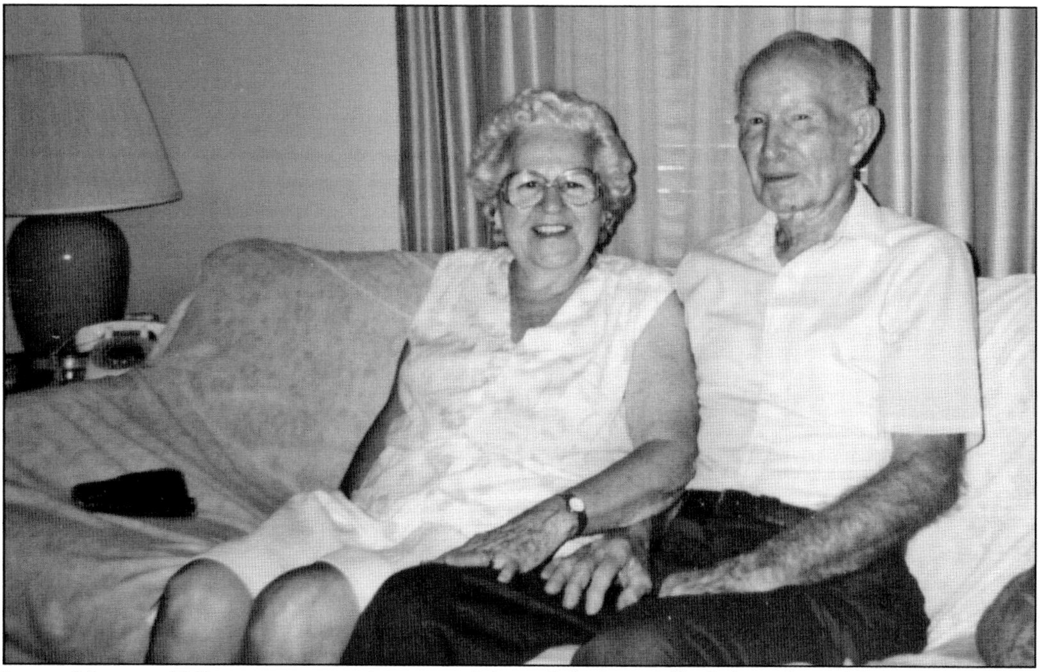

Joe and Juanita Hill were very much a part of Avondale. Joe Hill's father cleared land with mules; he called it mule-power not horsepower. Joe was a native Arizonian. He recalls the small stream of water trickling down the Agua Fria year-round. There were towering cottonwoods and large willows where families and Sunday school picnics were held. Joe reminisced about children digging in the sand till they reached water, as the water table was very shallow. Billy Moore did the same thing; he dug a cool water well and created a stage stop. (Courtesy author.)

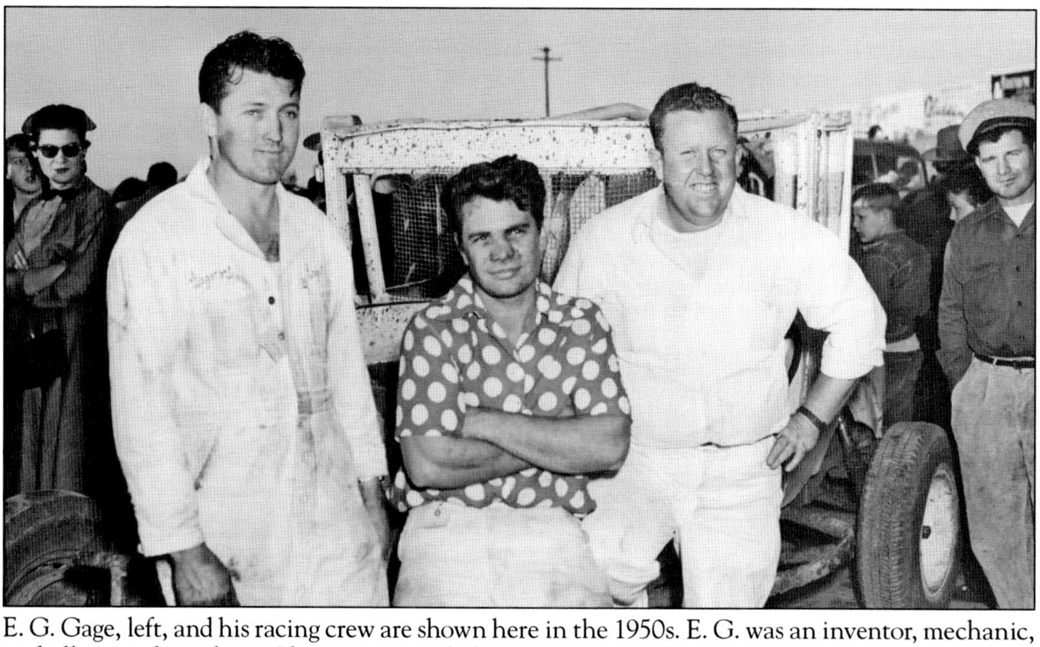

E. G. Gage, left, and his racing crew are shown here in the 1950s. E. G. was an inventor, mechanic, and all-around good guy. If someone needed a part fabricated or worked on, E. G was the go-to man. (Courtesy E. G. Gage.)

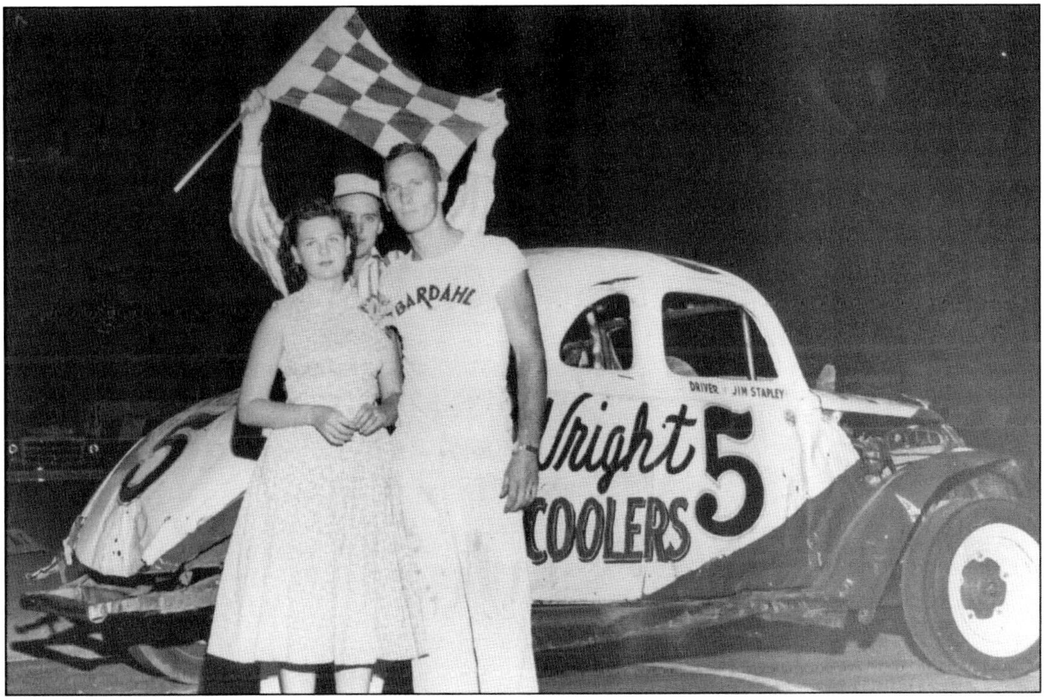

E. G. and Barbara Gage loved to race modified stock cars at a track located at the base of South Mountain. The daredevil track was in use before Manzanita Speedway was built. (Courtesy E. G. Gage.)

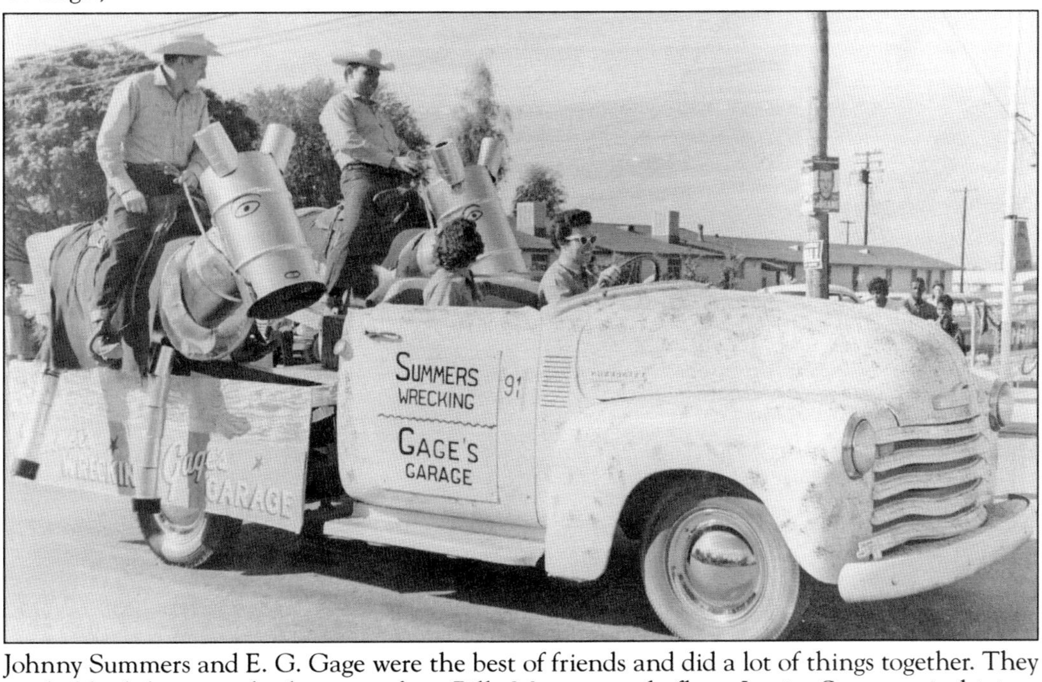

Johnny Summers and E. G. Gage were the best of friends and did a lot of things together. They used old oil drums and other parts for a Billy Moore parade float. Louise Summers is driving; Barbara Gage is in the passenger seat; and John Summers (left) and E. G. Gage (right) are in the back. (Courtesy E. G. Gage.)

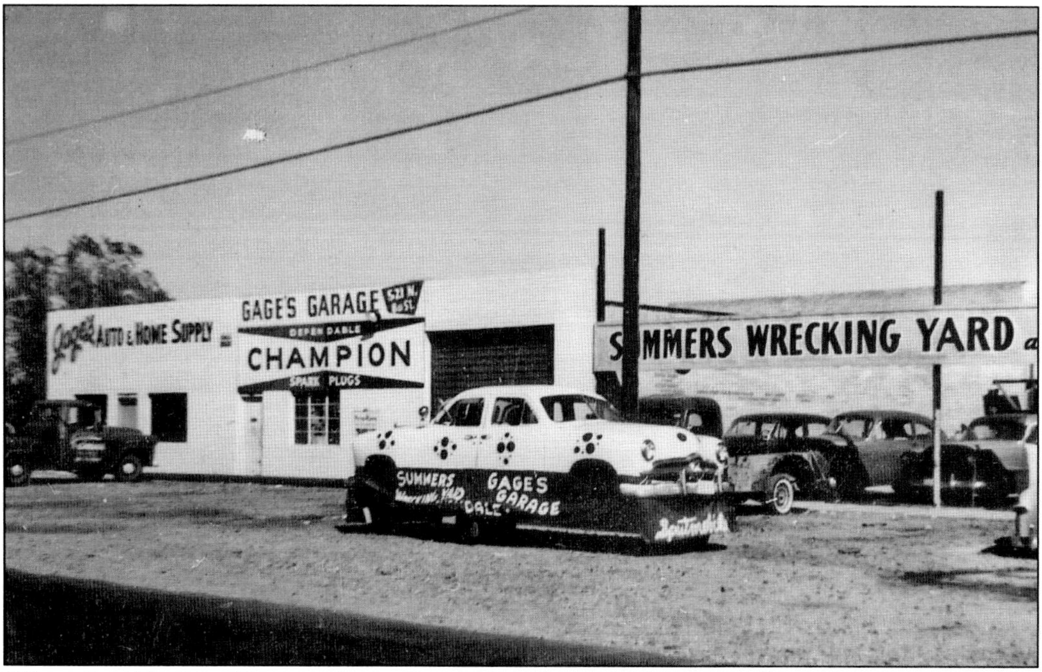

Where Paul Faith's office is today on Dysart Road was the business of Gage's Garage, and next door was Johnny Summers' Wrecking Yard. Together they concocted a "two-way car": it could go backward or forward and even sideways. The car was a hit during the Billy Moore Days parades. (Courtesy Pat and Corky Summer.)

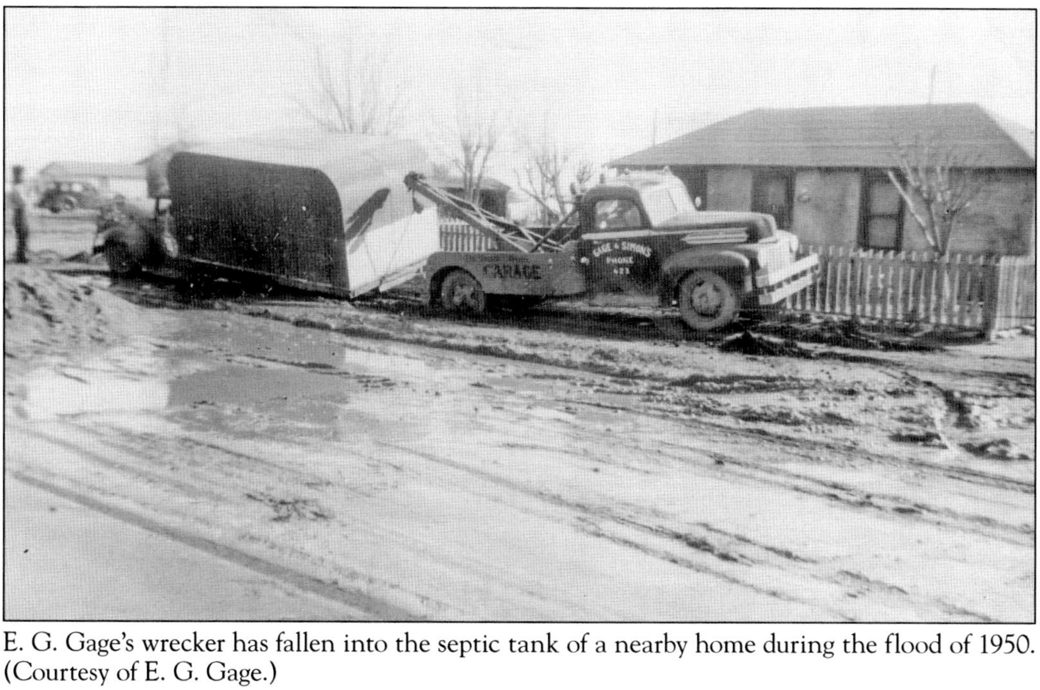

E. G. Gage's wrecker has fallen into the septic tank of a nearby home during the flood of 1950. (Courtesy of E. G. Gage.)

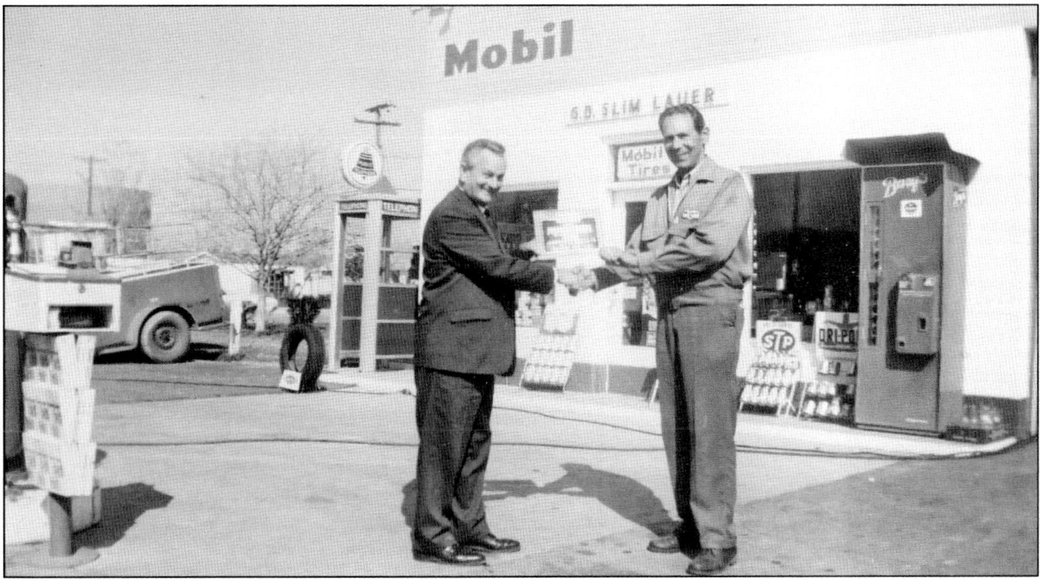

Slim Lauer's Mobil Station was one of Avondale's many gas stations. Cars were given gas and checked under the hood. The vintage Barq's Root Beer soda pop machine had a device built into the front to take the bottle cap off. Kids loved to collect the caps and attach them to their clothing with the cork lining. The public telephone booth was often used for emergencies given that mobile phones were not invented yet. (Courtesy *West Valley View* and the Lauer family.)

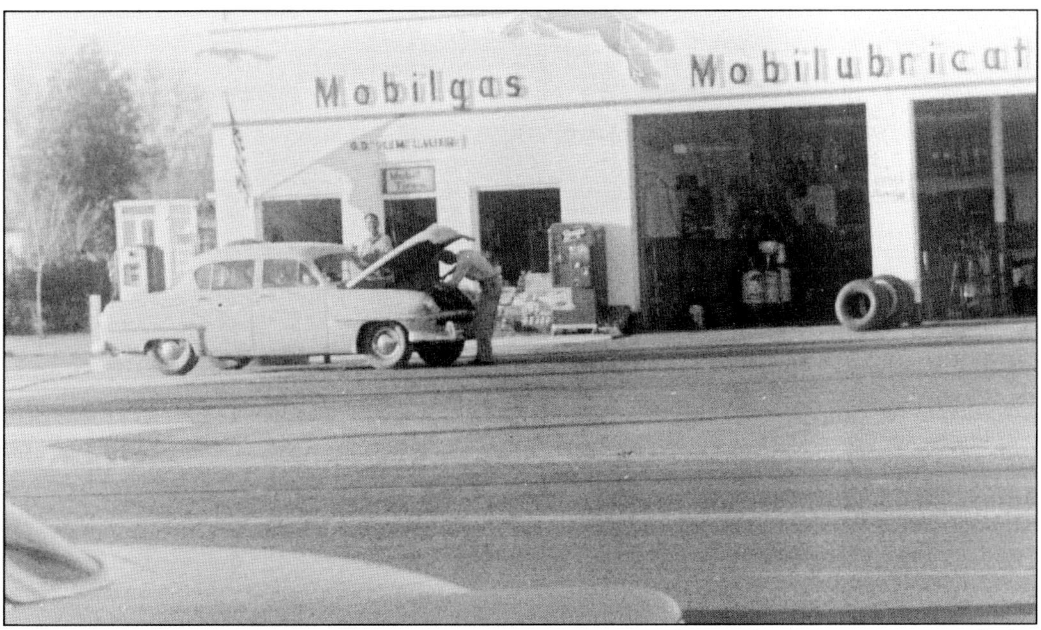

At Slim Lauer's gas station, patrons received full service. The attendant is checking a customer's oil after he has just washed the front windshield. (Courtesy *West Valley View* and the Lauer family.)

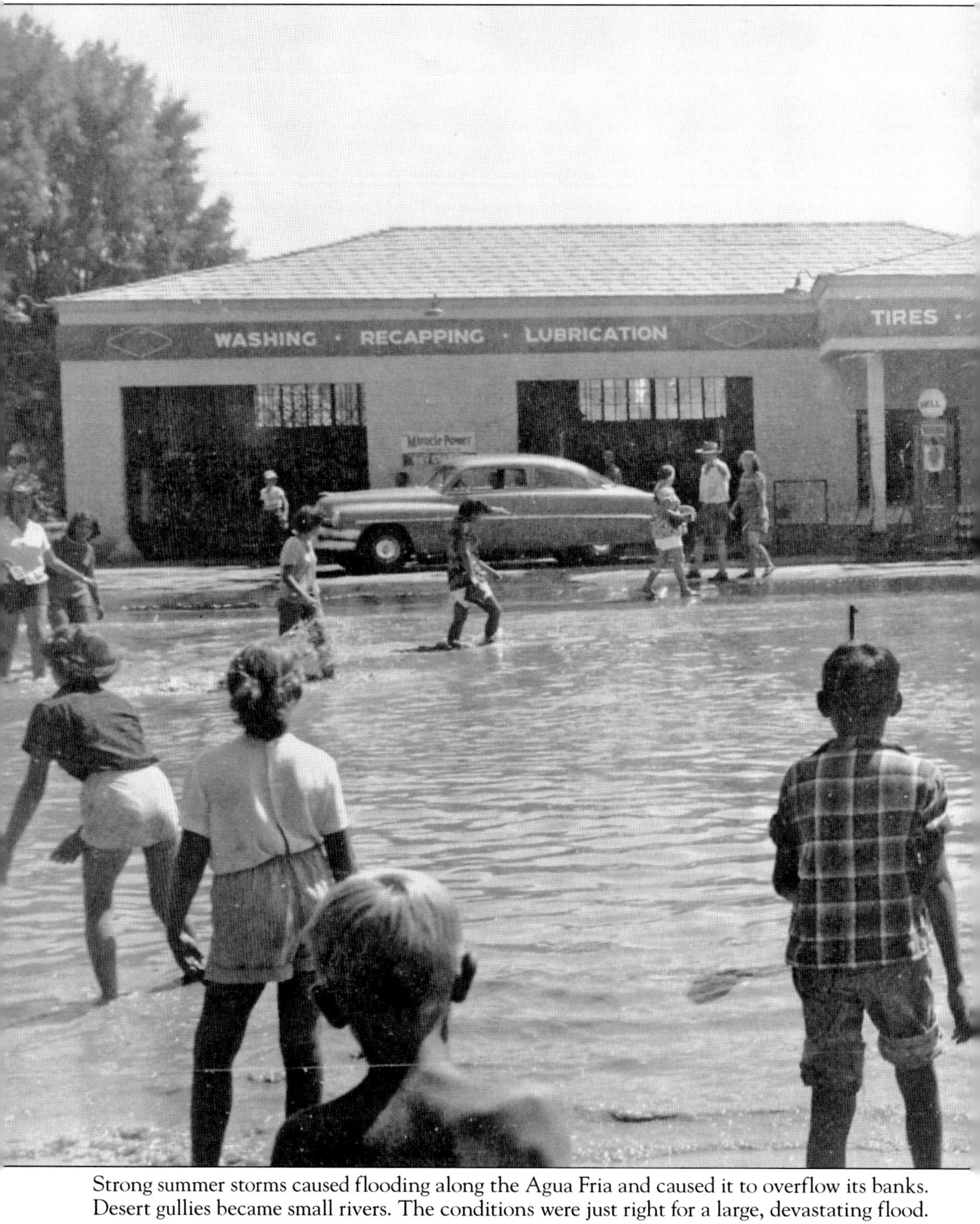

Strong summer storms caused flooding along the Agua Fria and caused it to overflow its banks. Desert gullies became small rivers. The conditions were just right for a large, devastating flood.

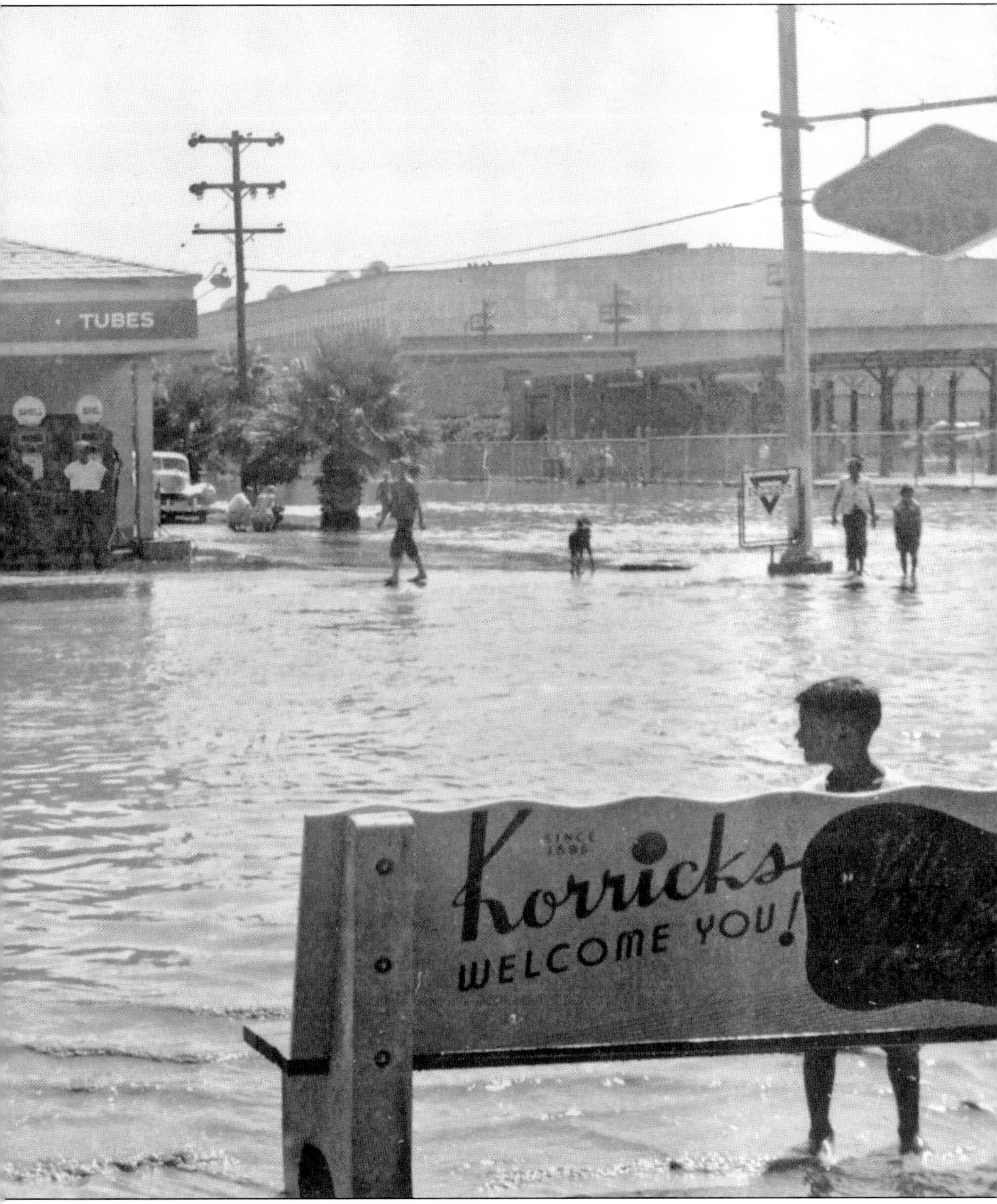

(Courtesy *West Valley View.*)

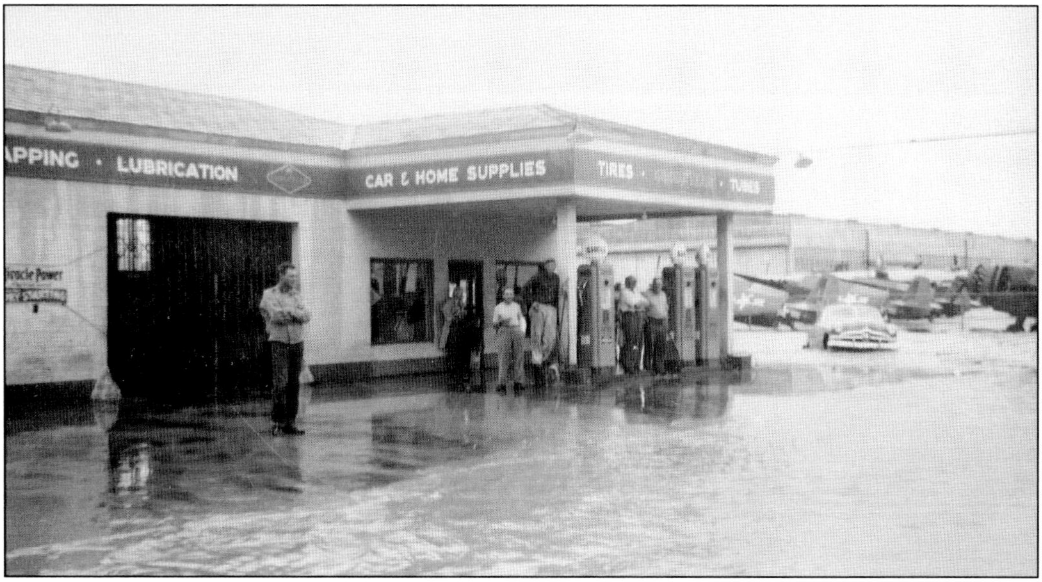

The Goodyear Tire Shop was flooded by way of the Agua Fria River and an earthen dam constructed along a canal north of Goodyear and Avondale. Water ran down Western Avenue and looked like a continuous lake from Avondale to Goodyear and beyond. (Courtesy *West Valley View.*)

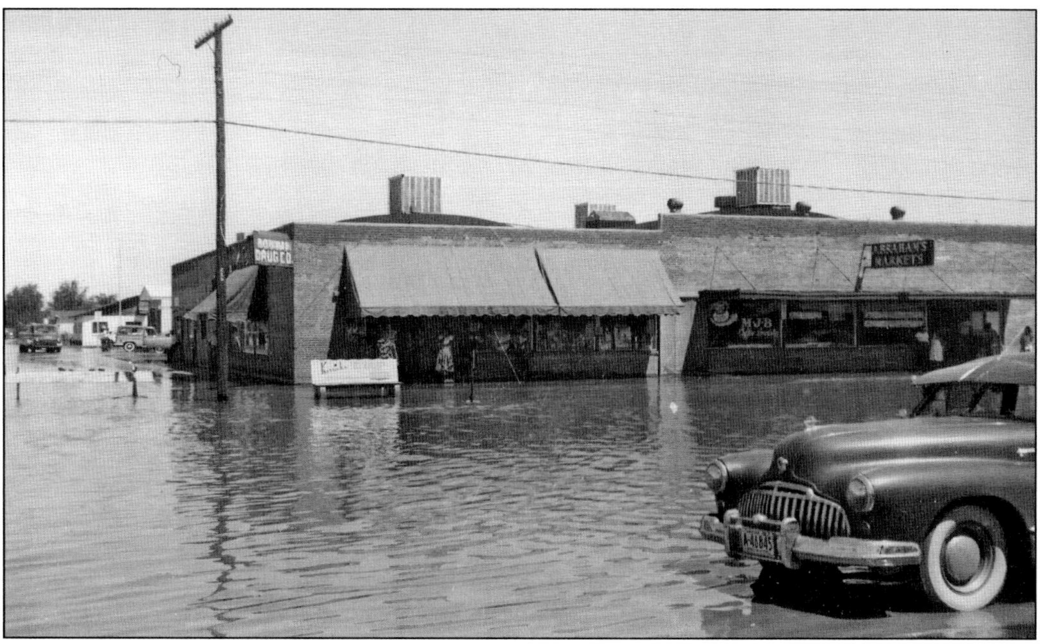

The flood of 1950 connected Goodyear and Avondale through a tragedy of Mother Nature. Citizens of both cities pitched in to clean up the rubbish and mud left by the flood. (Courtesy *West Valley View.*)

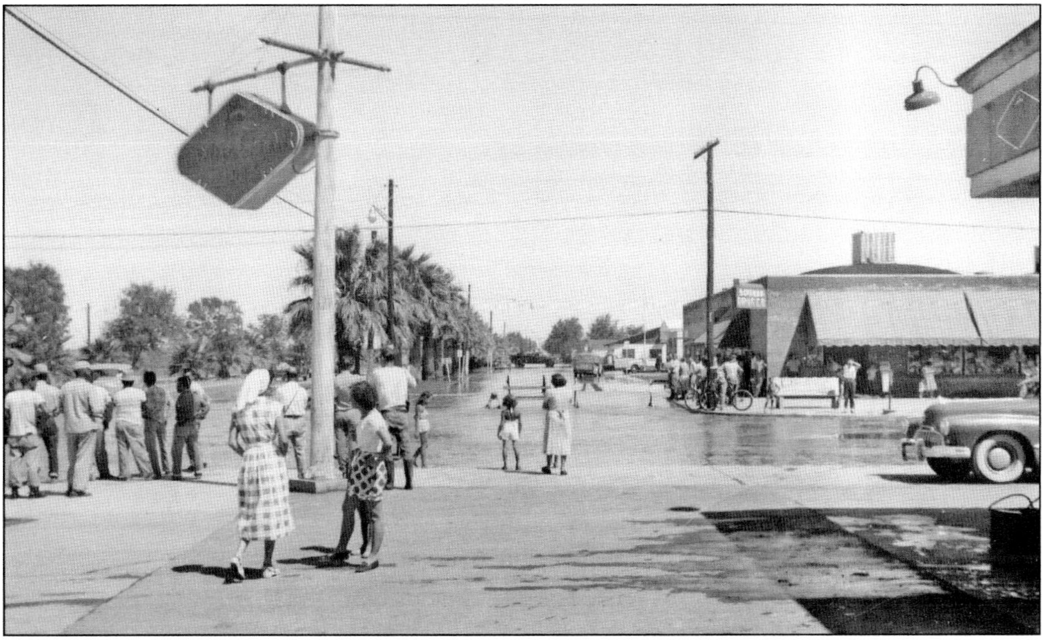

Avondale and Goodyear were not prepared for the great flood of 1950. The palm trees are much taller today and have lived through a good deal of history on Litchfield Road. (Courtesy *West Valley View.*)

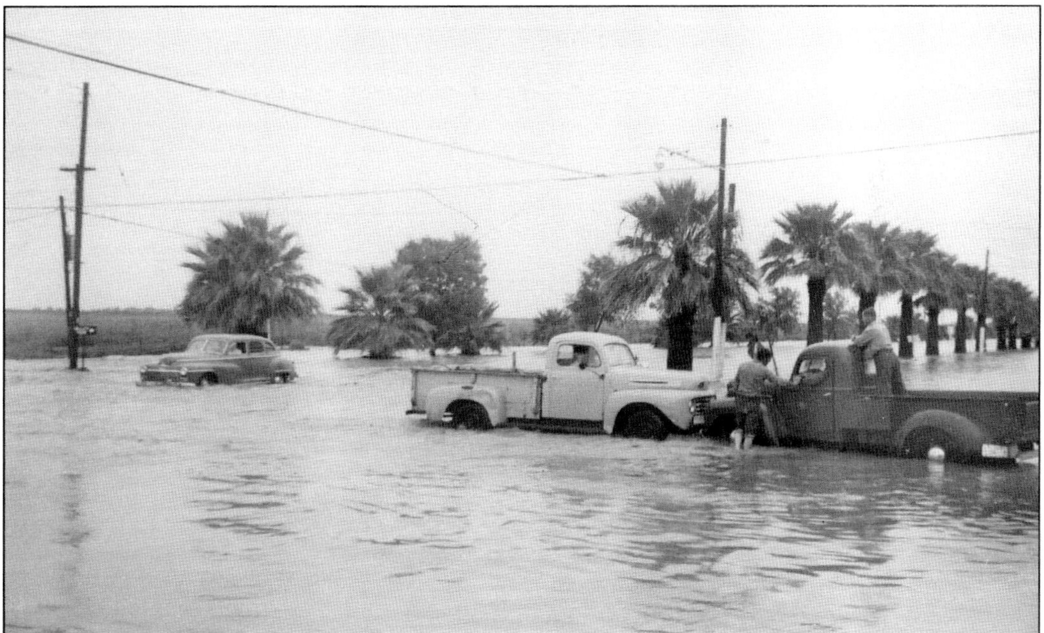

The old automobiles and trucks had a hard time traversing through the instant river. If water reached the distributor, the engine would shut down, the spark plug wire would short out, and the car would come to a halt. (Courtesy *West Valley View.*)

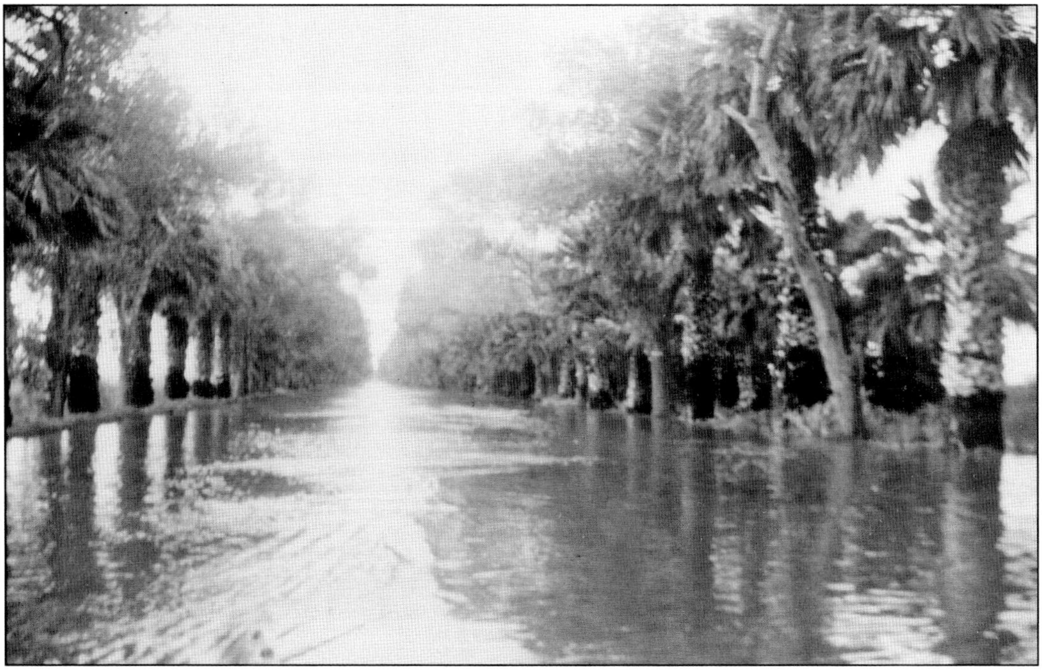

Litchfield Road was devastated after the 1950 flood. There were cottonwood, olive, and citrus trees planted on both sides of the road, and in places, the treetops touched from both sides of the road, making a tree tunnel. Oftentimes, one could see families picnicking under the shade. (Courtesy *West Valley View.*)

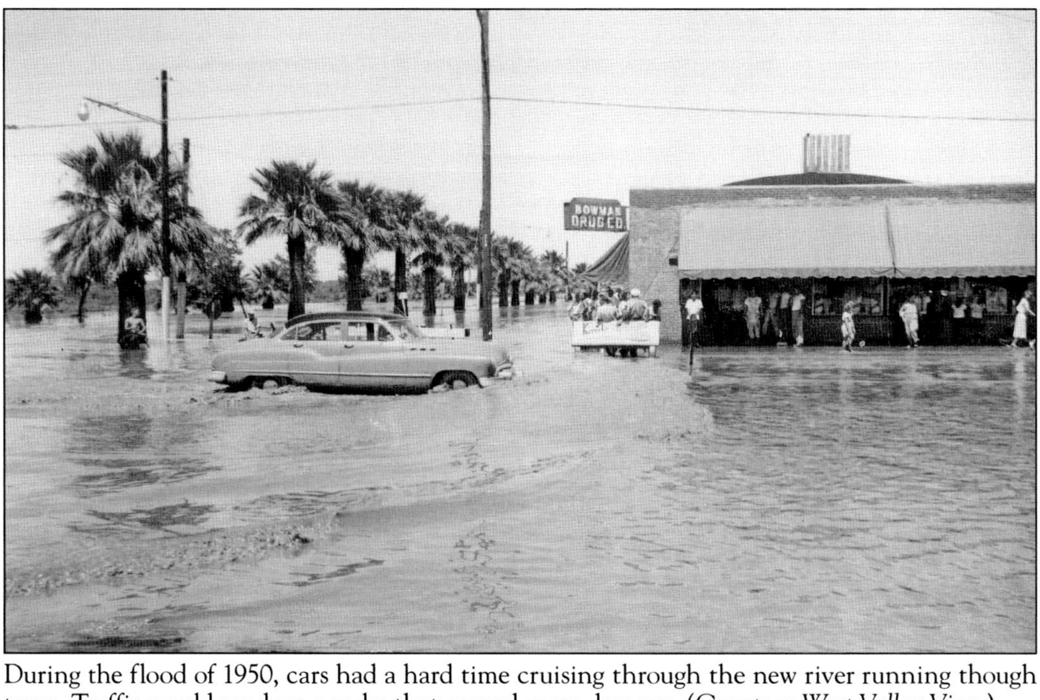

During the flood of 1950, cars had a hard time cruising through the new river running though town. Traffic would produce a wake that caused more damage. (Courtesy *West Valley View.*)

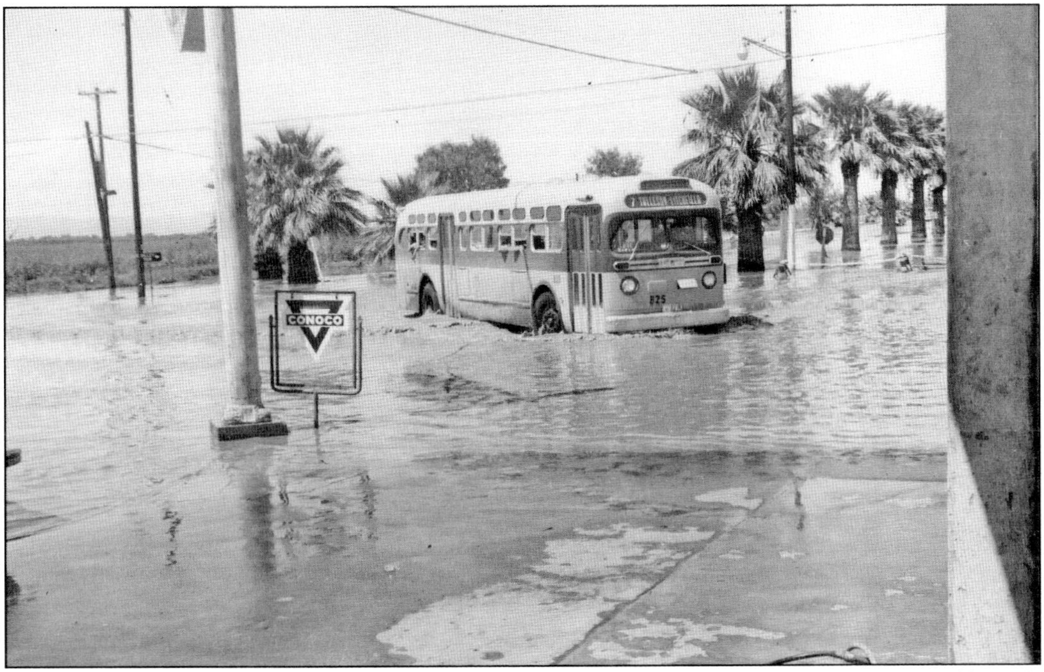

A bus route went from Tolleson to Goodyear and ran through Avondale. Passengers could catch a ride all the way down to the big city of Phoenix. A diesel bus could run through water with ease because there is no spark required to ignite the engine. (Courtesy *West Valley View*.)

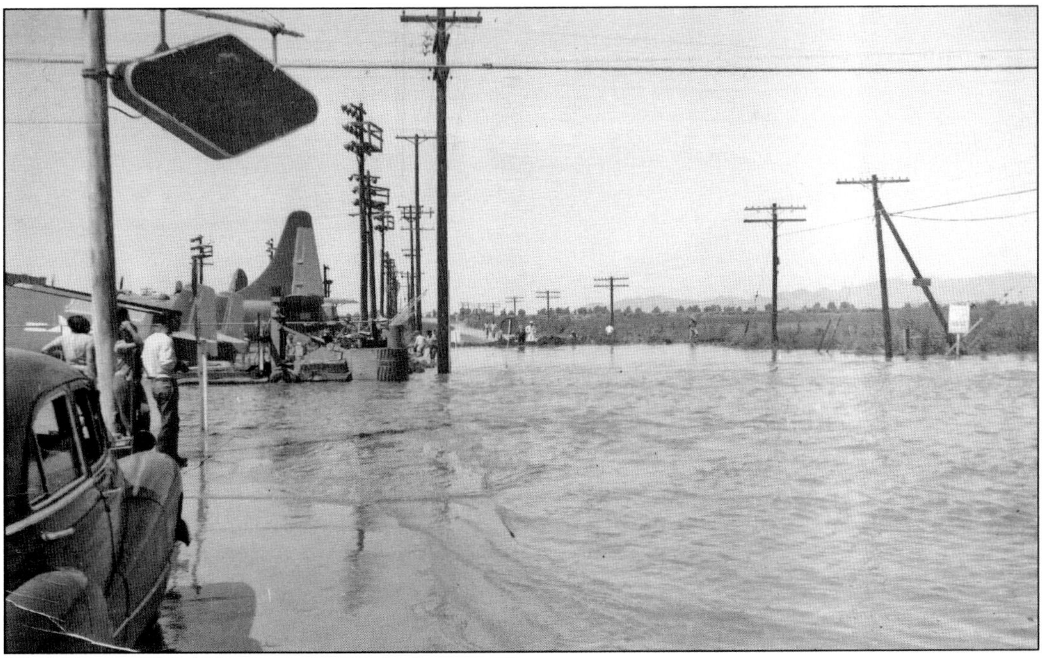

Just west on Yuma Road, a crew of many sailors were used to erect a temporary dam to salvage the navy base during the 1950s flood. (Courtesy *West Valley View*.)

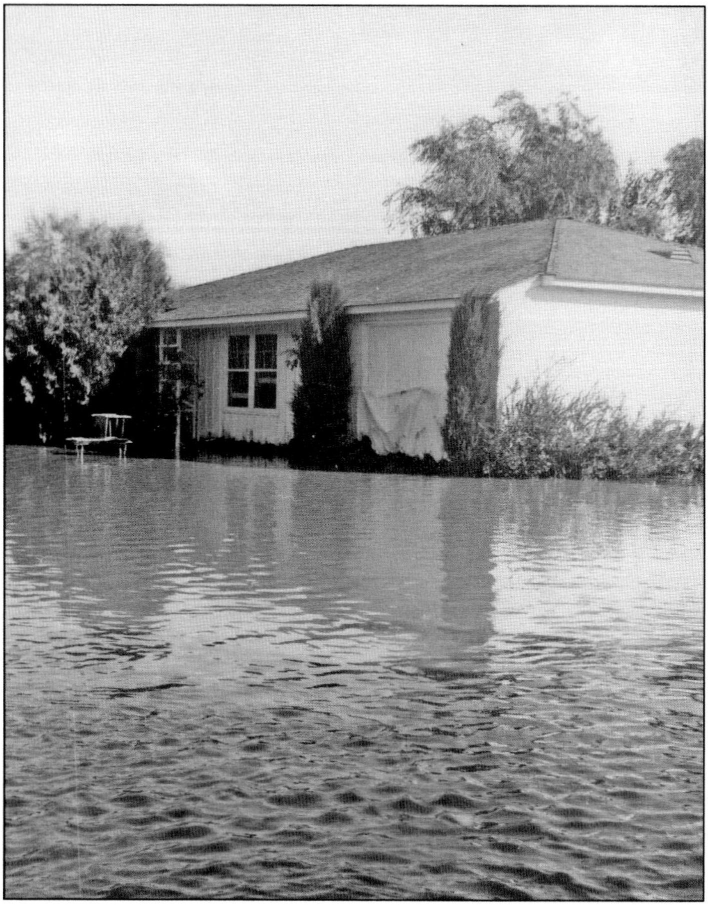

Many homes were damaged during the flood of 1950. Homeowners did all they could to salvage their homes and belongings. Mud was pushed up against the walls of homes in a desperate effort to dam the water. (Courtesy *West Valley View.*)

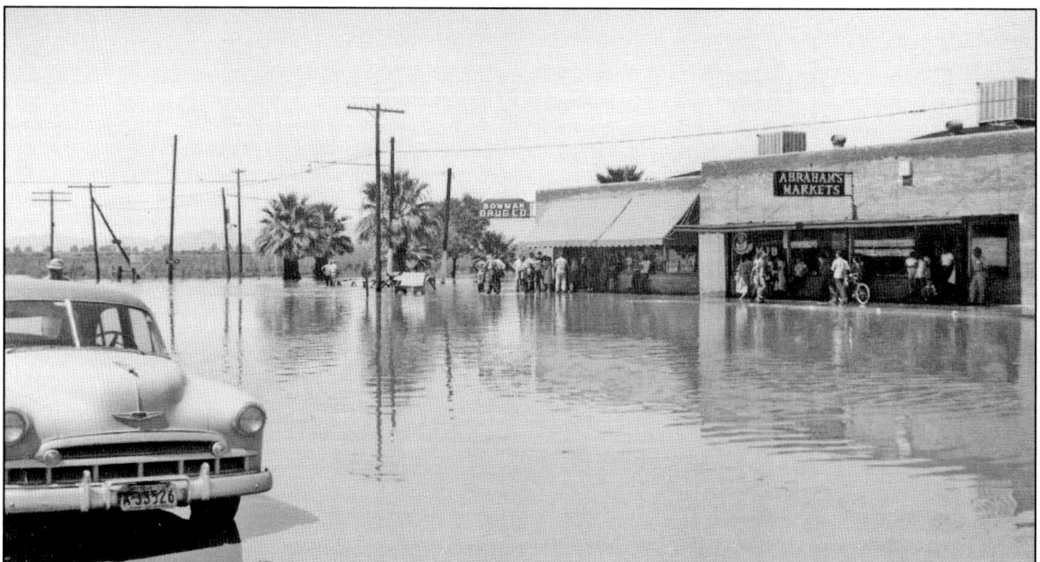

People were amazed to see the water; after all, it is a desert. Floods can happen almost anywhere, so people always need to be aware of the flood potential. (Courtesy *West Valley View.*)

Four

Freeways to Urbanization

After the Great Depression, Avondale and the economy were on their way up. Then along came World War II. It was unexpected, but after Pearl Harbor and the sinking of the USS *Arizona*, the nation rallied together.

The war effort was fought by many brave men and women and those civilians at defense plants. The navy base and Goodyear Aerospace provided employment and accommodations for their workers. Del Webb and Wing Foot Homes of Litchfield were among the builders who took on the job for the Avondale area. An abundance of builders came later, making today's Avondale the 12th largest city of Arizona.

Many of Avondale's immigrants settled here, such as Louise Manning's family in March 1927. The Manning family was from California. They traveled in a Model T Ford, and when they arrived, the bridge over the Agua Fria was washed out. Louise's parents, Verna and Melvin Manning, later bought 80 acres on Central Avenue and Van Buren. There was no electricity, and the children slept under large cottonwood trees next to where the busy Van Buren thoroughfare is today. There were only 50 children in the entire school. Today, with the rising population, there are eight schools in the Avondale School District. Two electric companies—APS and Salt River—provided services to Avondale. In the modern era, refrigeration units cool and heat homes.

Avondale's agriculture conditions were not overlooked by farmers. Irrigation made all this possible. Congress established the Bureau of Reclamation and authorized the Roosevelt Dam Project on the Salt River in 1902. Later other dams and man-made lakes would generate a vast irrigation network. The lakes were gravity fed from a higher elevation as dam after dam would collect and release the water. The water would eventually reach the valley below and was diverted to canal systems with headgates that could hold back water and release it when needed. At last, the canal water was sent to smaller ditches that flooded fields or backyards with just the right amount of precious water.

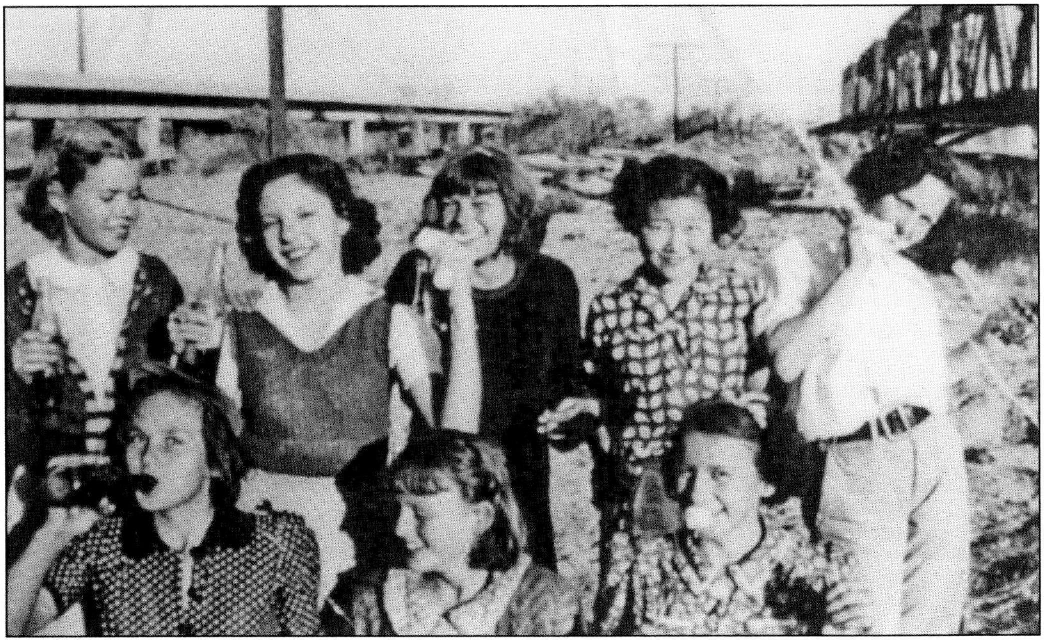

Avondale girls just want to have fun everywhere they are. This image was taken on the banks of the Agua Fria River between the train bridge and old Highway 80. (Courtesy City of Avondale.)

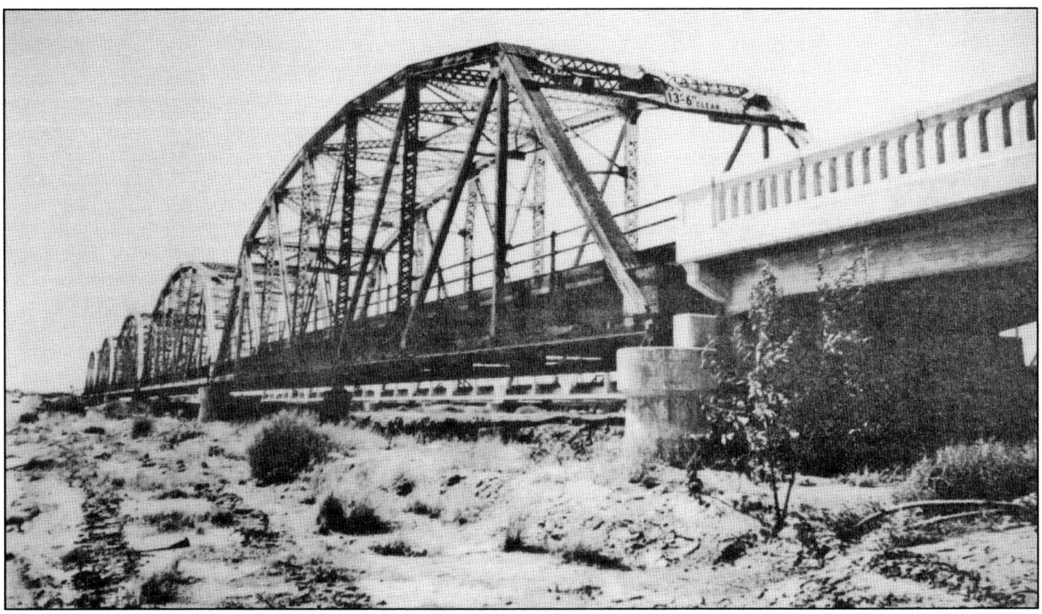

The Highway 80 bridge that carried Westsiders had to be demolished and replaced by the U.S. Department of Transportation. (Courtesy City of Avondale.)

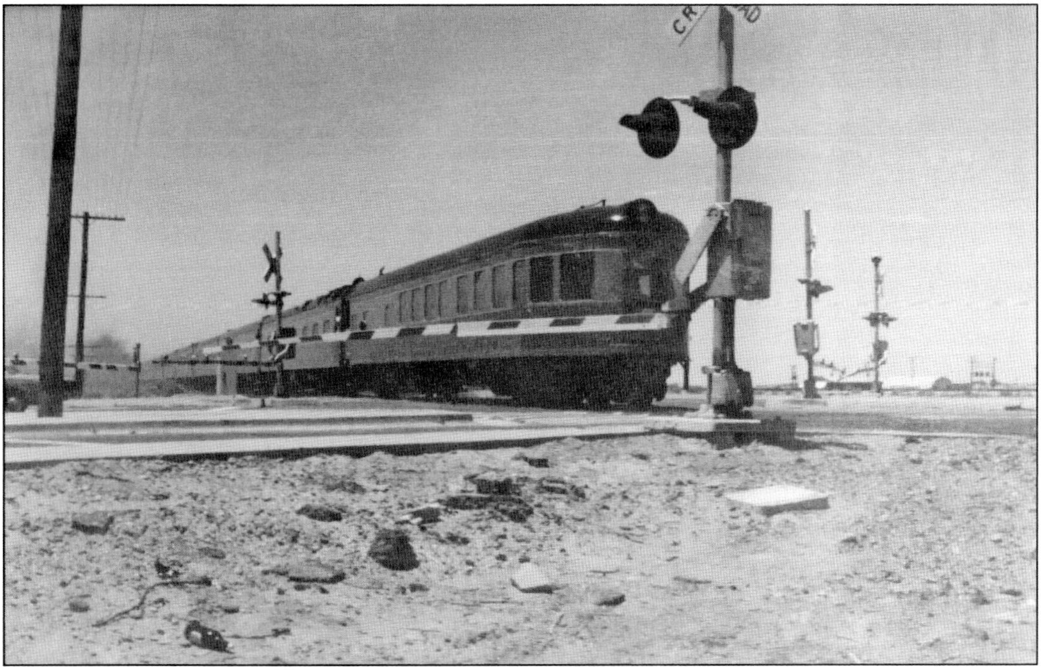

In the past, trains always had a caboose, but today there are none. This commemorative train passed through Avondale in 1984. (Courtesy Avondale City Library.)

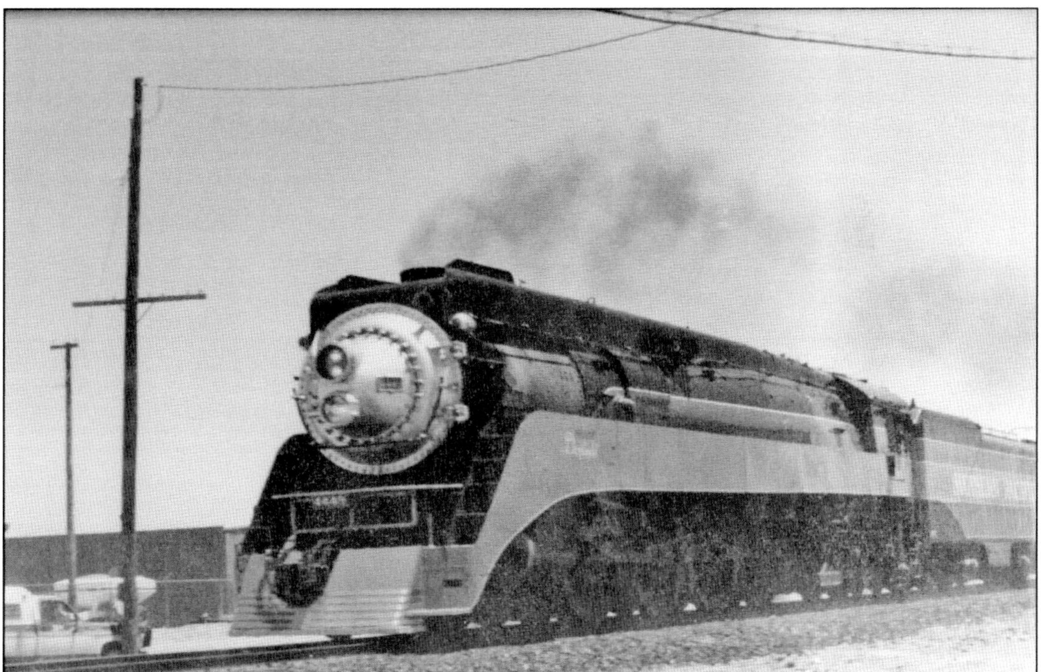

The Southern Pacific Railroad came through Avondale as a special edition in 1984. (Courtesy Avondale City Library.)

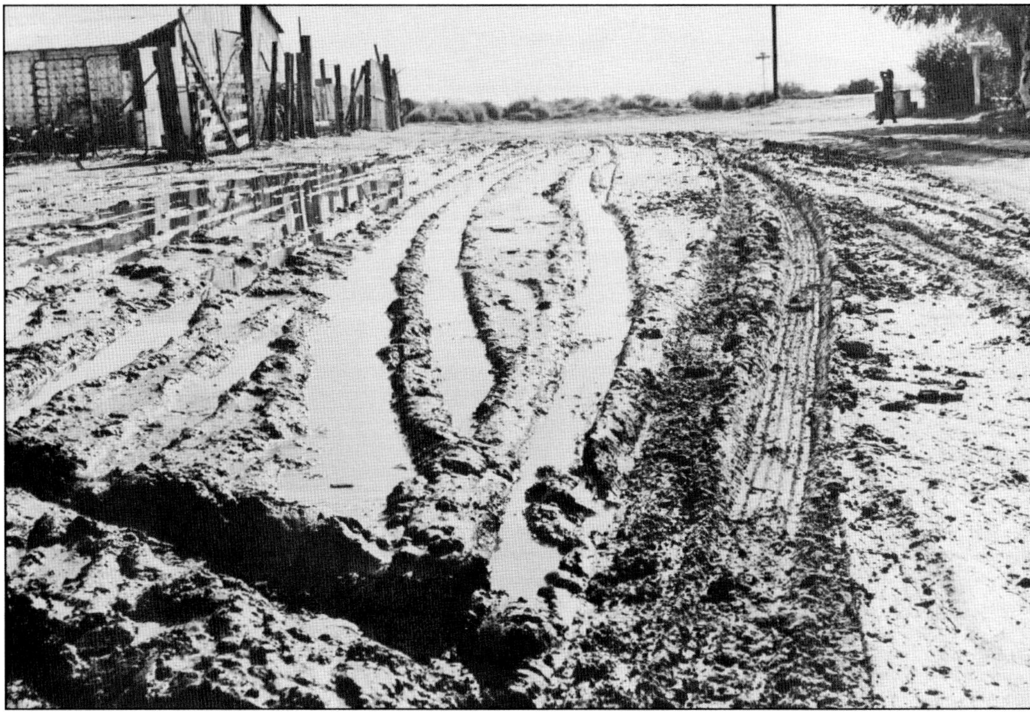

Unpaved dirt roads were slippery when wet and full of chuckholes. The desert soil is unpredictable. Dirt roads are easy enough to travel when they are dry, but once rain is added, it is a different story. (Courtesy City of Avondale.)

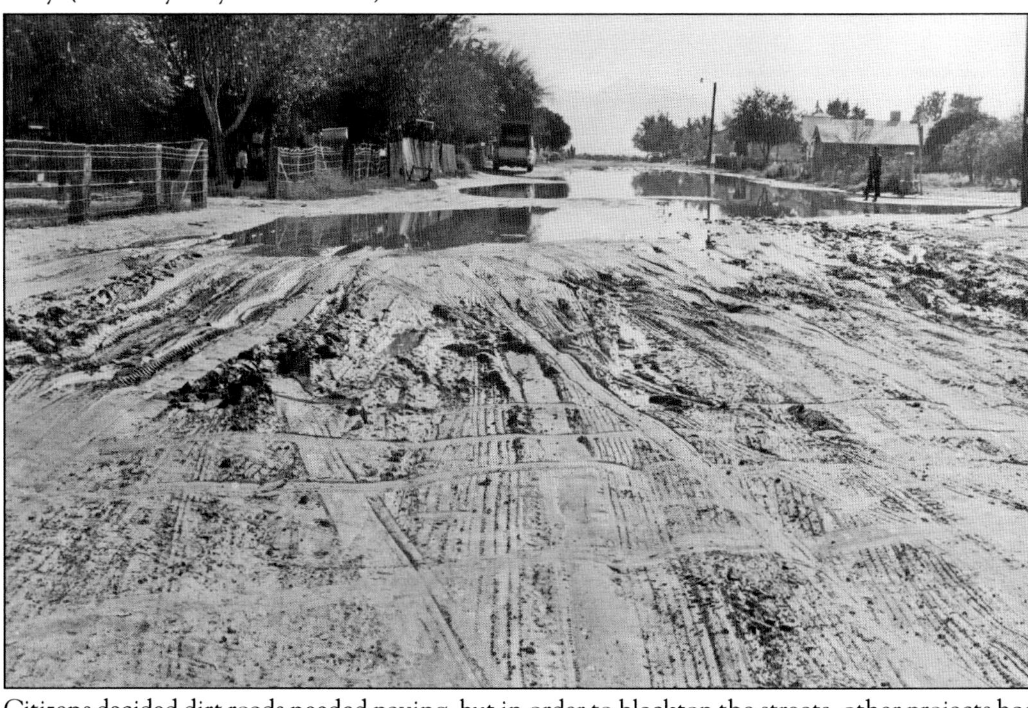

Citizens decided dirt roads needed paving, but in order to blacktop the streets, other projects had to be done first. (Courtesy City of Avondale.)

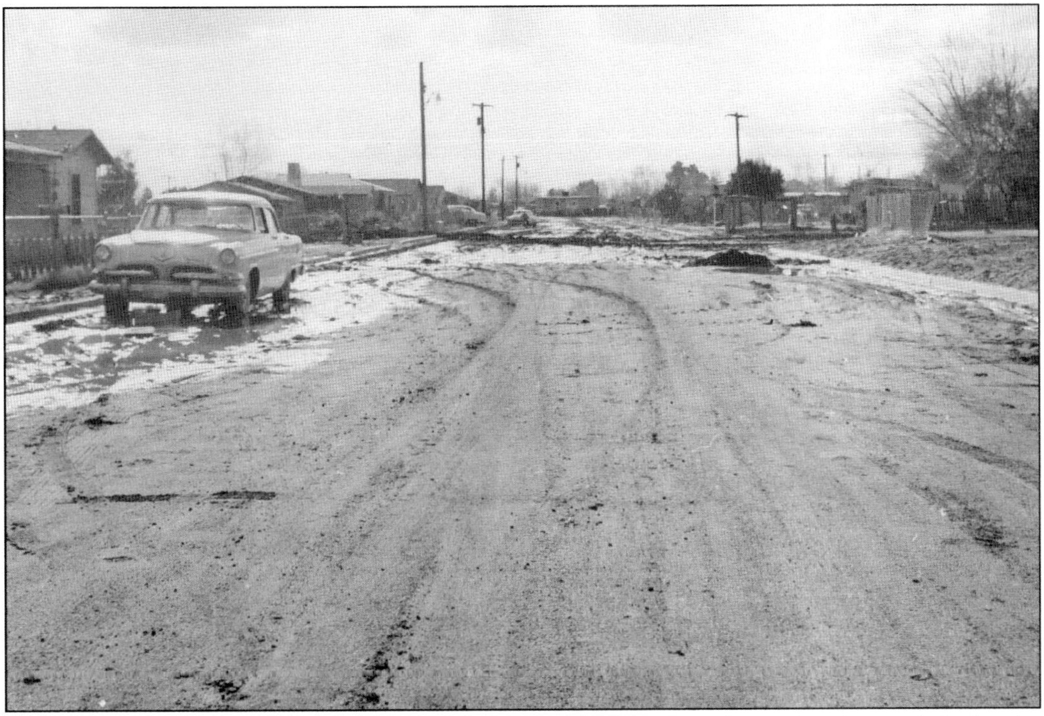

Blueprints needed to be engineered and gas lines and other obstacles under the earth had to be found, creating more jobs. (Courtesy City of Avondale.)

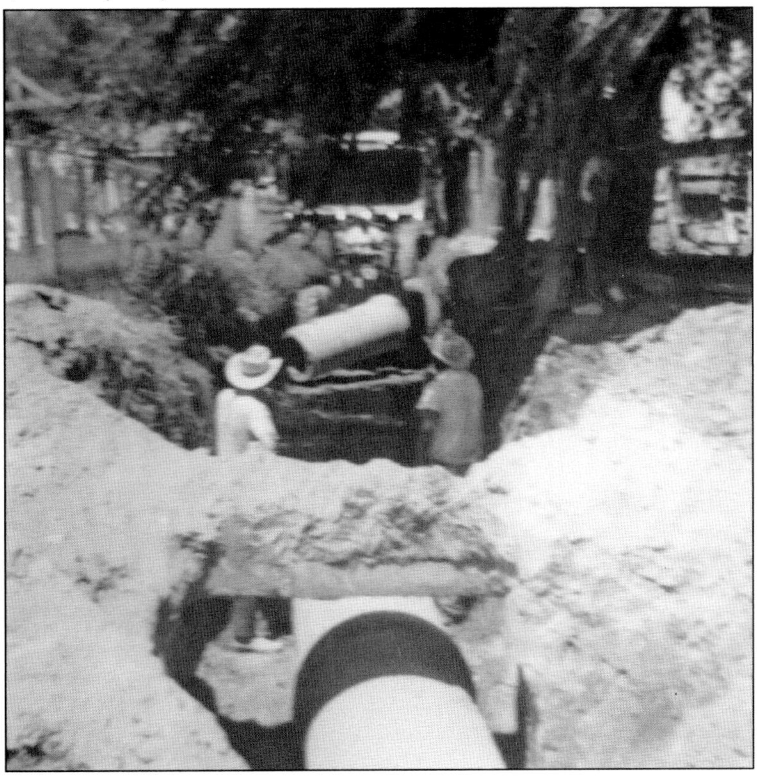

Water and sewer lines had to be located and dealt with before paving could begin. Some lines were replaced and other lines were added. Adding lines seemed to be a never-ending job. (Courtesy City of Avondale.)

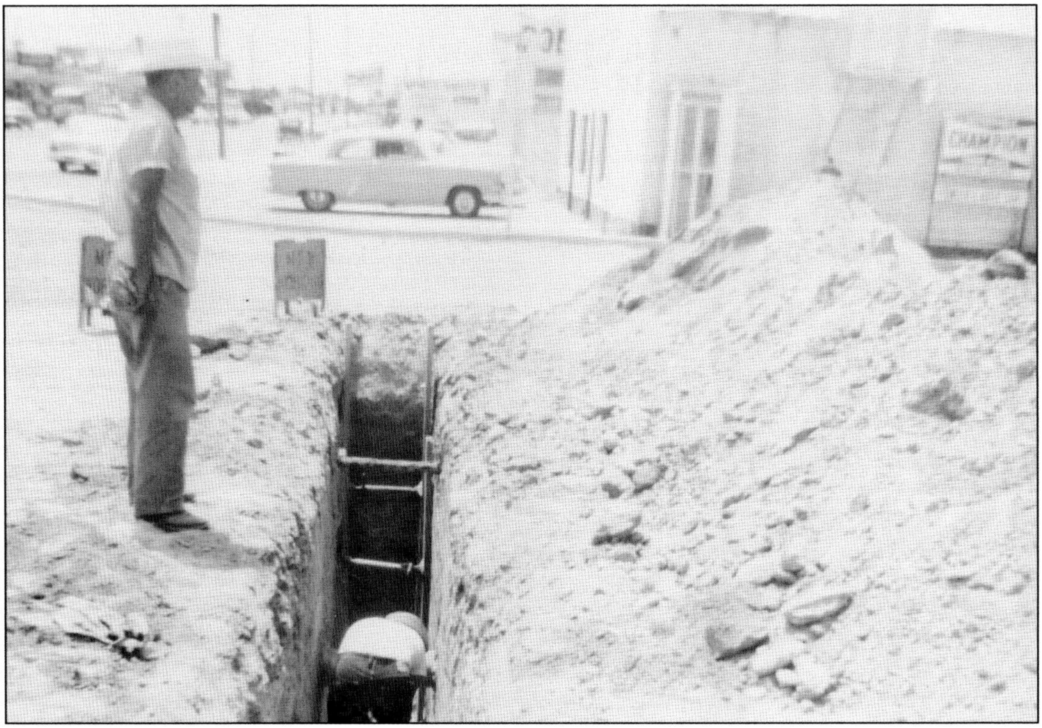

The Avondale public works department developed calculations and diagrams by their own minds without the modern convenience of computers. (Courtesy City of Avondale.)

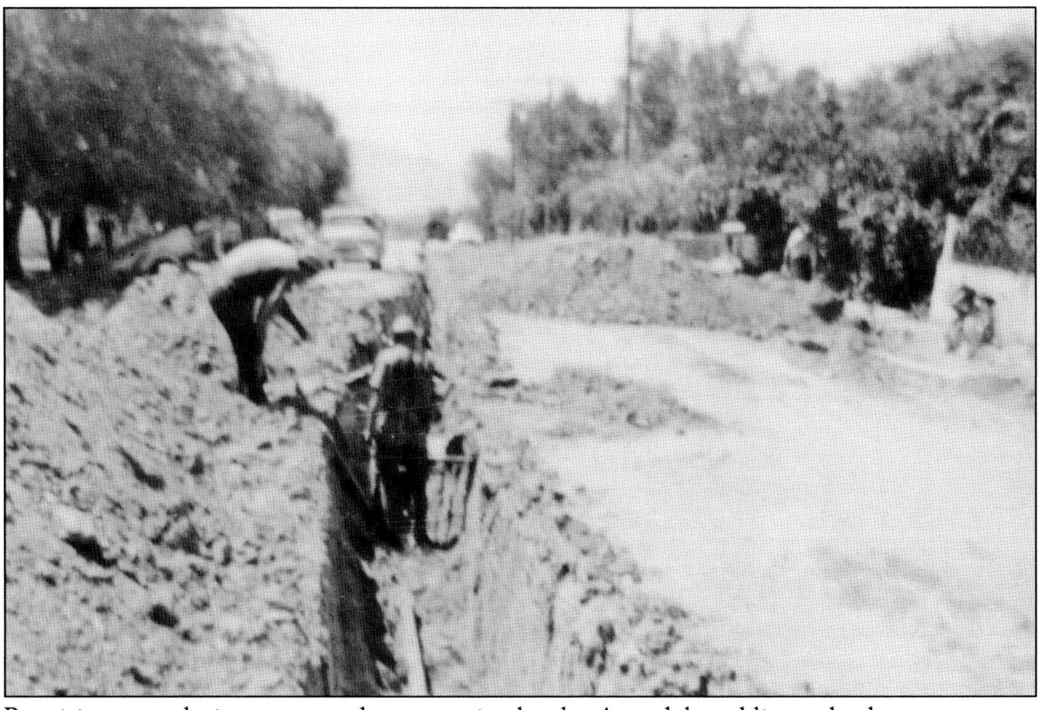

Repairing or replacing sewer and water mains by the Avondale public works department was required to keep up with growth. (Courtesy City of Avondale.)

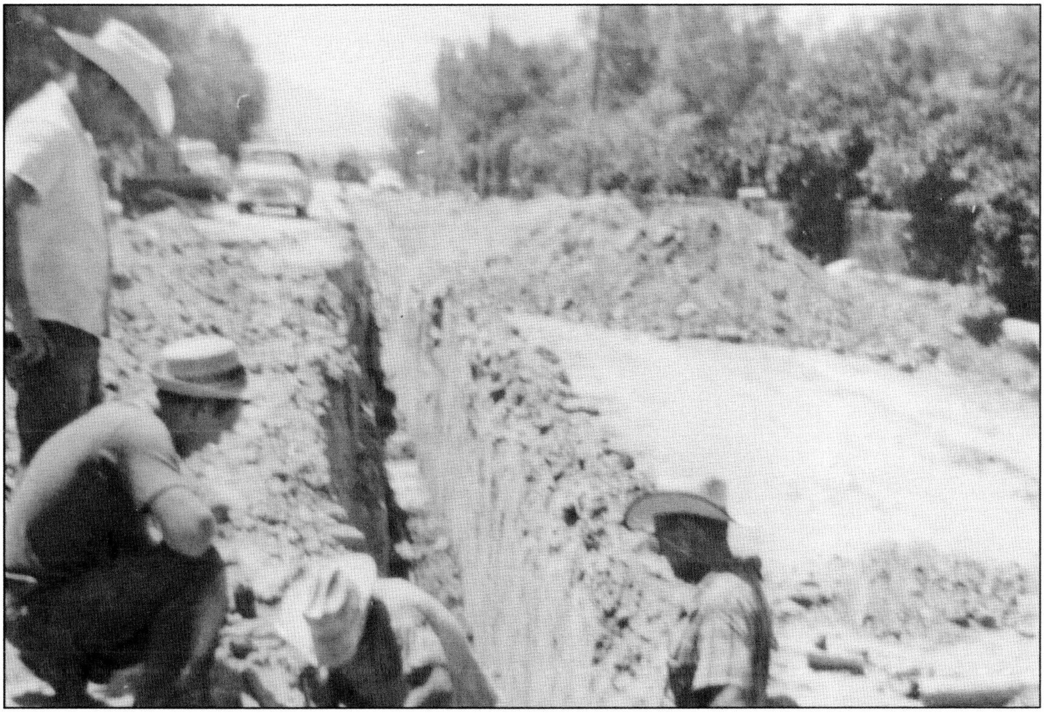

The Avondale public works department worked long and hard to make a small town blossom into the beautiful city of today. The work was hot and dusty but rewarding. (Courtesy City of Avondale.)

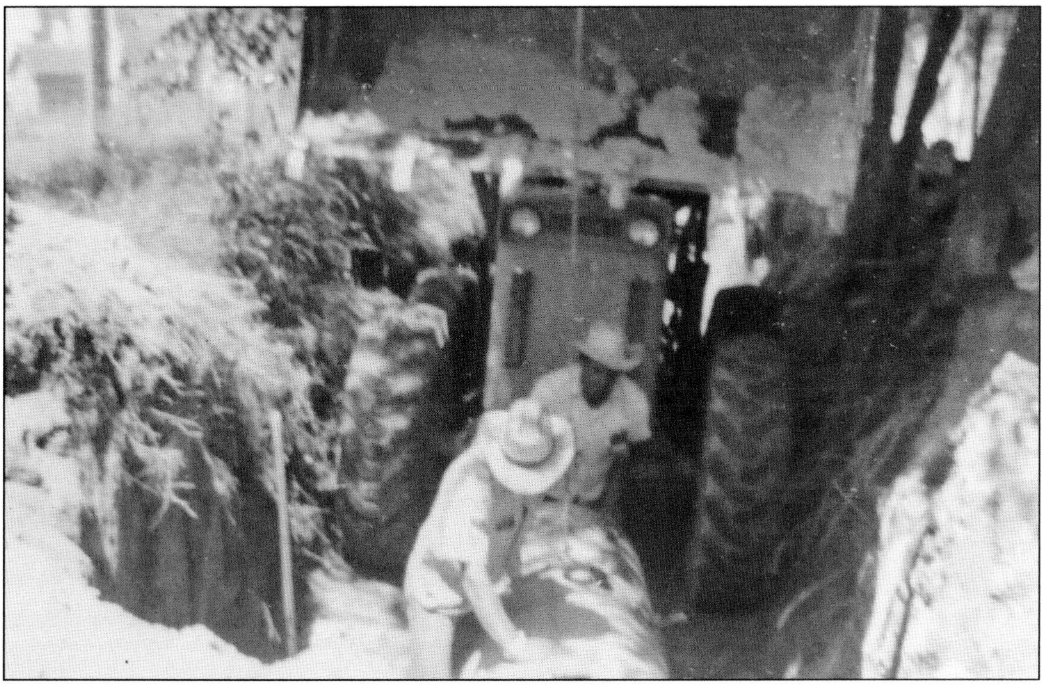

Sheer muscle power and some machinery were used at times to get the job done. The Avondale crew is installing sewer lines here. (Courtesy City of Avondale.)

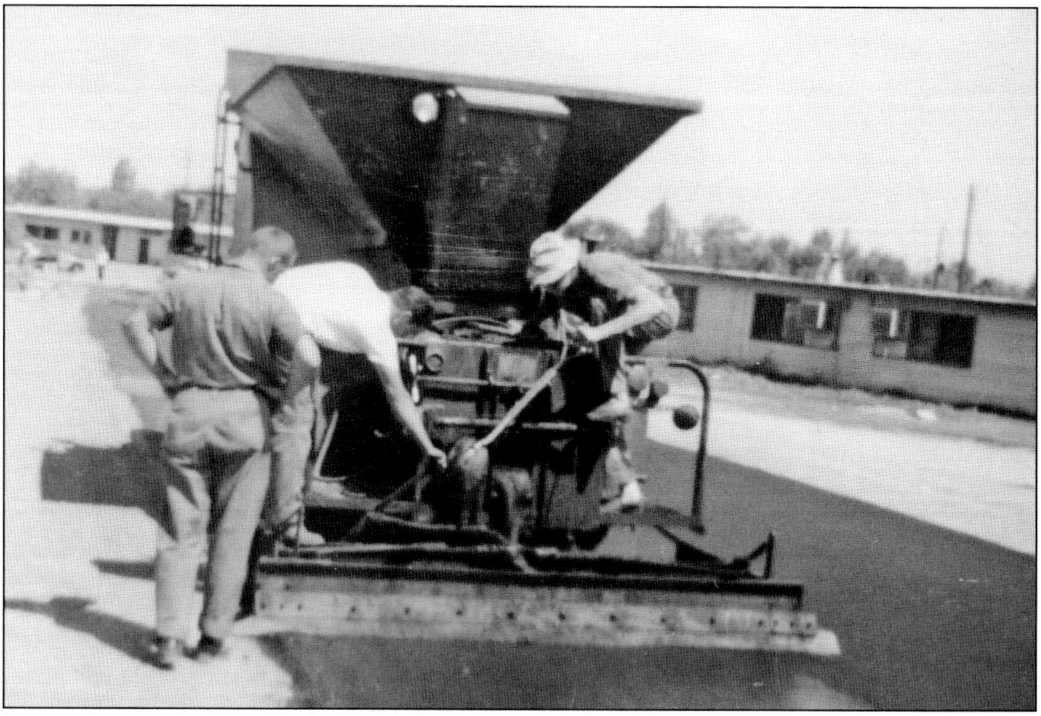

Paving the streets of the Circle neighborhood was needed on occasion, and a crew from Avondale did the job. (Courtesy City of Avondale.)

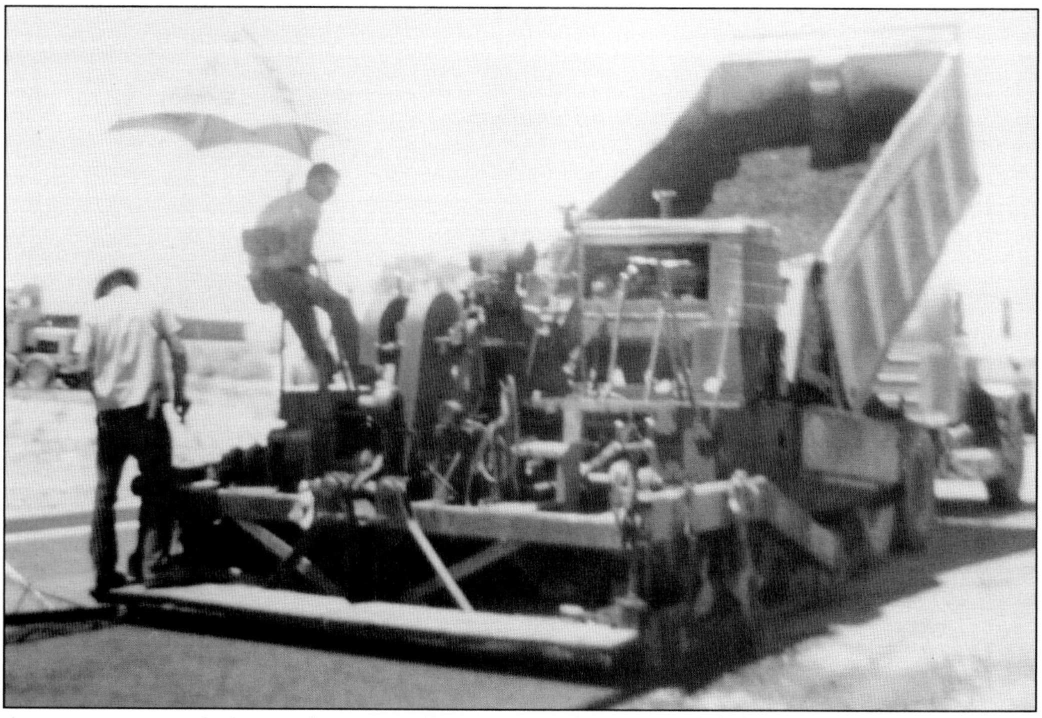

As time progressed, the machinery used to pave roads in Avondale became more sophisticated and fewer men were needed to do the project. (Courtesy City of Avondale.)

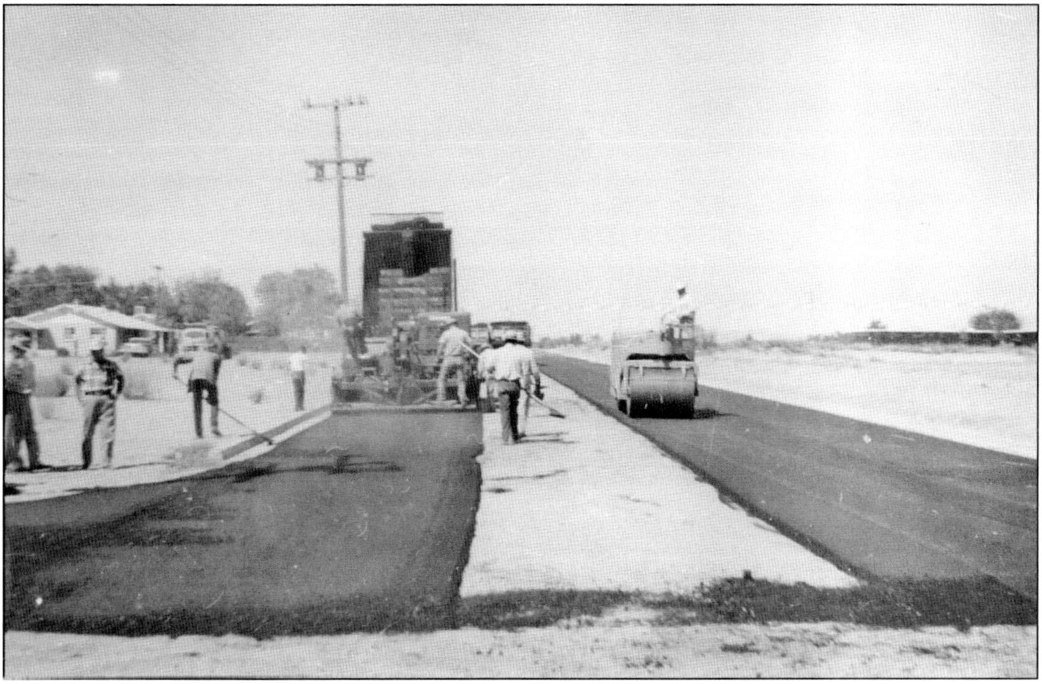

Paving projects were taken on by the City of Avondale near the Agua Fria River and throughout the city. Many roads needed to be paved, as most of the outlying areas had dusty dirt streets. (Courtesy City of Avondale.)

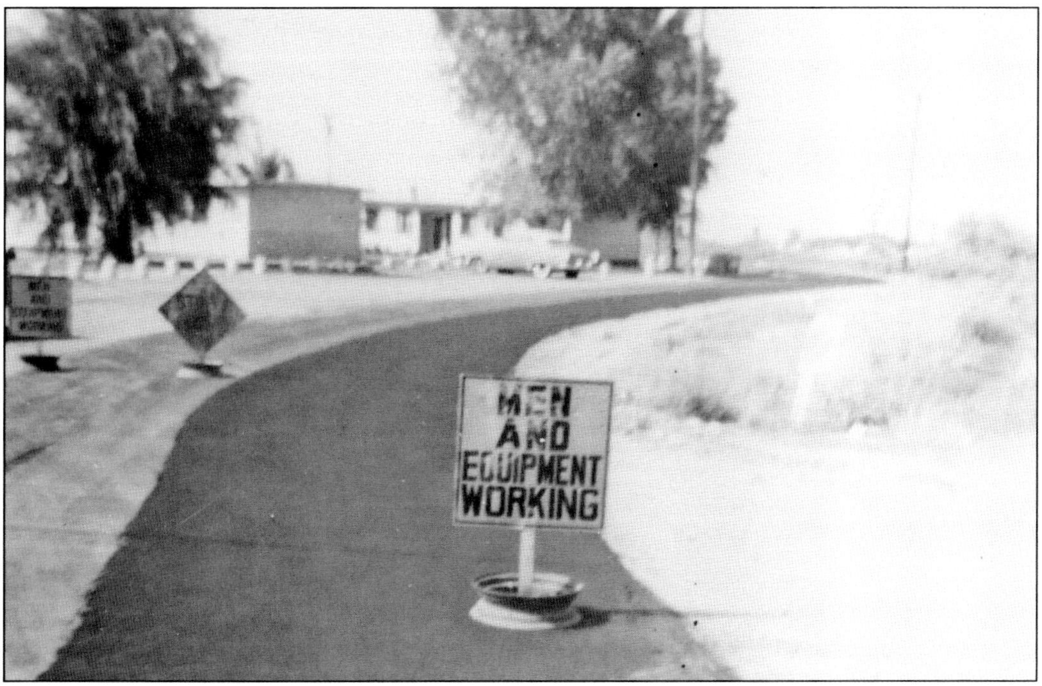

The Circle was a neighborhood built in a circle formation to house the employees of the Naval Air Facility and other government facilities. It was located on Western Avenue where the beauty college stands today. (Courtesy City of Avondale.)

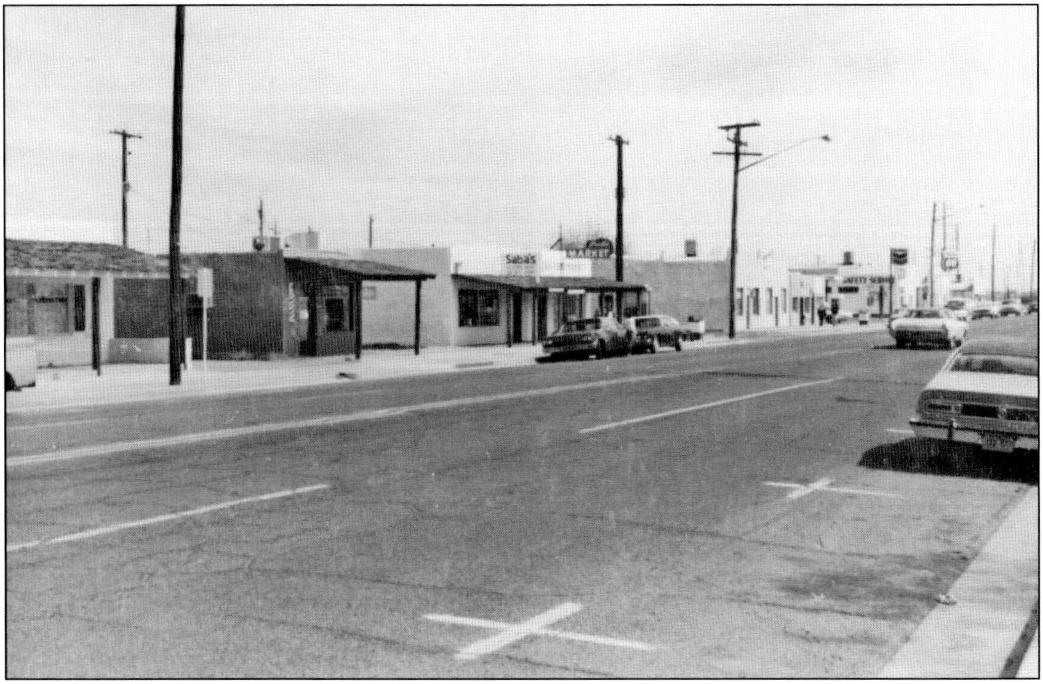

Western at one time had parallel parking, unlike today where parking is at an angle. Few people remember the island running down Western. New cement barriers are used today with the angle parking. (Both courtesy City of Avondale.)

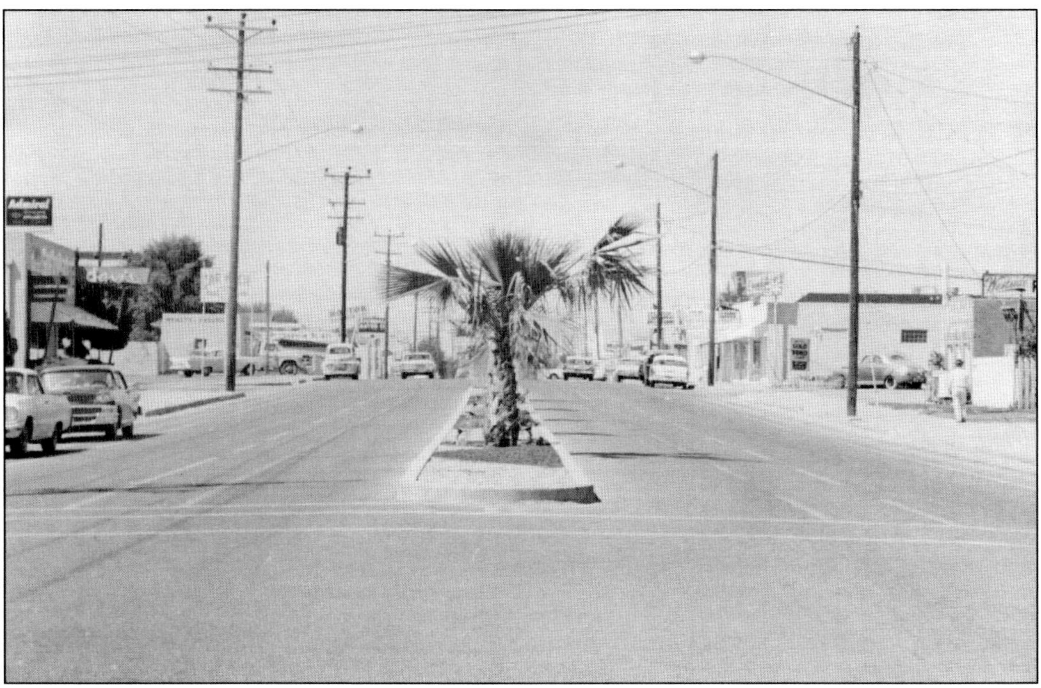

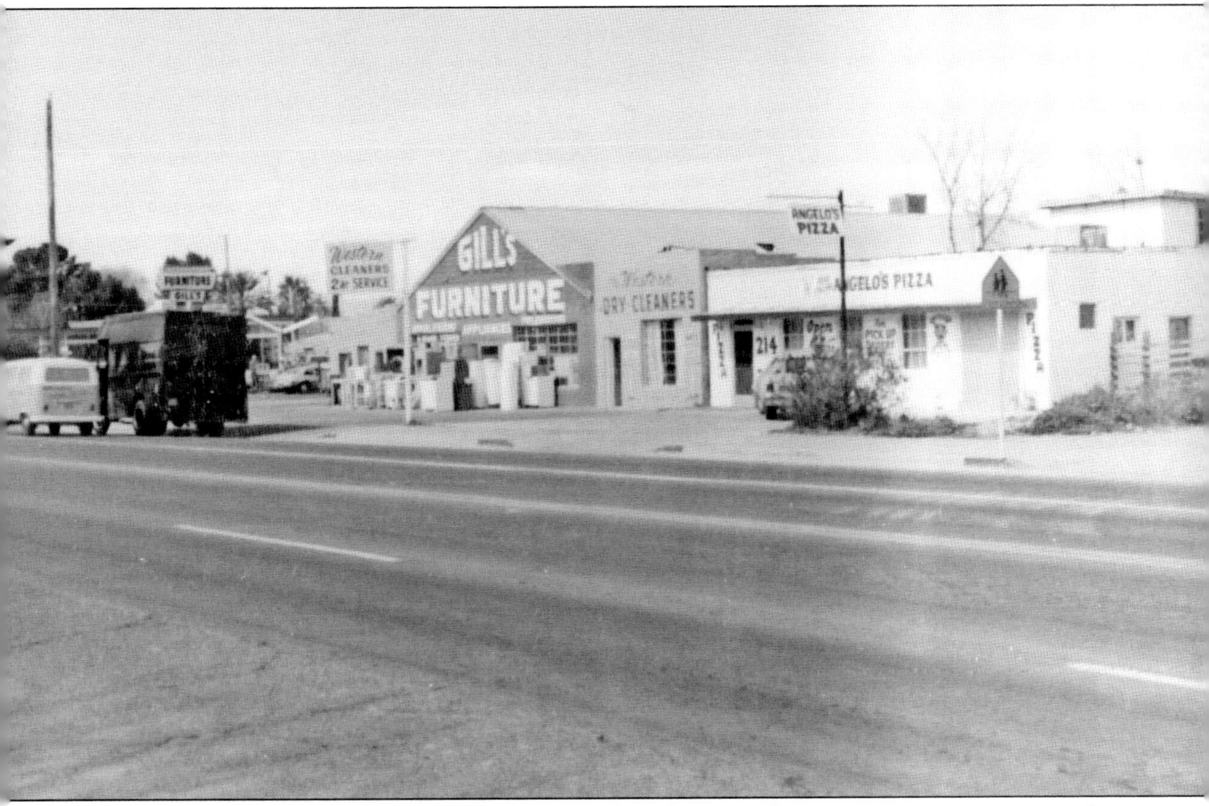

Gill's Furniture held new beginnings for many newlyweds. Large department stores were around 20 miles west in Phoenix. Locals did business with locals for the convenience, service, and loyalty. (Courtesy City of Avondale.)

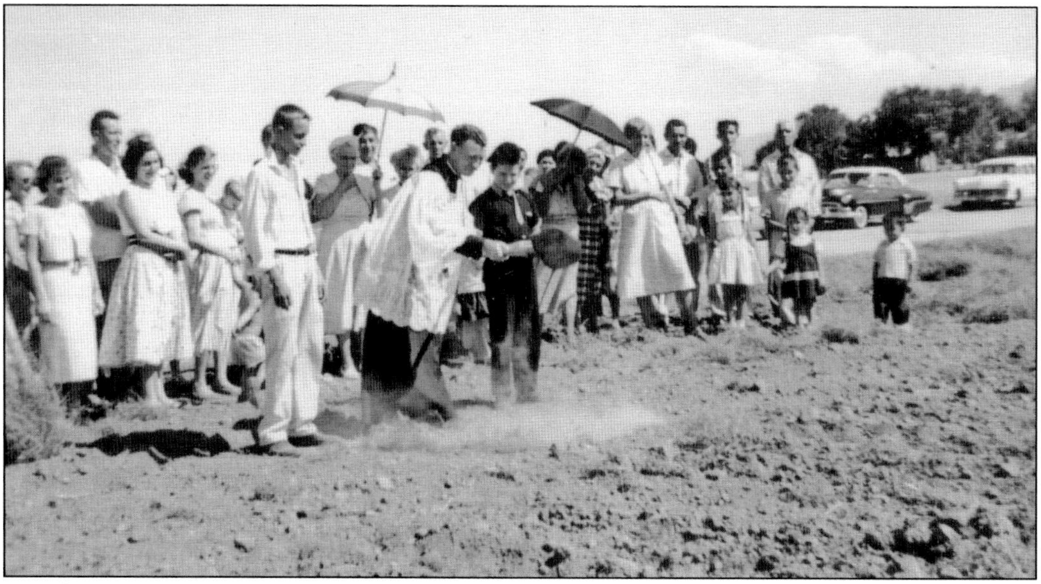

St. John Vianney Catholic Church had its ground-breaking and first blessing in 1958. (Courtesy Ken and Sally Kiko.)

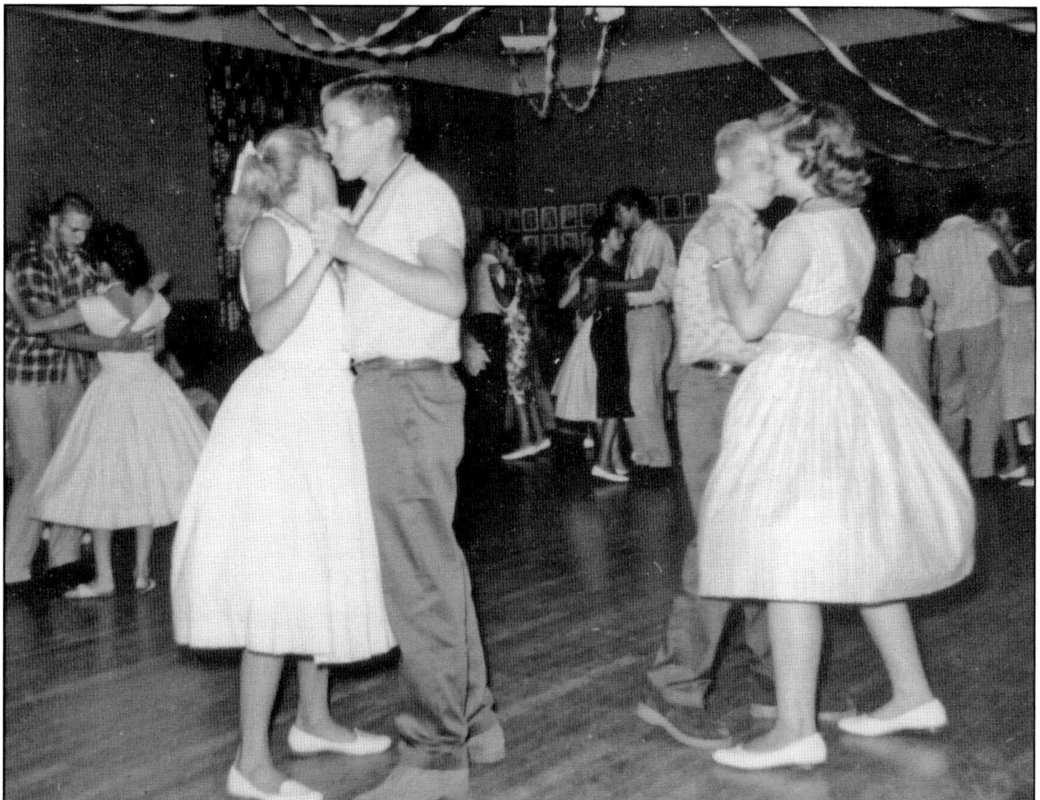

The Catholic Youth Organization (CYO) dance was popular with the younger crowd. This photograph shows, from left to right, Pat and David Falls, John Gast, and Rosemary Falls kicking up their heels. (Courtesy Ken and Sally Kiko.)

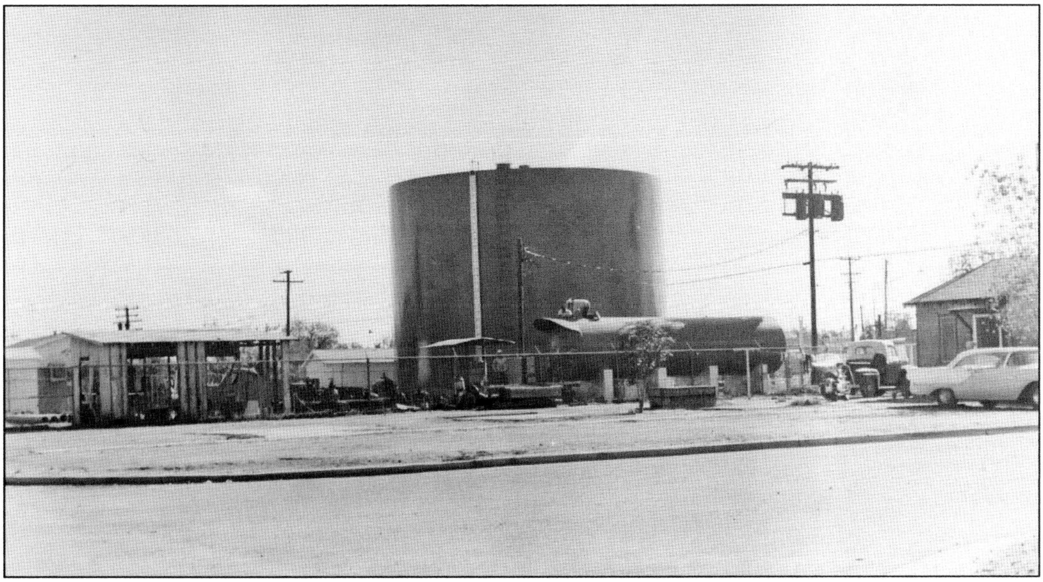

A large underground pump channels water from beneath the ground to a large holding tank, which is then pumped into a pressure tank. As the pressure builds, water is disbursed through mains to homes. (Courtesy City of Avondale.)

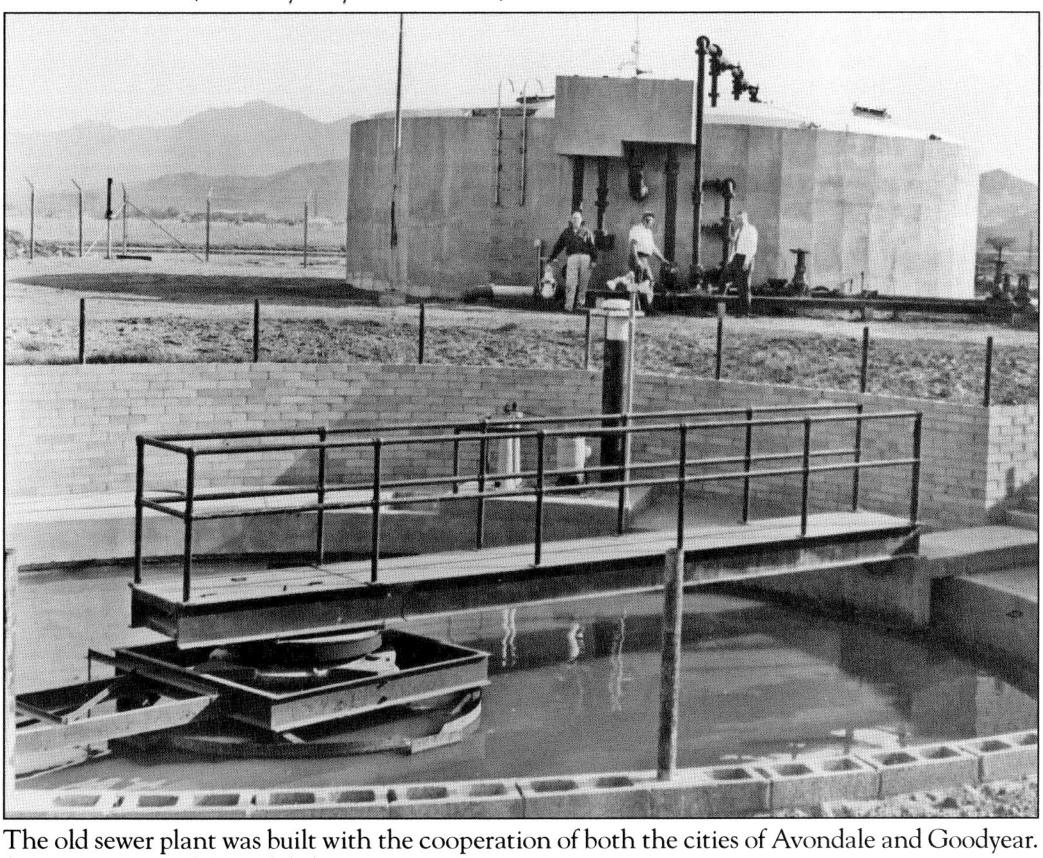

The old sewer plant was built with the cooperation of both the cities of Avondale and Goodyear. (Courtesy City of Avondale.)

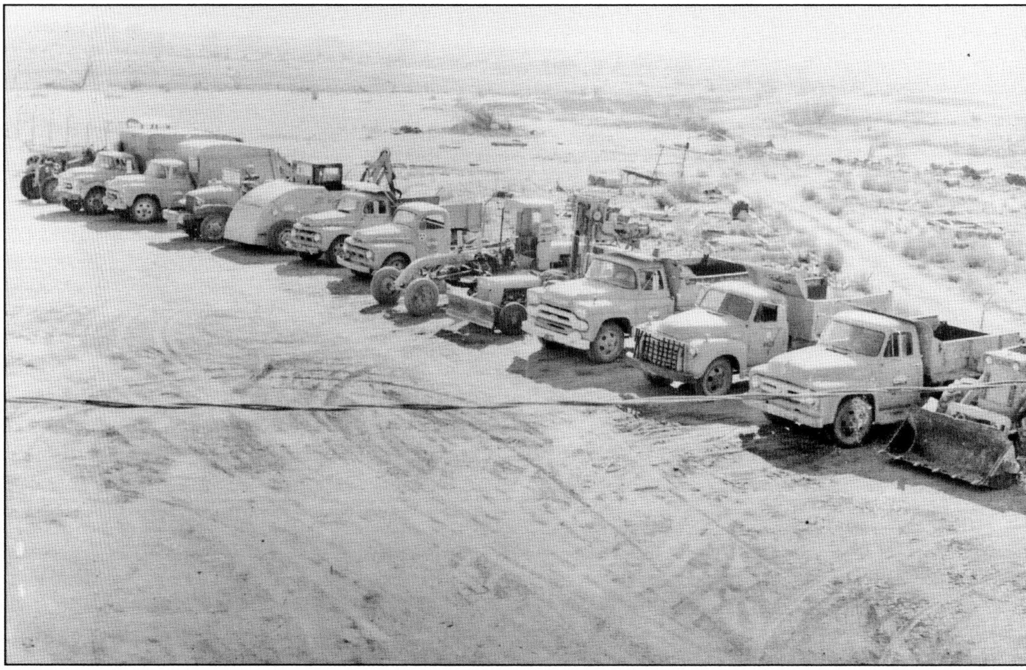

Avondale city equipment was stored in the old Public Works Yard on Lower Buckeye Road at the Agua Fria River. (Courtesy City of Avondale.)

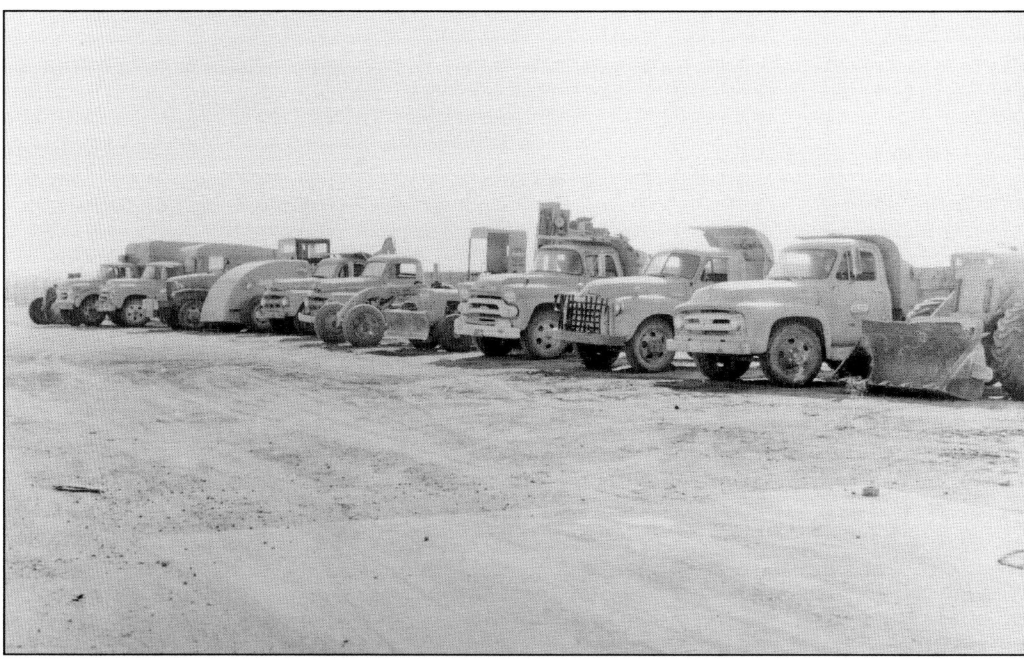

As Avondale grew, so did the amount of equipment needed to run the city. (Courtesy City of Avondale.)

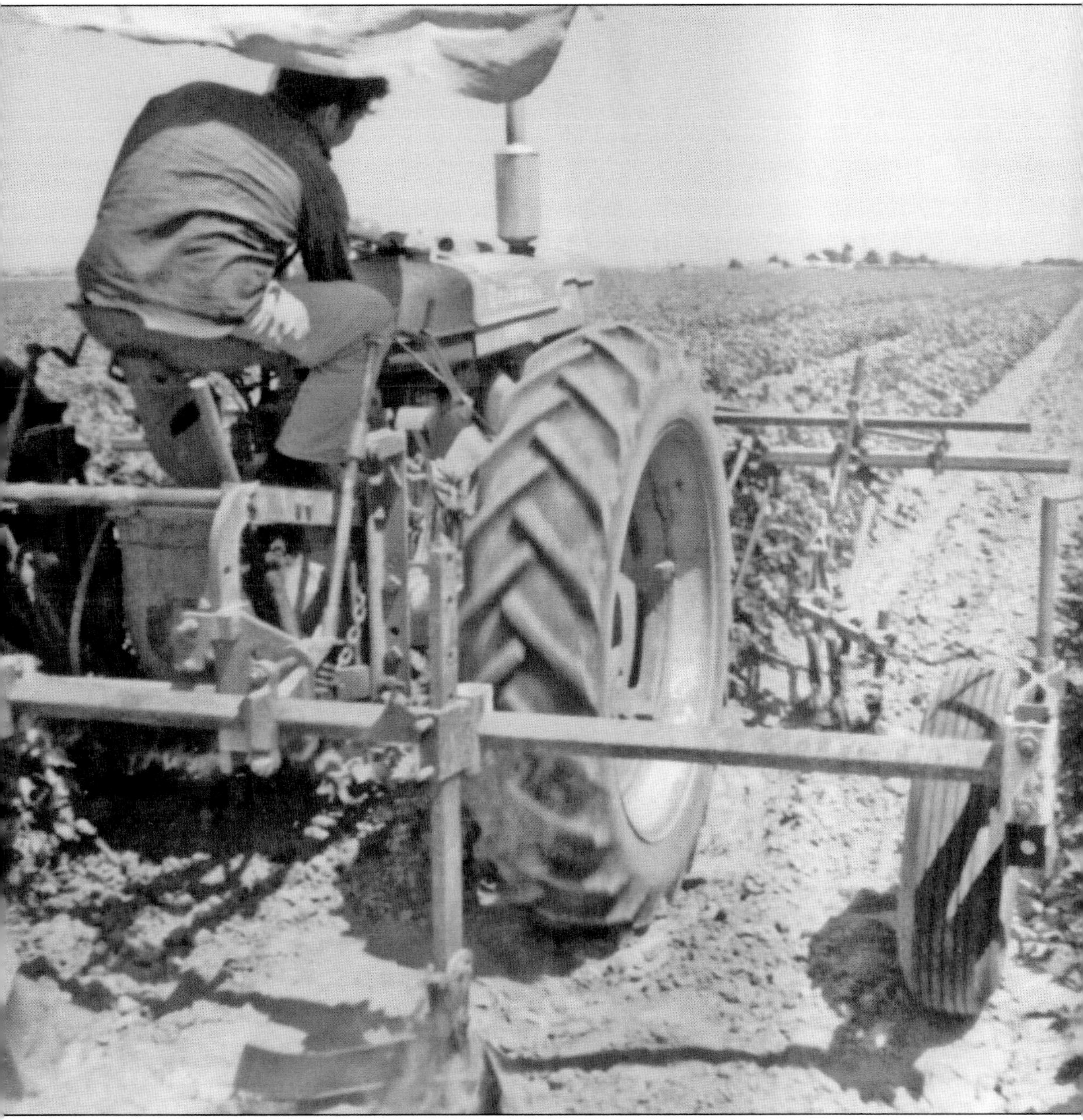

In the past, irrigation water was brought to a few individual homes and farms by way of hand-dug ditches. Some of the ditches once were built by ancient American Indian tribes using only sticks, rocks, their hands, and other primitive implements. With present-day heavy machinery, digging could take no time at all. Currently one of the ancient ditches can be spotted along 107th Avenue just south of Lower Buckeye. The view may not last long, for new homes are being built in the area at a rapid pace. (Courtesy the Schulkie family.)

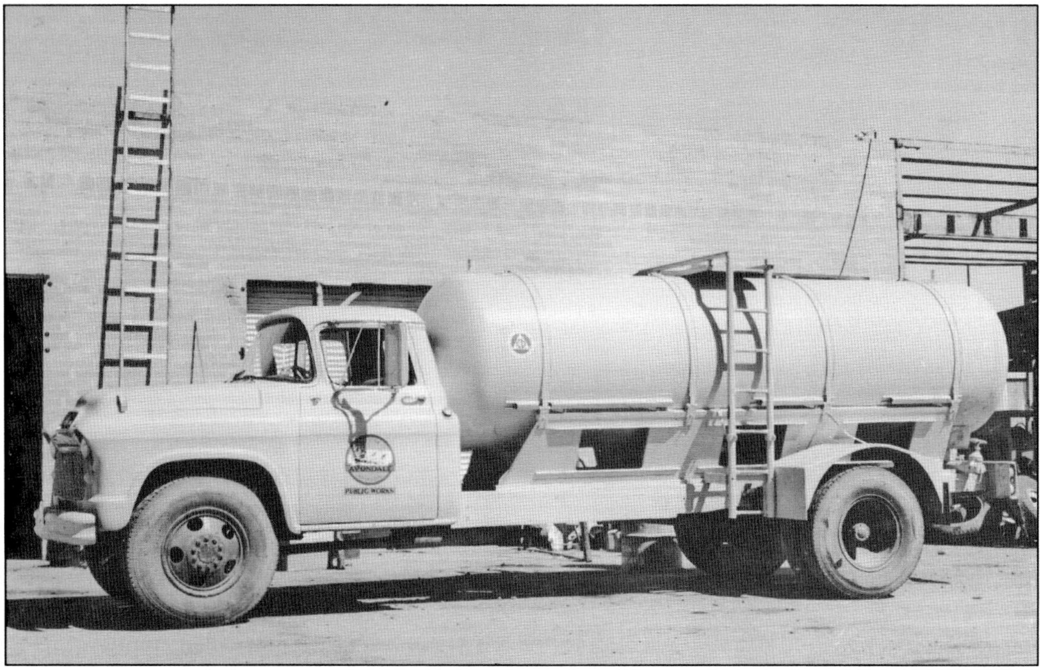

The city had to house the needed equipment and tools rather than keeping them in the open, so a maintenance facility was erected on Lower Buckeye Road and Fourth Street. (Courtesy City of Avondale.)

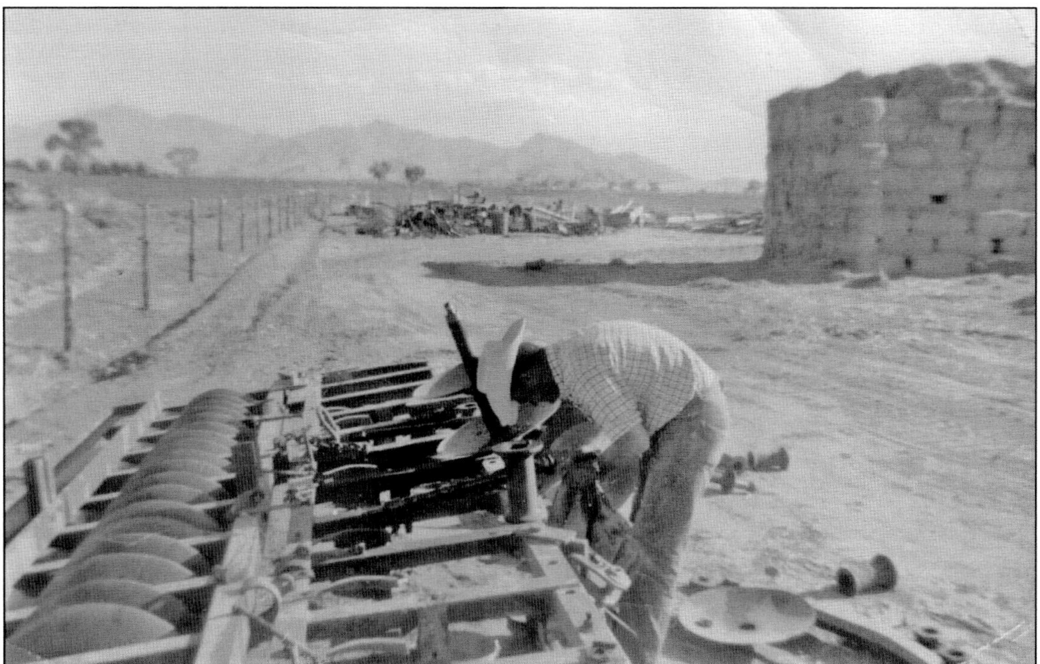

Bob Schulkie in 1959 worked on farm machinery. The Estrellas are looming in the background; today Cold Water Crossing with its lovely homes sits on the property. (Courtesy the Schulkie family.)

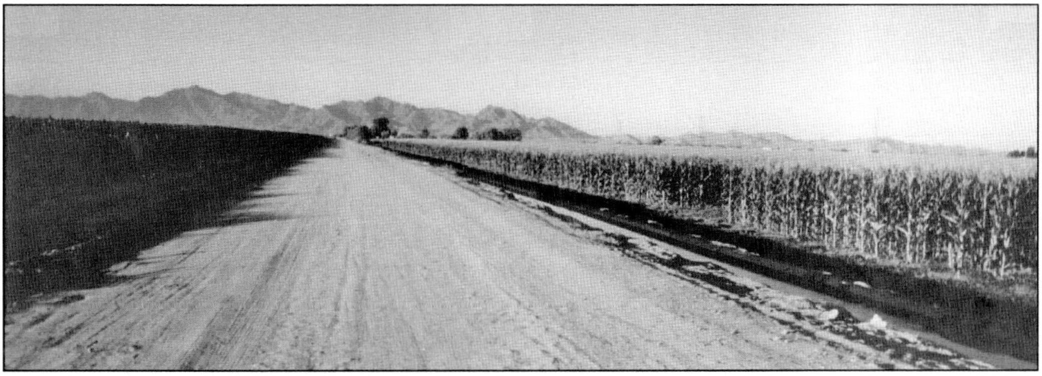

At the Schulkie farm, looking south from McDowell Road near El Mirage Road, a good corn crop was growing on either side of the dirt trail. There wasn't much to obscure the horizon at that time. Today there are subdivisions. (Courtesy the Schulkie family.)

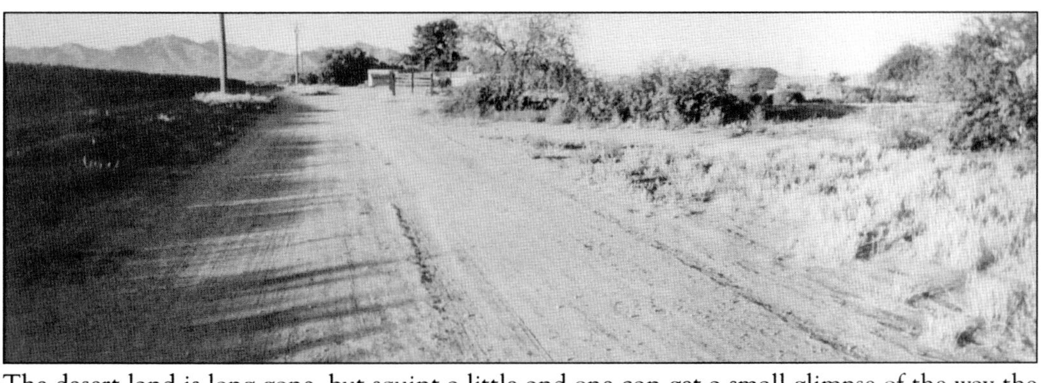

The desert land is long gone, but squint a little and one can get a small glimpse of the way the area looked at one time. (Courtesy the Schulkie family.)

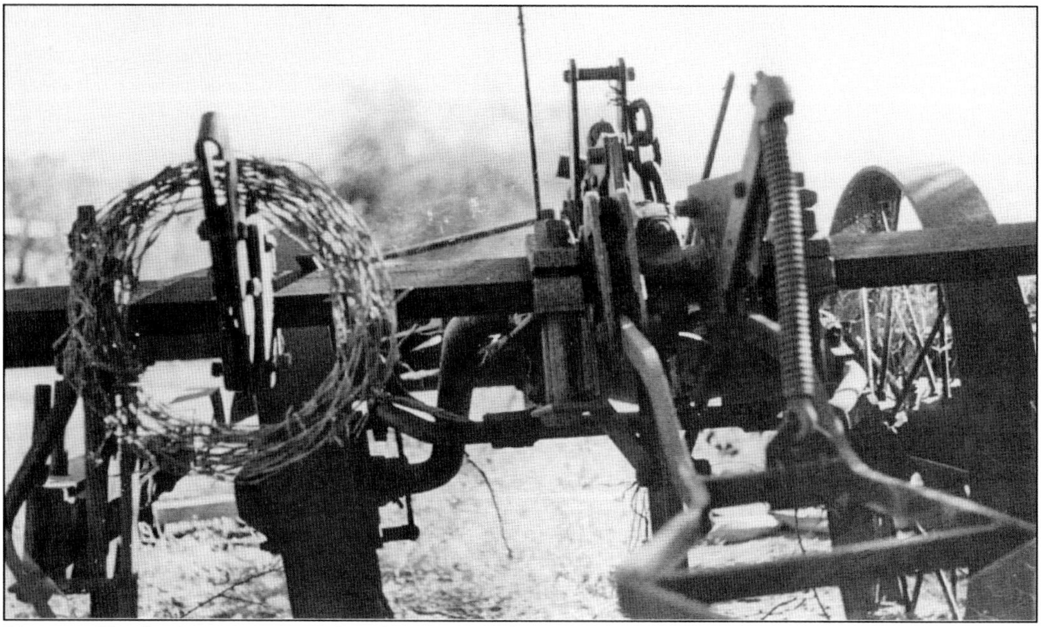

Plenty of barbed wire was used to keep animals from the fields, and that includes the human kind as well. The wire would designate ownership and boundaries. A few lawsuits have been argued as to how long the barbed wire fencing was used to designate property lines. (Courtesy the Schulkie family.)

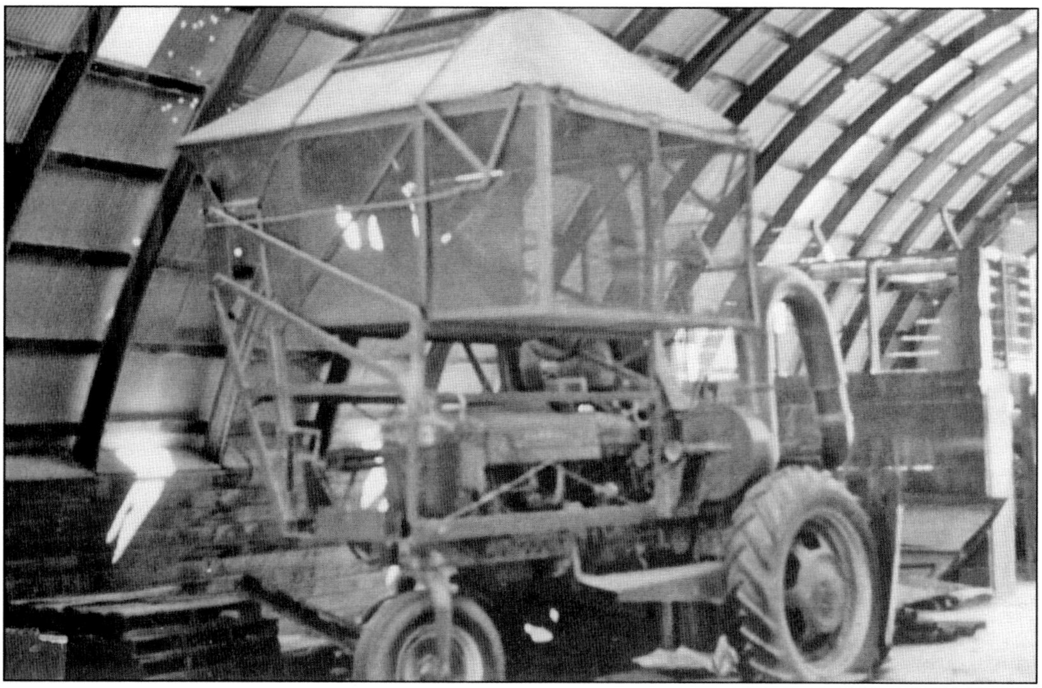

A cotton picker is parked in the old metal barn. The round metal barn was a landmark on the Collier farm until the farm was sold. As people traveled near the railroad tracks on Buckeye Road from Cashion to Avondale, the Quonset hut glistened as the sun struck the bright metal shed. (Courtesy the Collier family.)

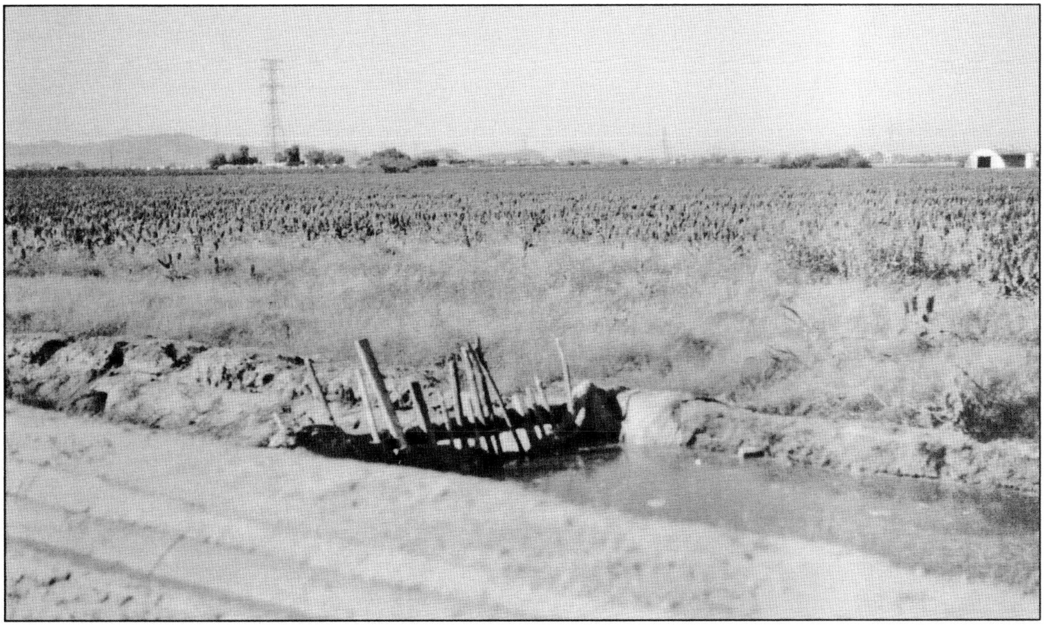

The original ditches that brought water to the valley were hand-dug by hardy pioneers. Headgates were constructed of twigs and anything that would prop up against them to dam irrigation water. The water then was released into a parched field of a large plot of land. This method controlled how much water would be used. (Courtesy the Collier family.)

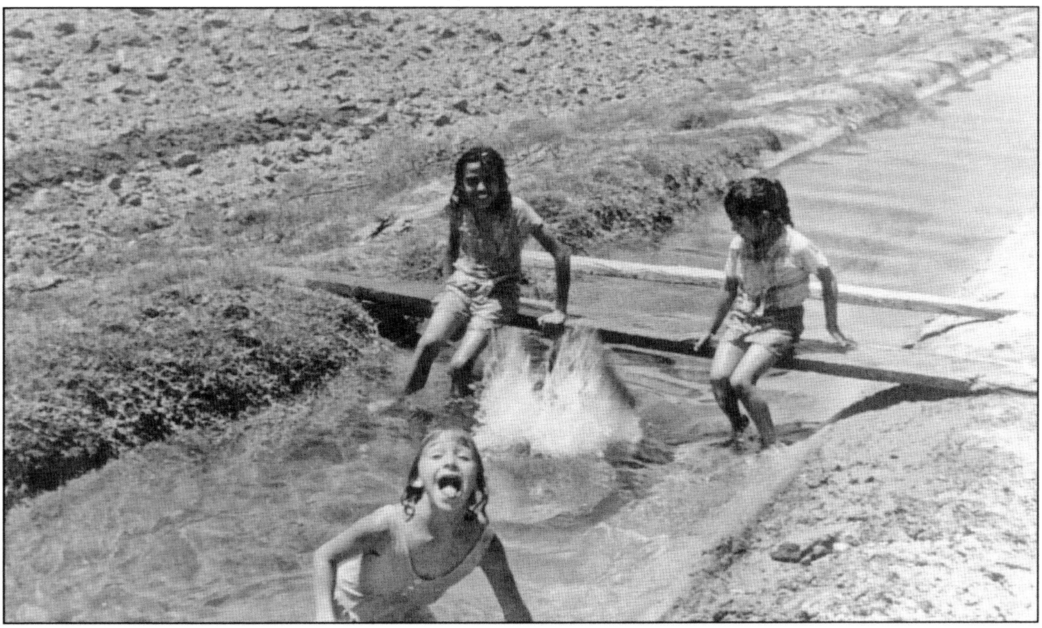

During the long hot summers, loads of children had no pools nearby, so they would look forward to irrigation days. Kids could sneak a cool swim from farmers' ditches or canals. Ditches were smaller than the large canals and a lot more prevalent. Ditches were similar to today's game pools but with swift, cool water running though them. One could catch a good ride for quite a distance. To know where the good spots were, follow the children; they always knew. (Courtesy the Schulkie family.)

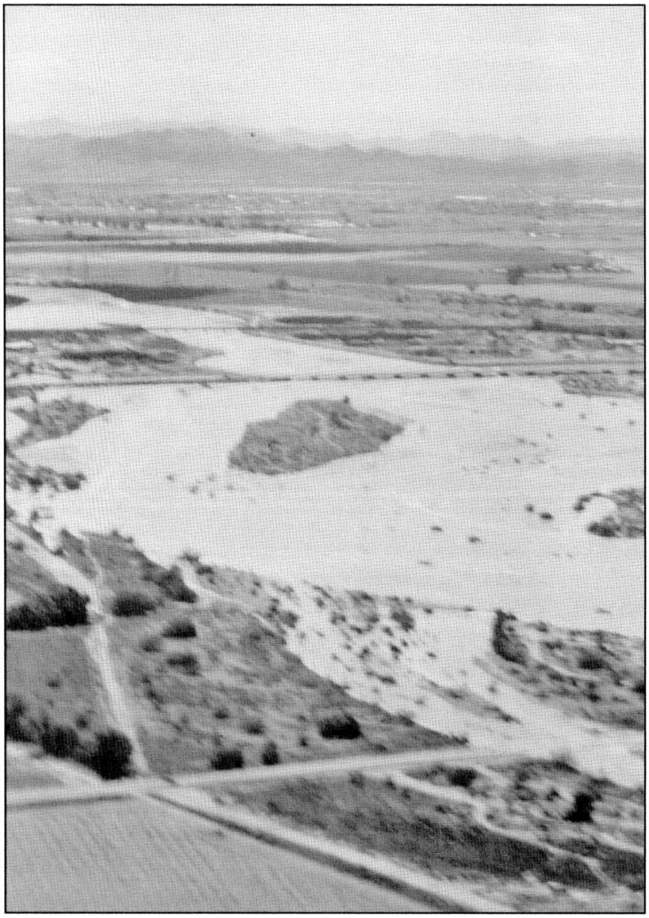

The back of this photograph—titled "Just another Agua Fria River flood"—reads, "Taken from Leverton's Helio." Not only had the Agua Fria flooded but New River as well. They merge just north of Camelback. The picture was taken in 1980. The Agua Fria River has another tributary, New River, which meets near Camelback Road. When the two meet during flood stage, they can be a destructive force. (Courtesy Sally Schulkie Marcotte.)

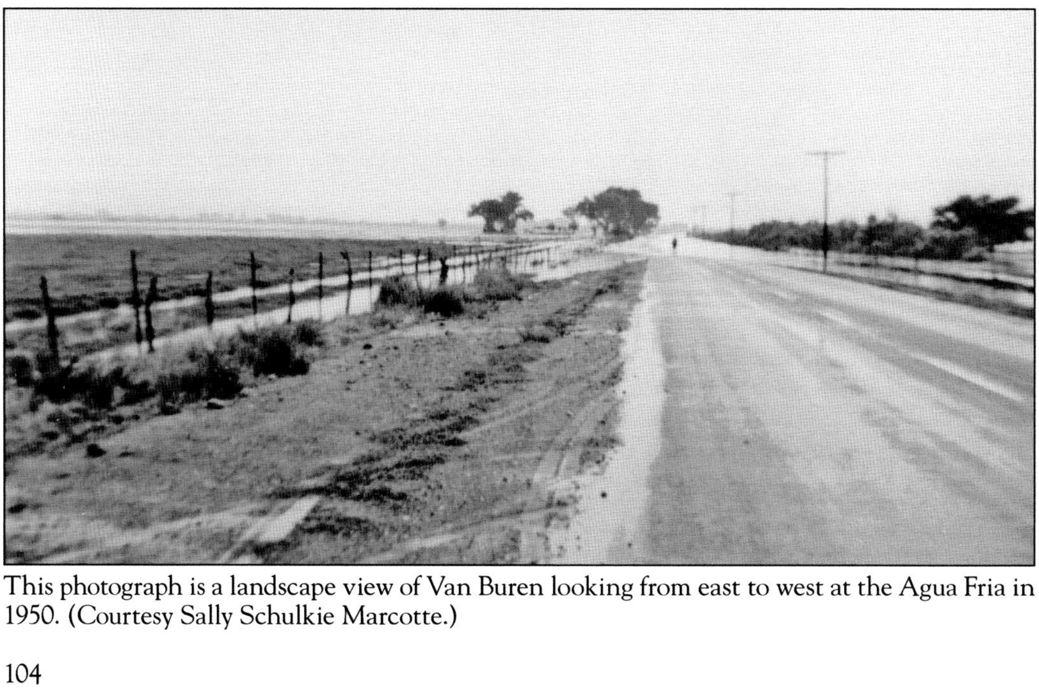

This photograph is a landscape view of Van Buren looking from east to west at the Agua Fria in 1950. (Courtesy Sally Schulkie Marcotte.)

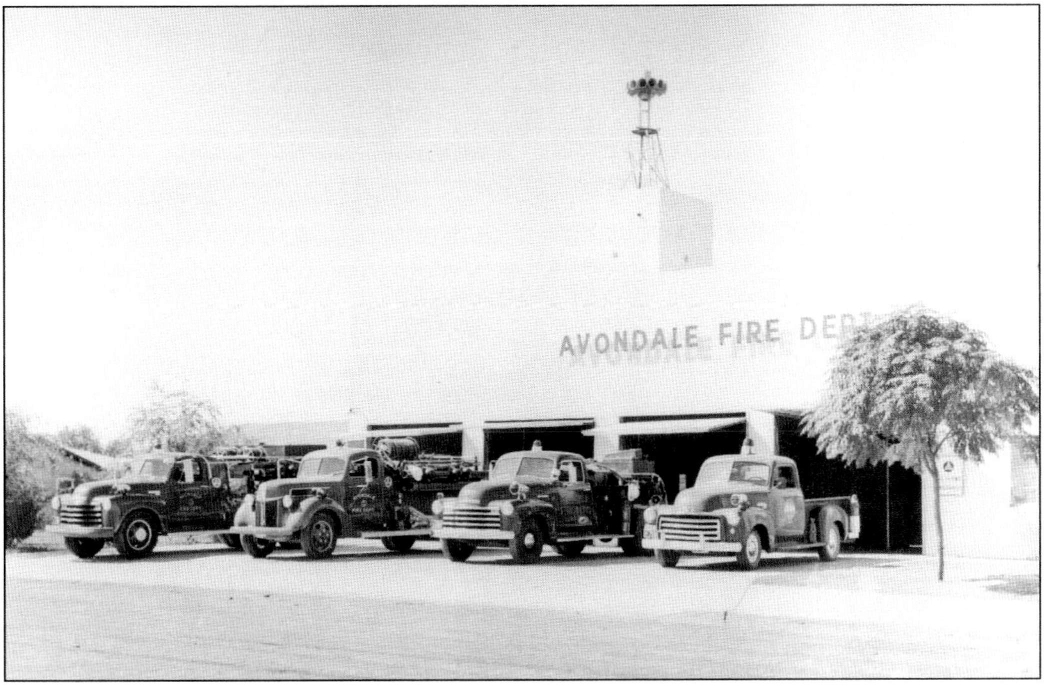

The old fire station remains on the original site. Other stations are disbursed throughout the city at needed locations. The vintage fire truck was on standby for the dedication of a new and improved library in 1985. The current library is located on Western Avenue but will have a new home a little farther west soon. The first library was in a small building at the Circle across the street from where it is currently. The librarian was Eleanore Stanton, who volunteered Tuesdays and Thursdays. At present, the computer room is the most popular spot in the building, and there is always someone anxiously waiting to use them. (Both courtesy City of Avondale Library.)

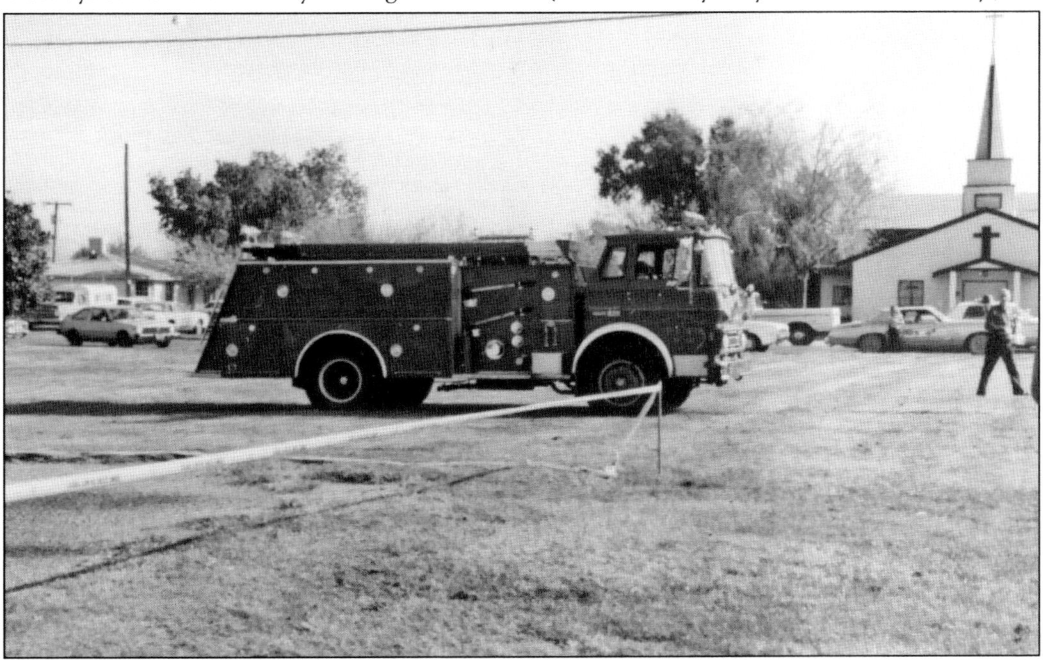

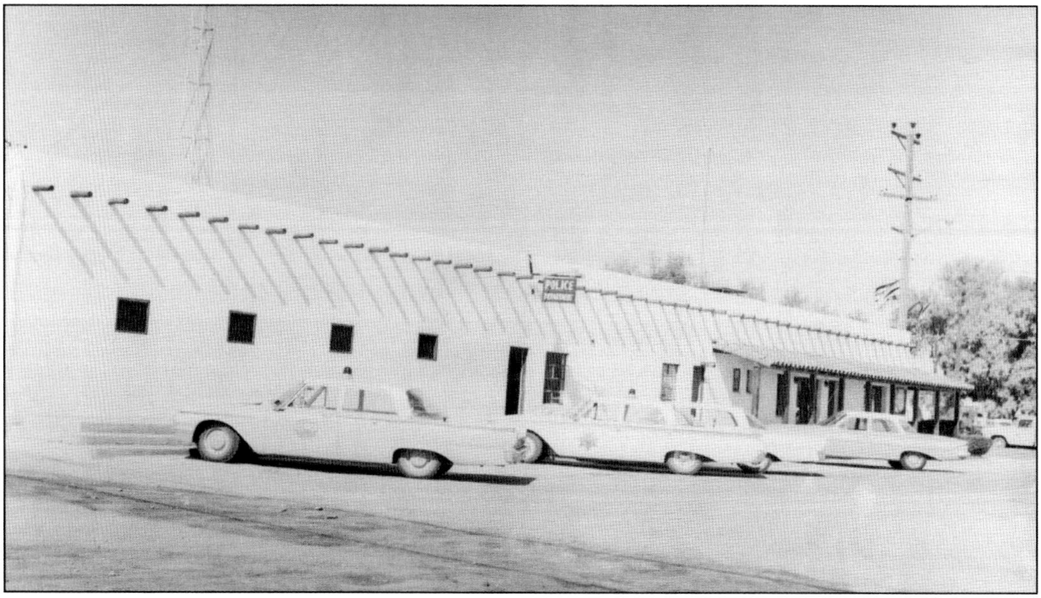

The police department on Western Avenue (above) had only two patrol cars and two officers in 1960. This was another era, and not much crime was perpetrated, but the police were always there when needed. The Avondale city limits covered the Agua Fria River to Central and Van Buren to Lower Buckeye. Below, Mayor John F. McCauley presents a plaque for enduring service to Avondale. The ceremony took place in the old city hall building on Western Avenue. Seated from left to right are Councilman Warner, Emory R. Evans, and Dessie Lorenz (who would become the first female mayor of Avondale). The vice mayor was John Summers. The logo at the bottom of the desk was the old stagecoach image still used today. (Both courtesy City of Avondale.)

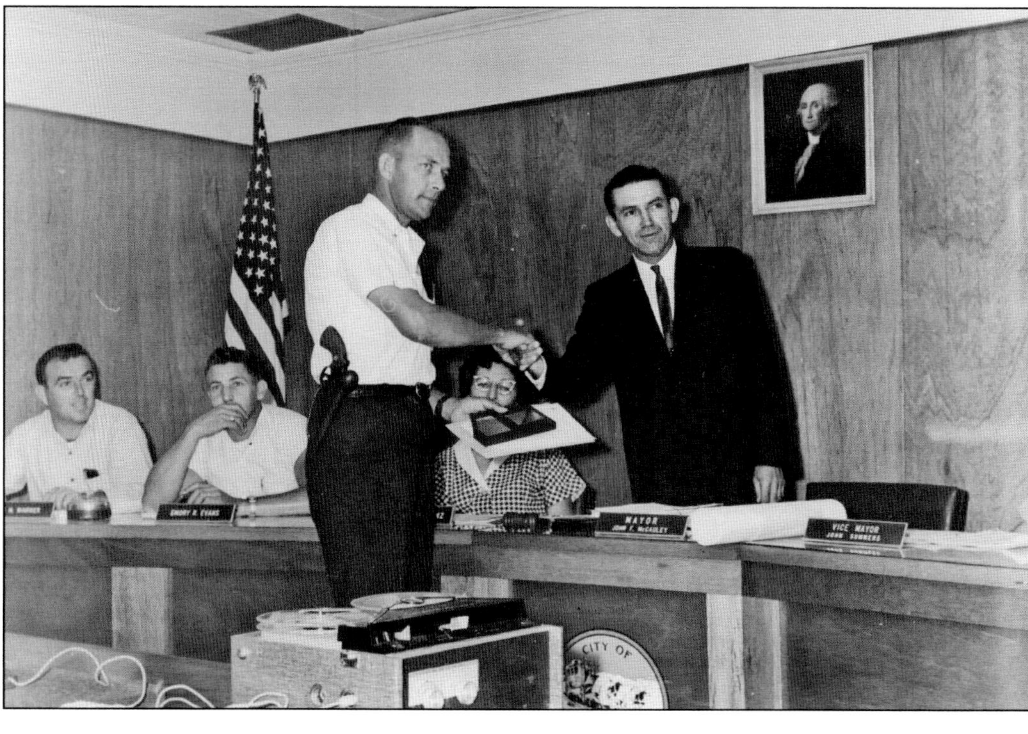

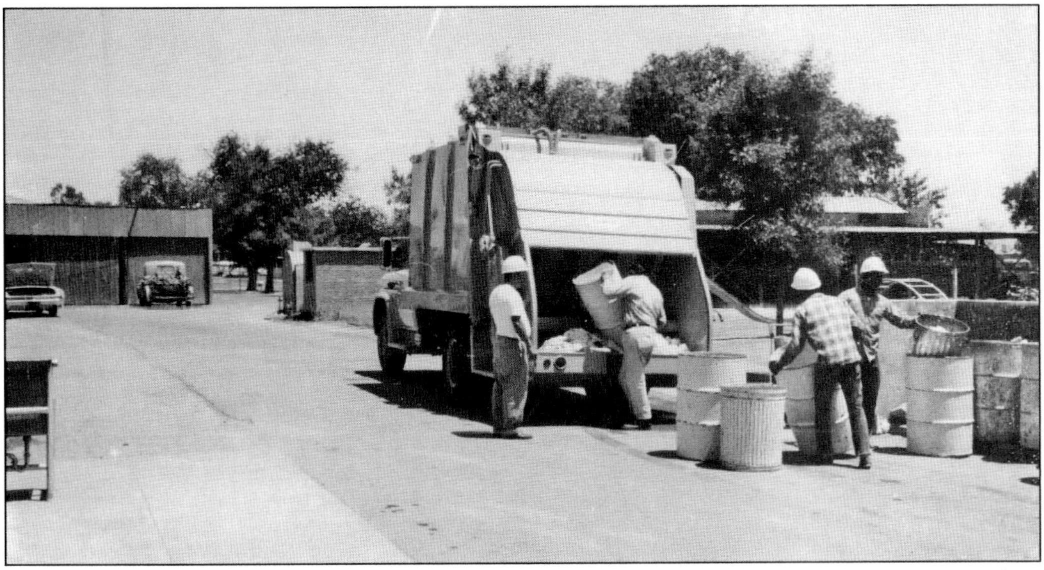

Garbage days of the past were not technical by today's standards. Men hopped out of the truck to gather garbage cans with gloved hands. They would heft them into a large bin with a hydraulic mechanism that could crush garbage as they moved along. When the vehicle was full, off to the dump they went; today dumps are called landfills. One of the dump sites used is the current Phoenix International Raceway parking lot. (Courtesy City of Avondale.)

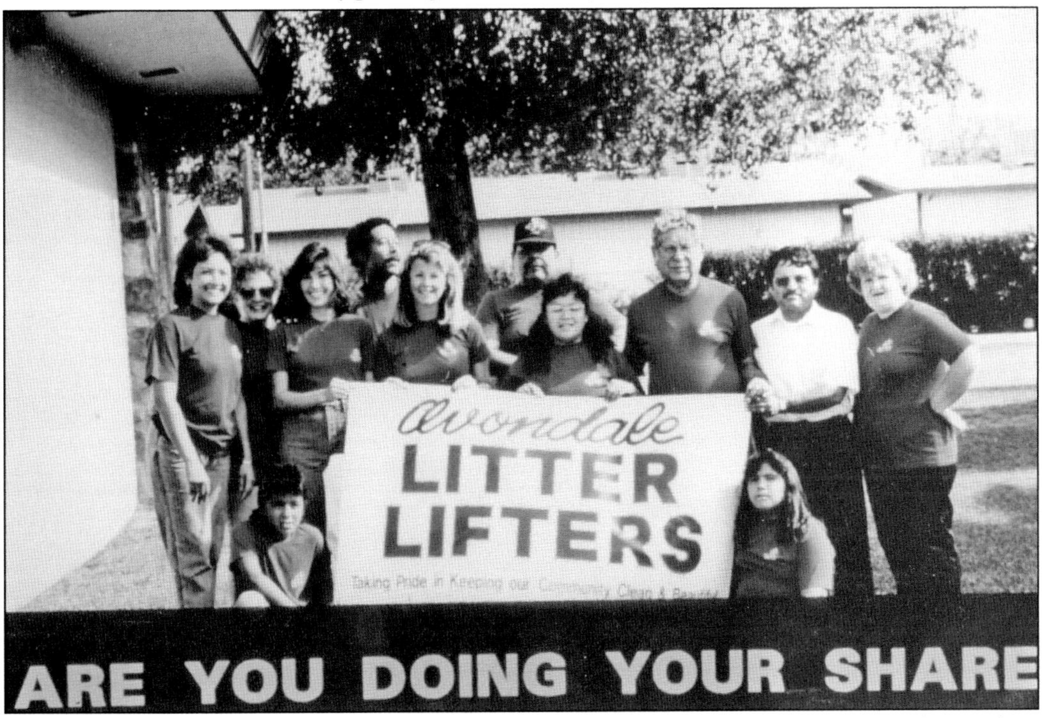

This is Litter Lifters, a volunteer community group that meets the first Thursday of each month to pick up litter in Avondale. Pictured from left to right are (first row) two unidentified; (second row) Irene Aguirre, unidentified, Sophia Johnson, Harold Branch, Linda Farris, unidentified, Juanita Rodriquez, Bill Bedoya, Tom Morales, and unidentified. (Courtesy Sally Schulkie Marcotte.)

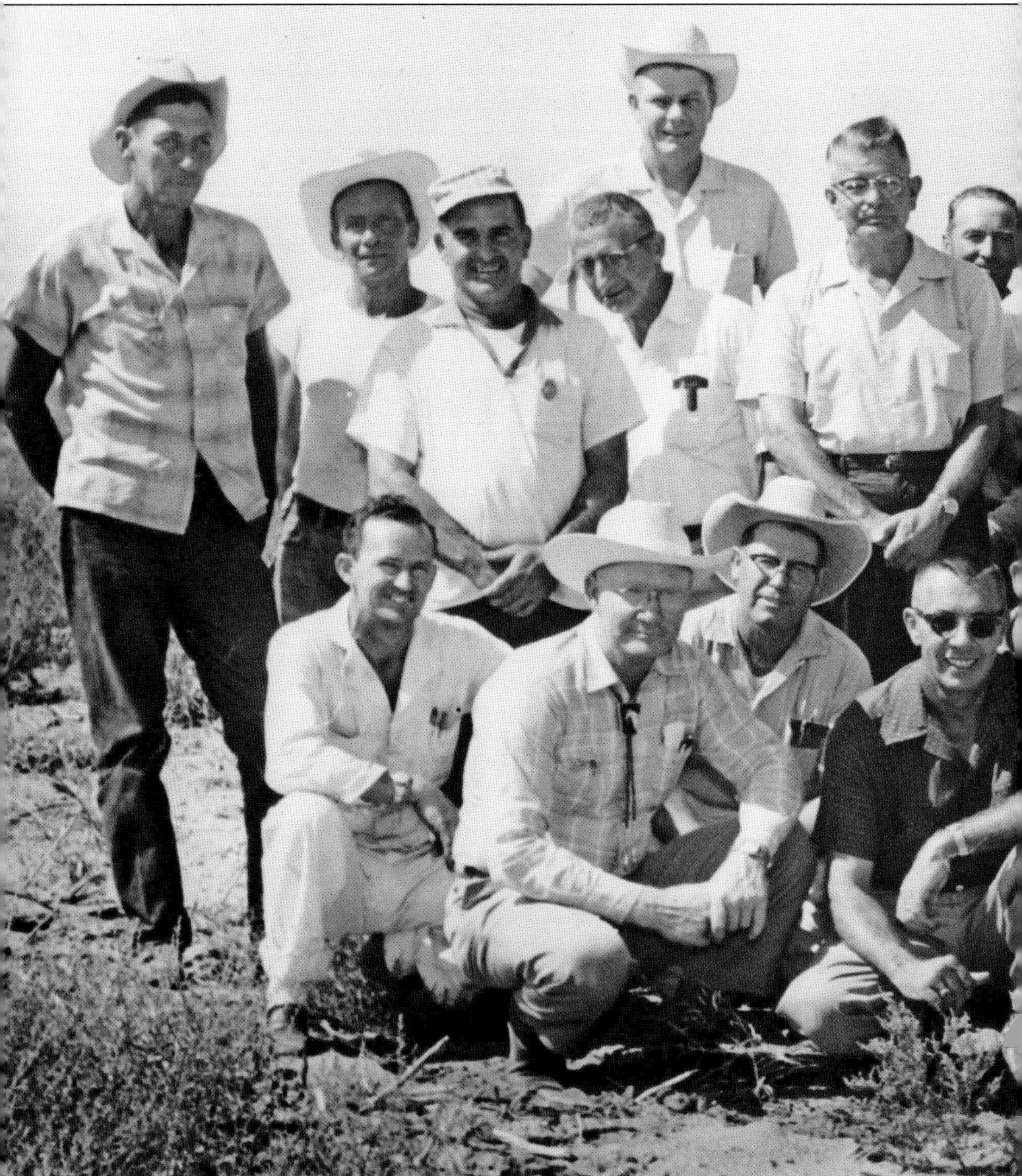

A community Waste Water Treatment Facility was constructed on Lower Buckeye Road and Fourth Street in Avondale for both Avondale and Goodyear. City officials, guests, and project engineers attended the groundbreaking ceremonies for the plant in September 1958. Pictured from left to right are (first row) Homer Tyler, Tex Stewart, Adrian Stewart, two unidentified, Russ Brinker (mayor of Avondale), unidentified, George Leftwich, Bill Rhodes, Dory Snydal,

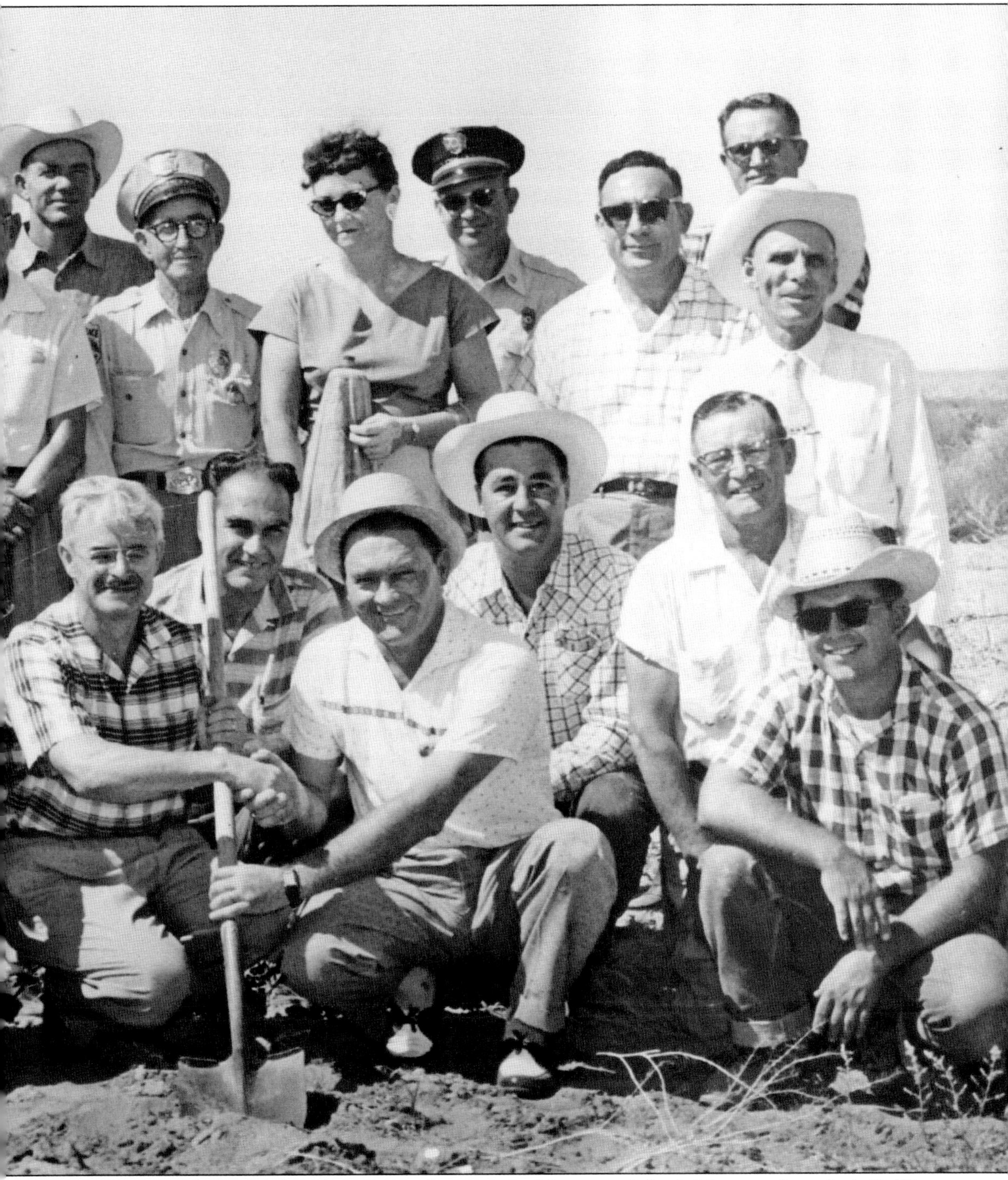

and unidentified; (second row) Earl Vaughn, Leonard Lawson, John Mabis, unidentified, O. T. Nall, unidentified, Bernard Ferguson, unidentified, Ollie Howard, Bill Lynn (Goodyear chief of police), ? Turner, George Watson (Avondale chief of police), two unidentified, and Blackie Buttes. (Courtesy City of Avondale.)

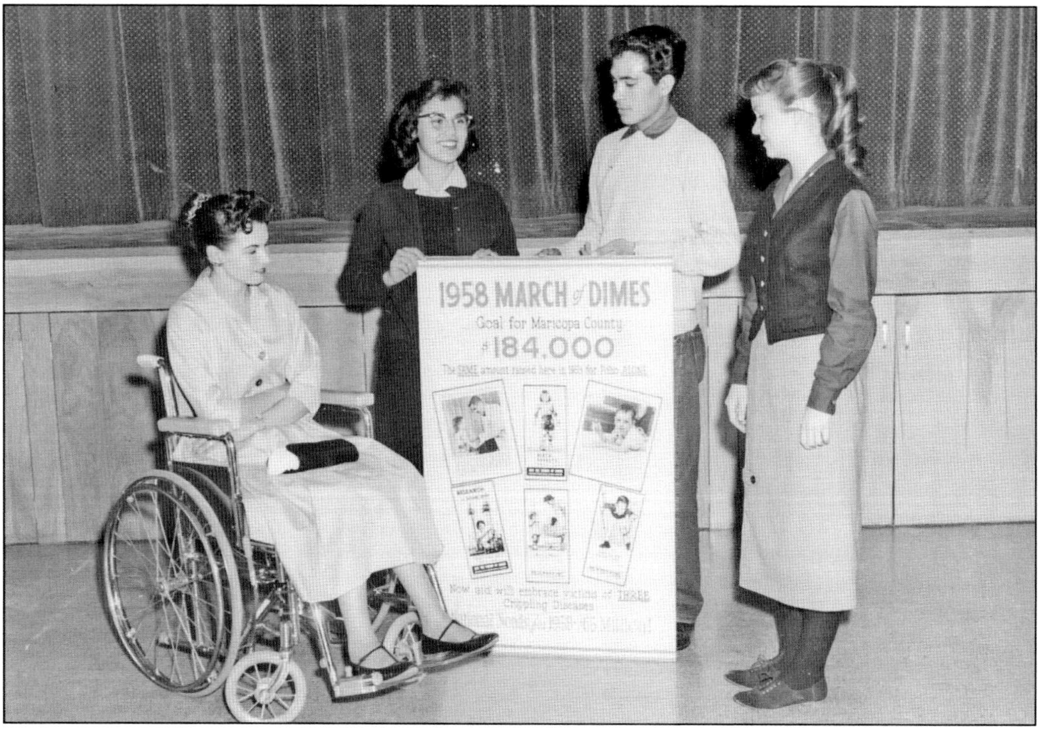

Avondale was and still is a giving community. The local March of Dimes was headed by three Agua Fria High School students—Olivia Luque, Ernie Garcia, and Penny Stapleton. (Courtesy City of Avondale.)

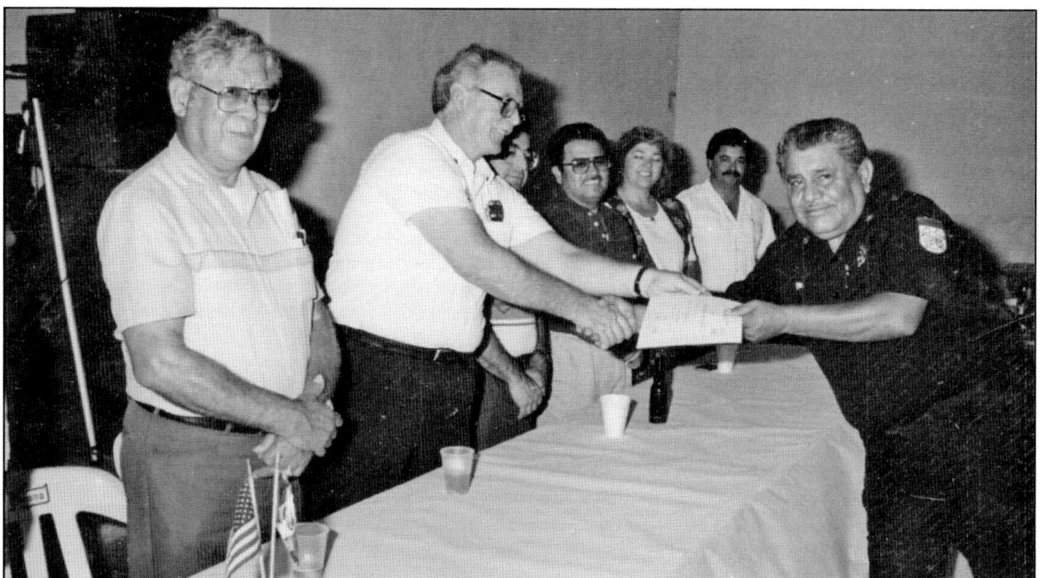

Raymond "Bill" Bedoya was the mayor of Avondale in the 1990s and hosted many city awards ceremonies during his service. Pictured here are Raymond "Bill" Bedoya (first from left), John Walter (second from left), Tom Morrales (fourth from left), and Oralia Contrreas (fifth from left). (Courtesy City of Avondale.)

Bill Bedoya (center), mayor of Avondale in the 1990s, admired the annual decorations for Billy Moore Days. (Courtesy City of Avondale.)

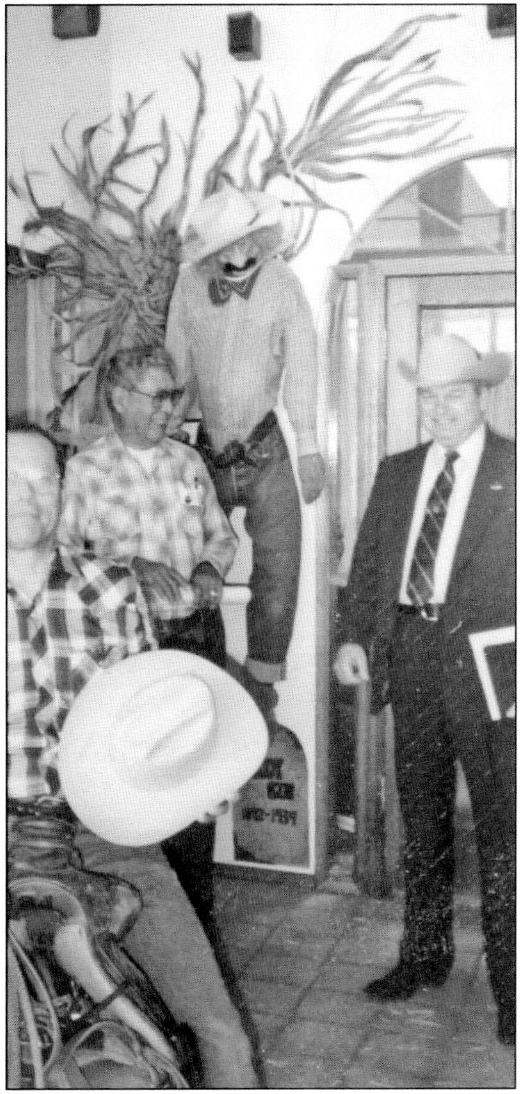

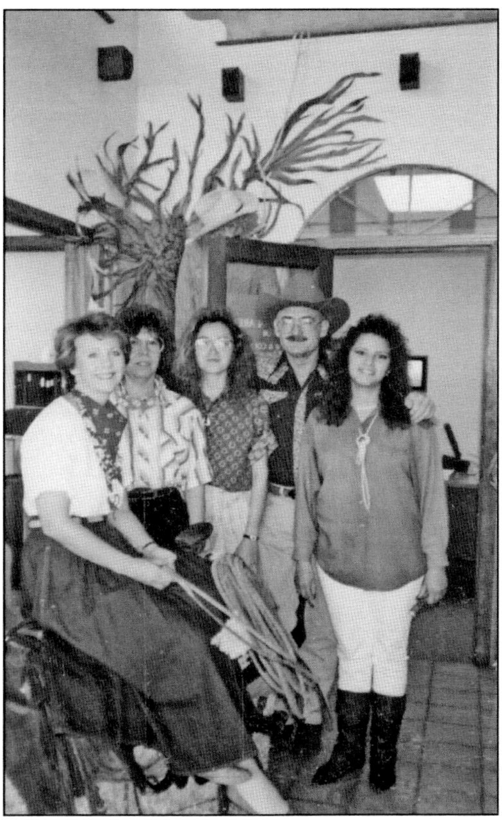

From left to right, Linda Farris, Mary Ellen Carr, unidentified, Don Graham, and Lori Pariga pose with an old saddle and lasso for a Billy Moore Days celebration. (Courtesy City of Avondale.)

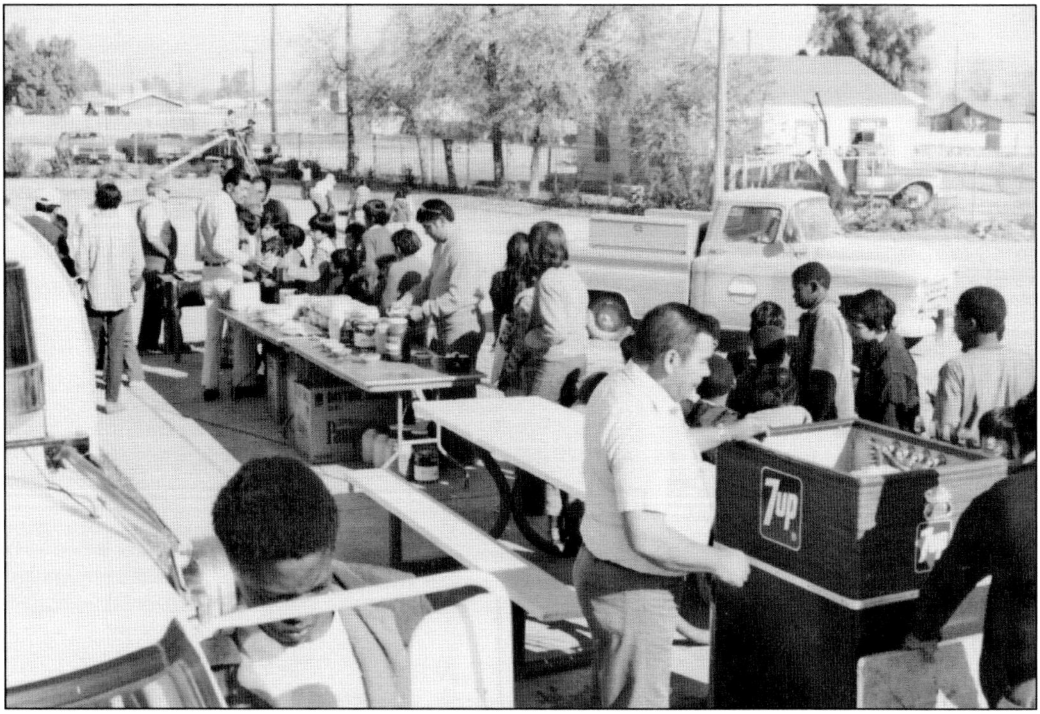

The police chief, John Lopez, often gave back to his community, such as at this Christmas party. Doing so, he showed his great spirit. (Courtesy City of Avondale.)

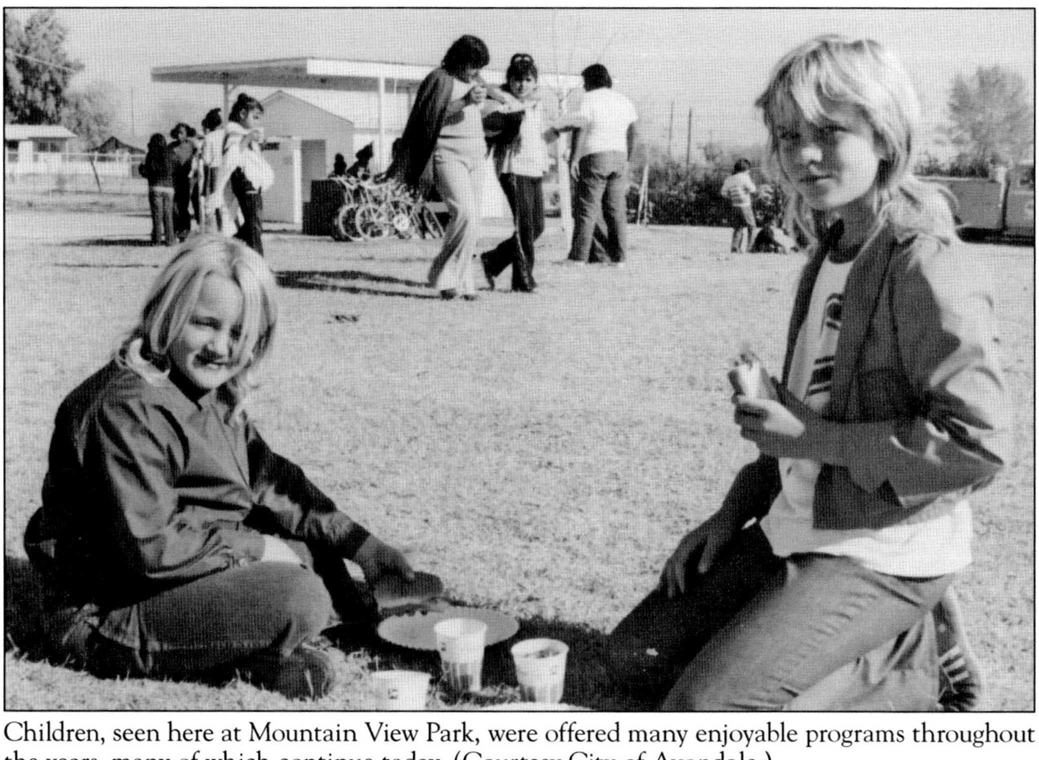

Children, seen here at Mountain View Park, were offered many enjoyable programs throughout the years, many of which continue today. (Courtesy City of Avondale.)

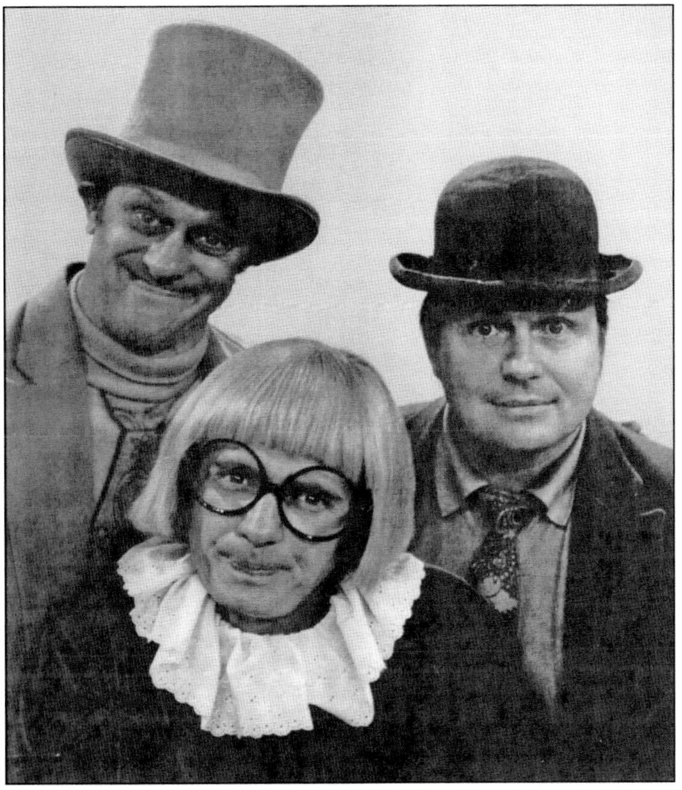

Good old Wallace and Ladmo were part of the longest-running kids' program in the state of Arizona. The show also included Gerald. If you were a child growing up in the Valley during the 1960s, 1970s, or 1980s, you were watching the *Wallace and Ladmo Show* on television. (Courtesy City of Avondale.)

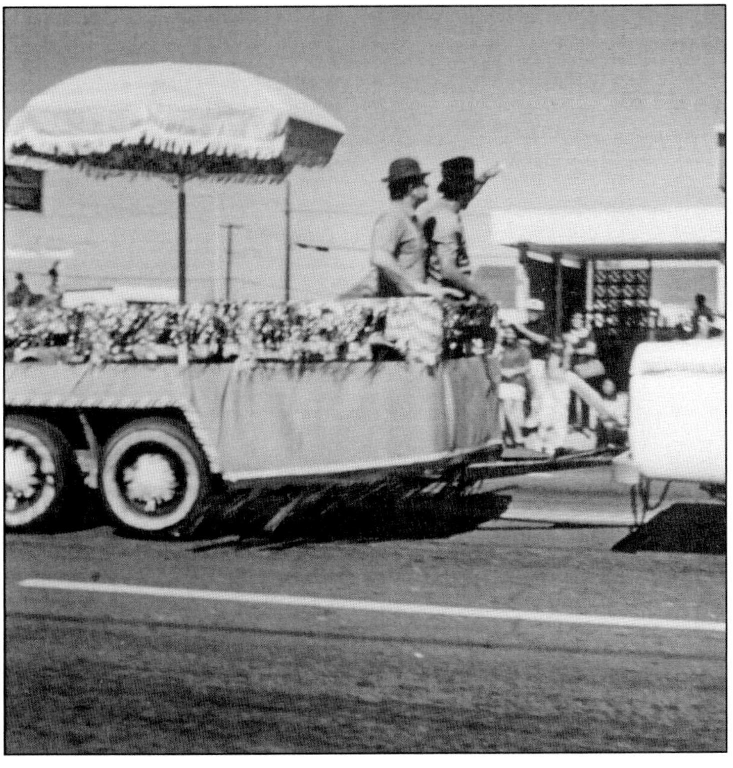

The slapstick funny men Wallace and Ladmo were always a hit at any parade in Arizona and often were included in the Billy Moore Days parade. (Courtesy City of Avondale.)

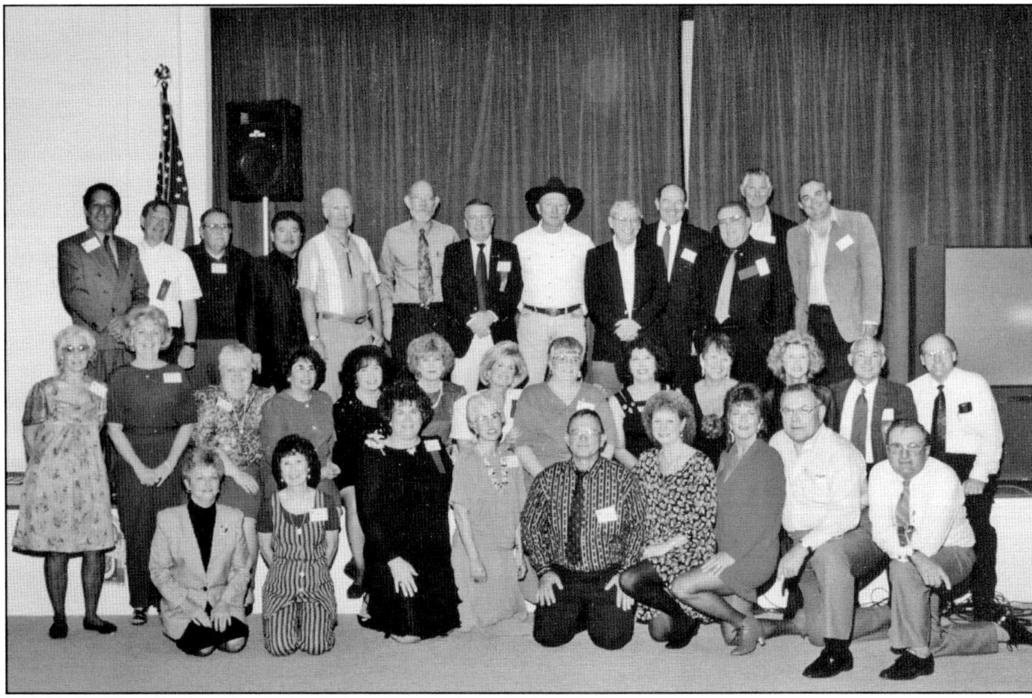

The Agua Fria High School reunion in 1999 took place on the stage of the school. From left to right are (first row) Francis Stinett, Vivian Belcher, Lenore Semmler, Peggy Jenkin, Dennis Wood, Hazel Schreffel, Earline Darnell, Ron Boatwright, and Stu Anderson; (second row) Judy Parenteau, Gwen Laravia, Carolee Stanley, Alice Garcia, Connie Watkins, Yvonne Heenan, Jeanne Ingerson, Gloria Jacobson, Cruz Dominguez, Janet Wilt, Carolee Feltch, Roger Harris, and Bill Russell; (third row) Richard Gomez, Richard Manley, David Falls, Ruben Kellingsworth, Harley ?, Tom Kampert, Mack McCarley, John Green, Ken Kiko, Larry Baker, John Craft, Roy Colbert, and Bill Armstrong. (Courtesy Ken and Sally Kiko.)

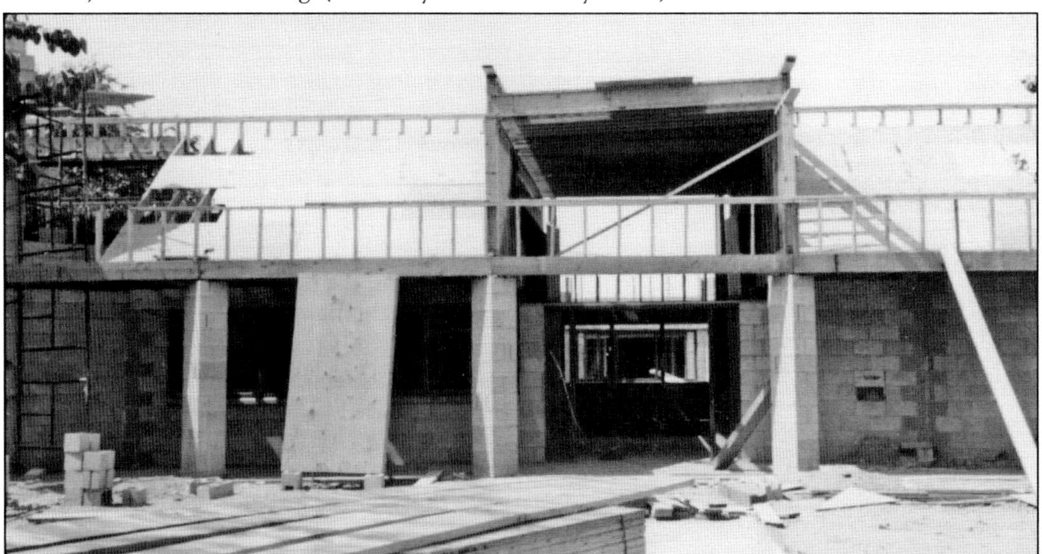

Sturdy construction was added to the library in 1985. (Courtesy City of Avondale.)

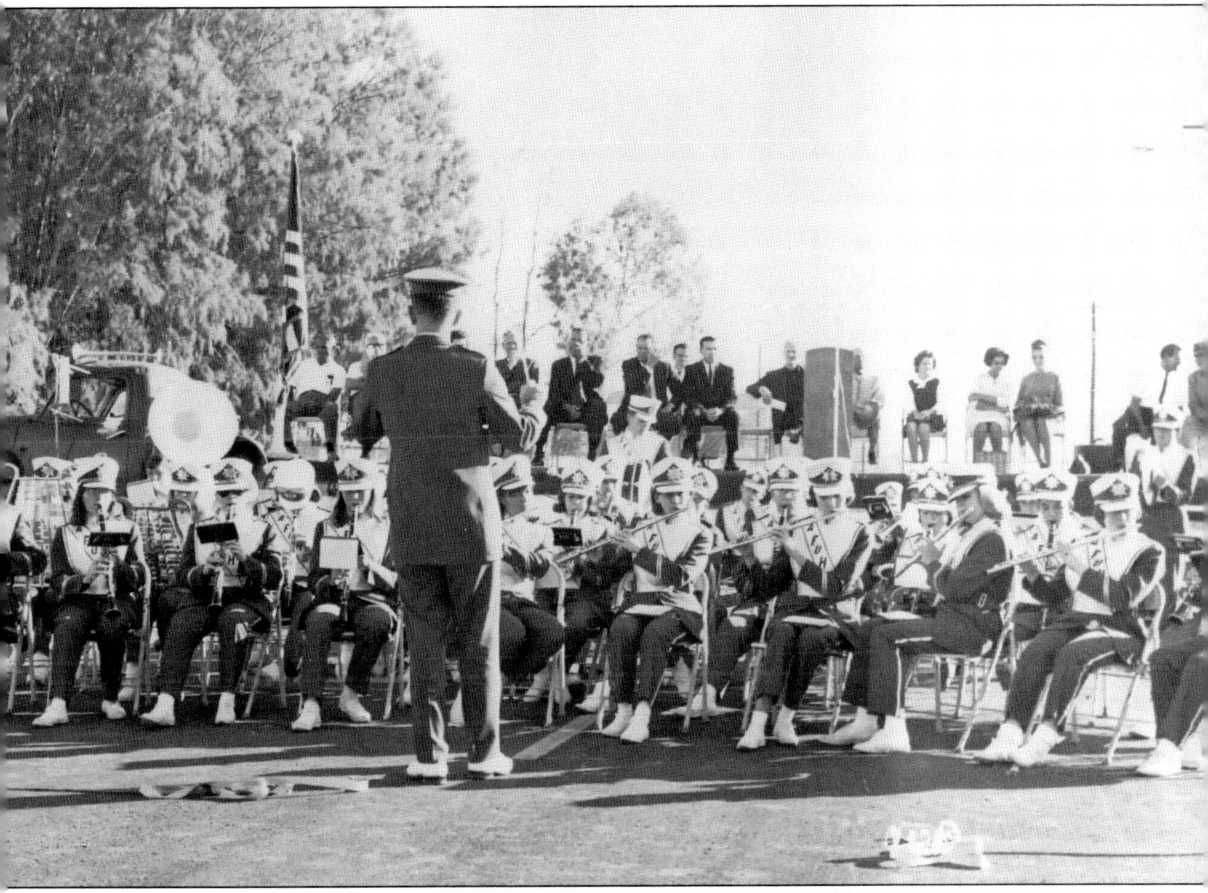

The Agua Fria High School Band played at the grand opening of the library's new addition in 1985. (Courtesy City of Avondale.)

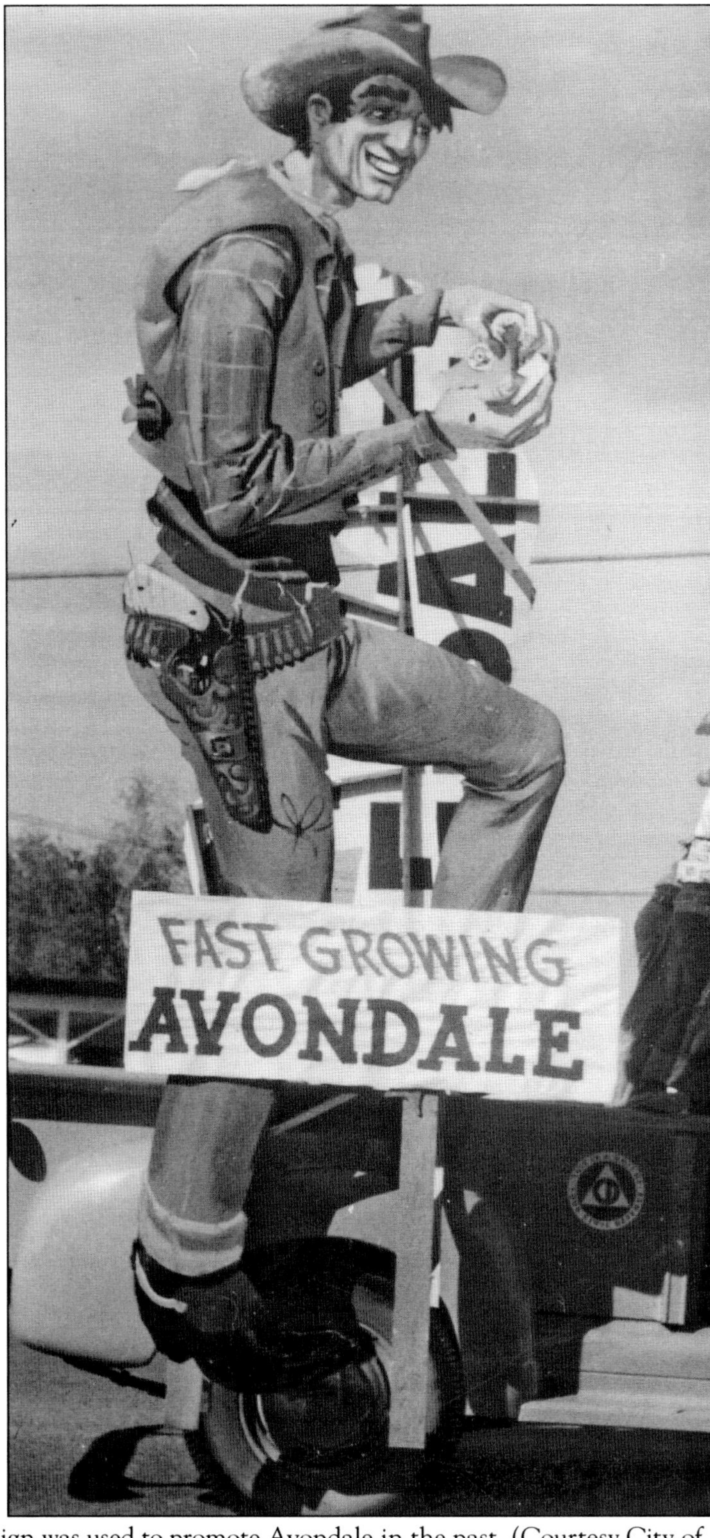

A whimsical sign was used to promote Avondale in the past. (Courtesy City of Avondale.)

Five

Avondale Today and Tomorrow

In 1975, Carlos Palma was Avondale's city manager. At the time of his appointment, the city of Avondale was 3.5 miles in size, with a population of approximately 7,000. All residents of the city lived west of the Agua Fria River. The only bridge over the Agua Fria was the Buckeye Road Bridge. In 1996, the population was a mere 23,000. Avondale's incorporated area was 24 square miles, and city hall's address was 325 North Central Avenue. The mayor was Raymond "Bill" Bedoya, and the city manager was still Carlos Palma.

Today Avondale has a population of 69,356. City hall is located in a beautiful structure at 11465 West Civic Center Drive. The city encompasses 54.8 square miles and has a budget of $267,975,710.

Avondale is still positioned for greater growth and prosperity well into the future. A wide range and variety of cultural, economic, and educational advances have been set in place to support the growing population. Resources range from the top-notch educational programs such as the West Valley Arts Council to Estrella Mountain Community College and technological advances in education at the Universal Technical Institute. Avondale's recreational activities become a city within a city overnight with the growing popularity of the Phoenix International Raceway (PIR). PIR is known as the world's fastest one-mile paved oval and is the open venue of multiple NASCAR events annually, each attracting nearly 400,000 enthusiasts and hundreds of race teams, contributing hundreds of millions of dollars to the state and local economy of Avondale.

Avondale's next step into tomorrow will meet the growing local demand for city employment; the emerging medical field has attracted many great minds of the Southwest and office buildings are sprouting up as fast as business parks and light-manufacturing facilities. The City of Avondale has designated over 400 acres in the General Plan, which is currently in various stages of design approval. Avondale is growing to become a competitive metropolis of Maricopa County but will never forget its roots.

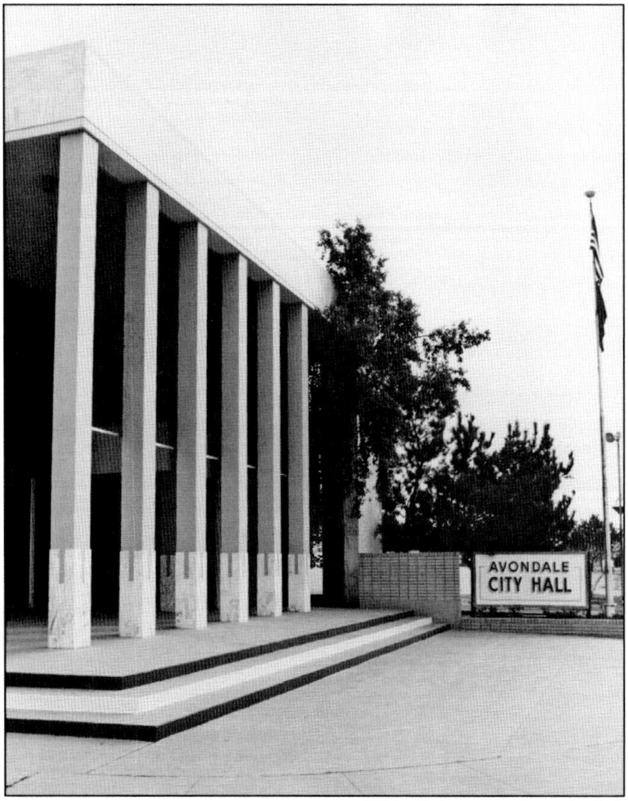

The first city hall was located on Western Avenue. The second location of the city hall was on Central in the Bank of Gibralter building. (Courtesy City of Avondale.)

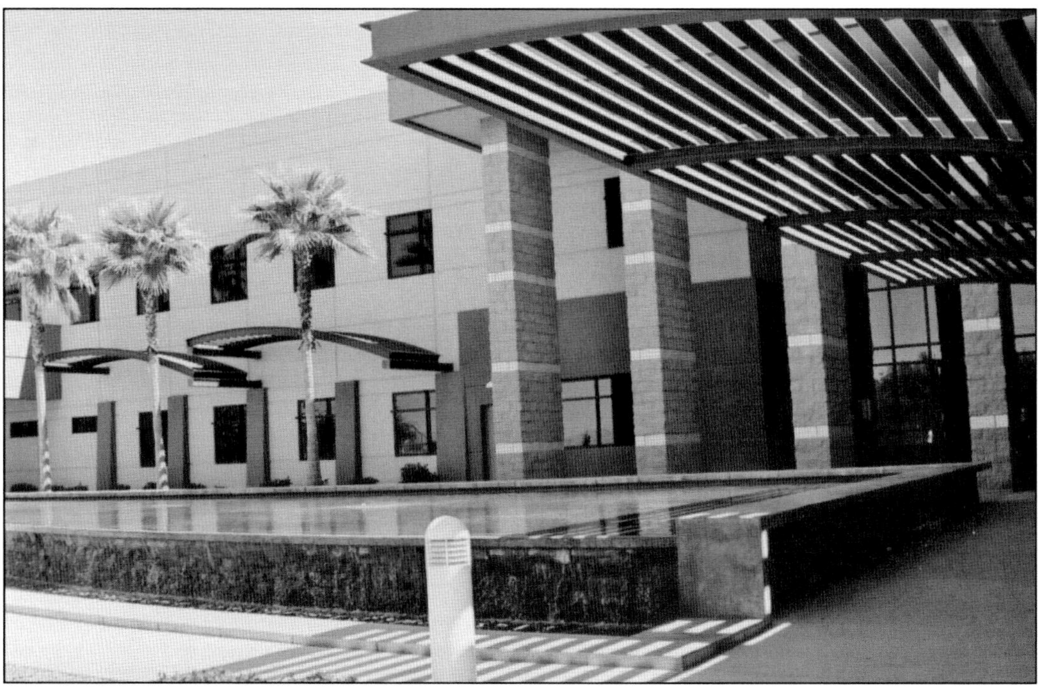

The new contemporary city hall's address is 11465 West Civic Center Drive; it sits at the corner of Avondale Boulevard. (Courtesy author.)

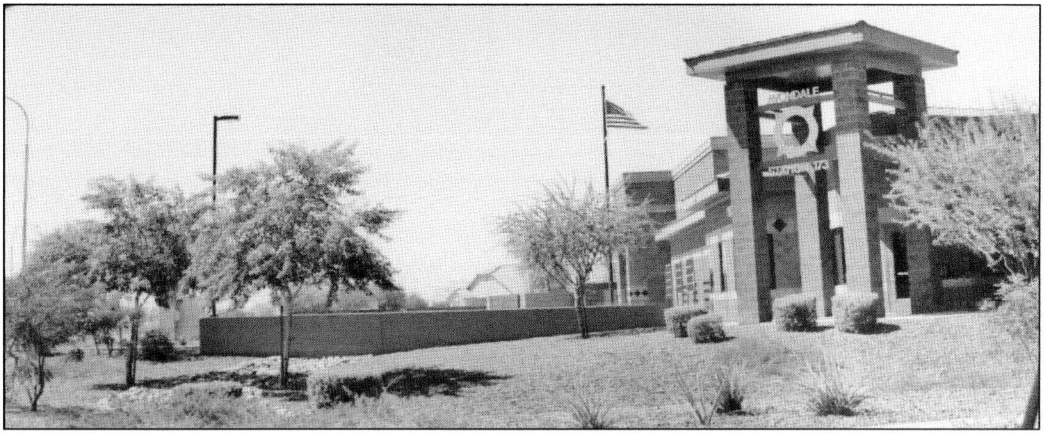

One of the newest fire stations, built in 2006, is on Avondale Boulevard and Durango Street. (Courtesy author.)

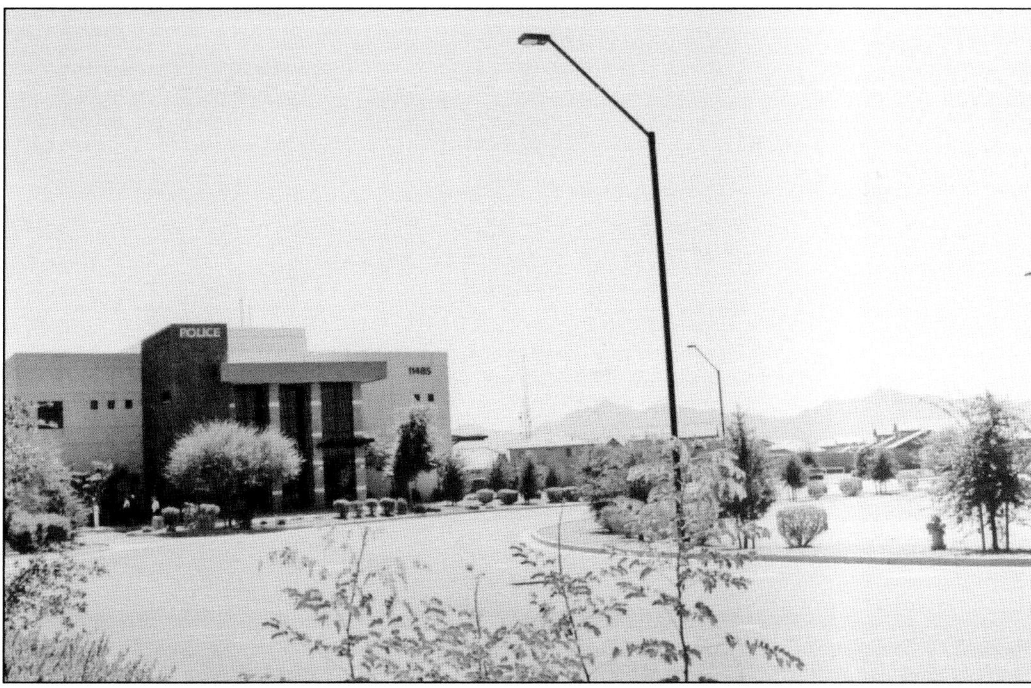

Avondale has two police stations; the newer one is a multi-story structure next to the modern city complex. (Courtesy author.)

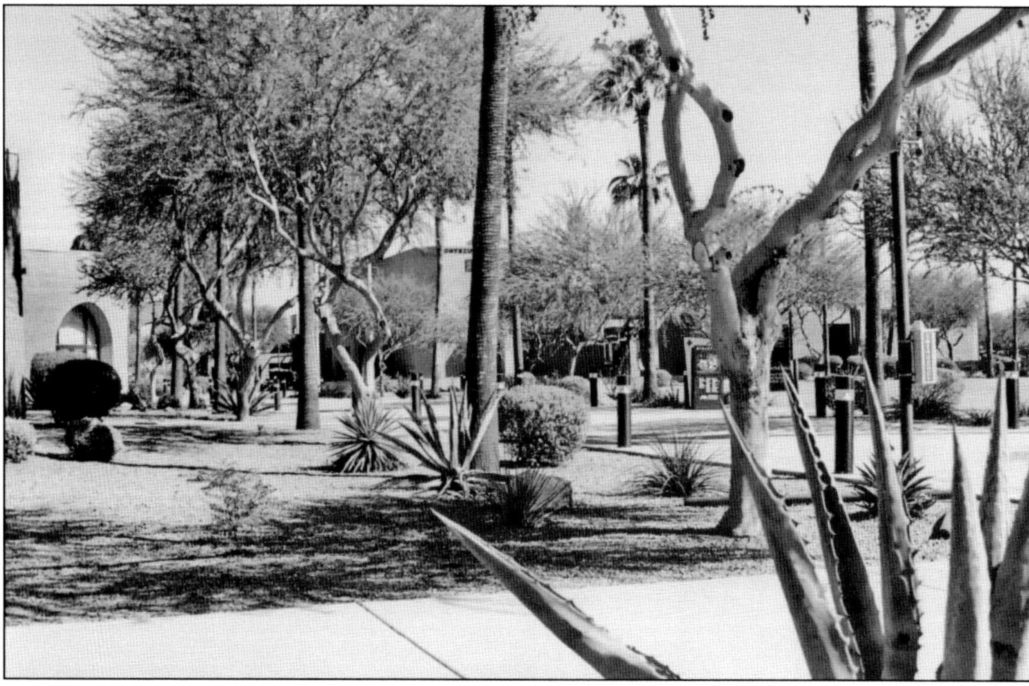

Avondale has a fine junior college. Estrella Community College has innovative classes for everyone. (Courtesy author.)

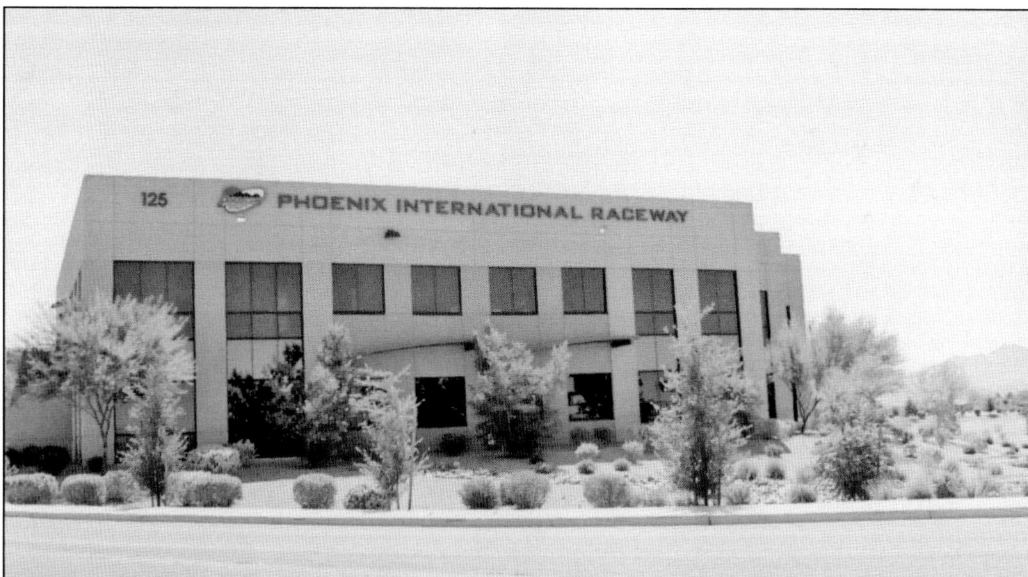

The site of Phoenix International Raceway began as a dirt go-cart track, and then in 1963, it became a one-mile paved oval. After name changes and new owners, the track's fortune would change. Dennis Wood sold the track to Buddy Jobe. Jobe improved the track and attracted NASCAR in 1988. In 1997, Phoenix International was purchased by International Speedway Corporation, who owns and operates it now. (Courtesy author.)

Phoenix International Raceway is the largest corporation in Avondale and creates a great deal of revenue for the city. (Courtesy City of Avondale.)

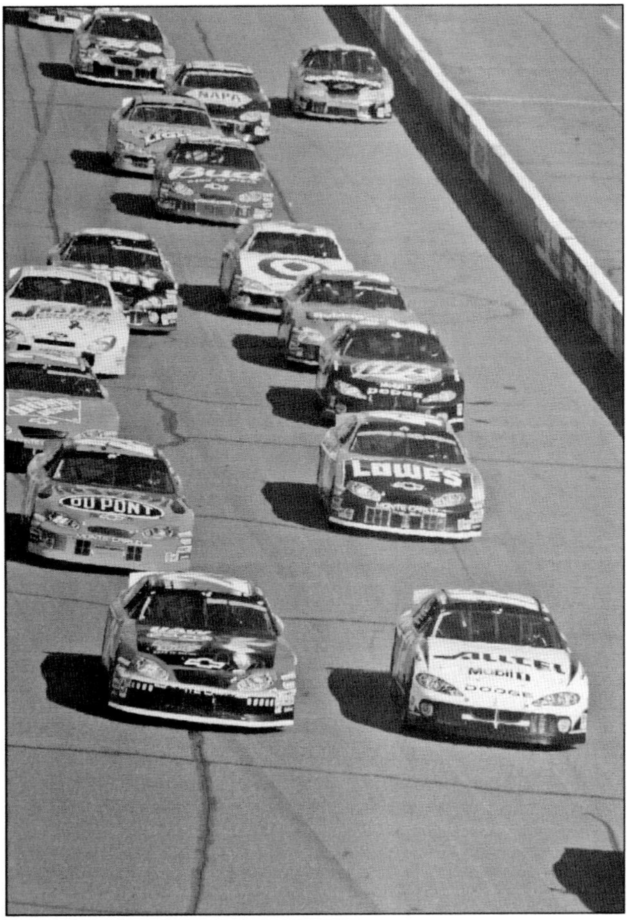

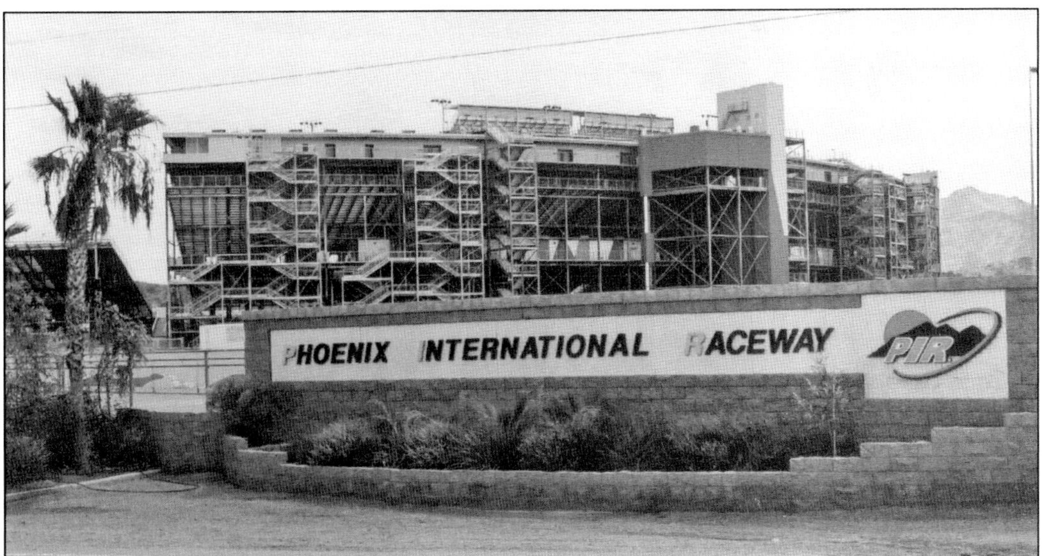

Today the racetrack is fondly known as "The Jewel of the Desert." Its location at the base of the Estrella Mountains provides breathtaking views. (Courtesy author.)

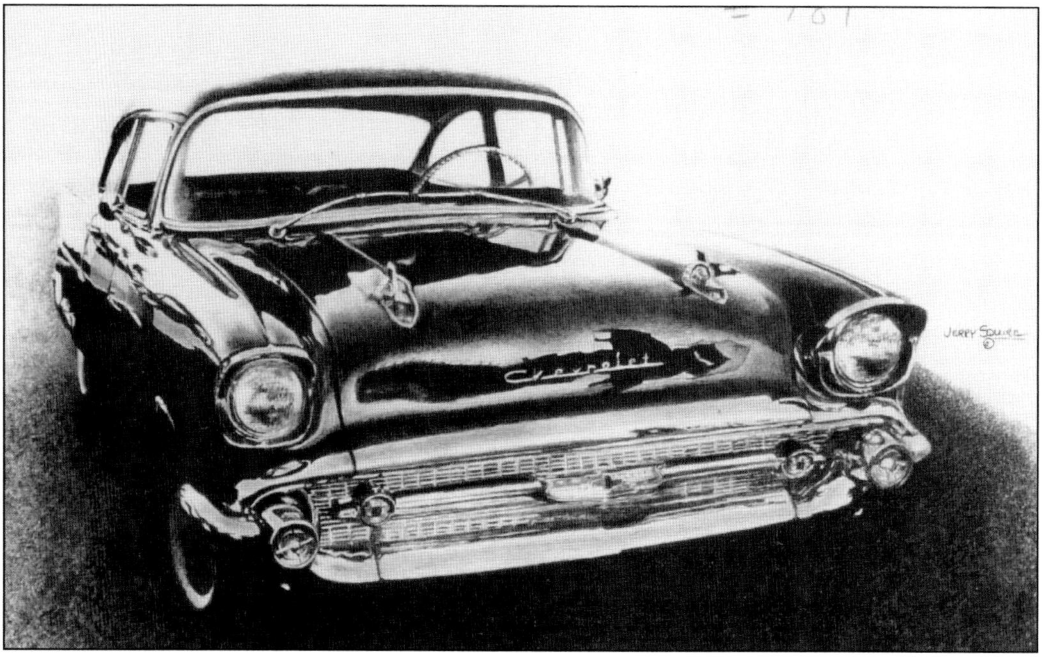

The picture was drawn by the author, Jerry Squire. If you look closely, you can see the last turn with the grandstands of Phoenix International Raceway in the reflection. The picture is titled "The Last Turn." (Courtesy author.)

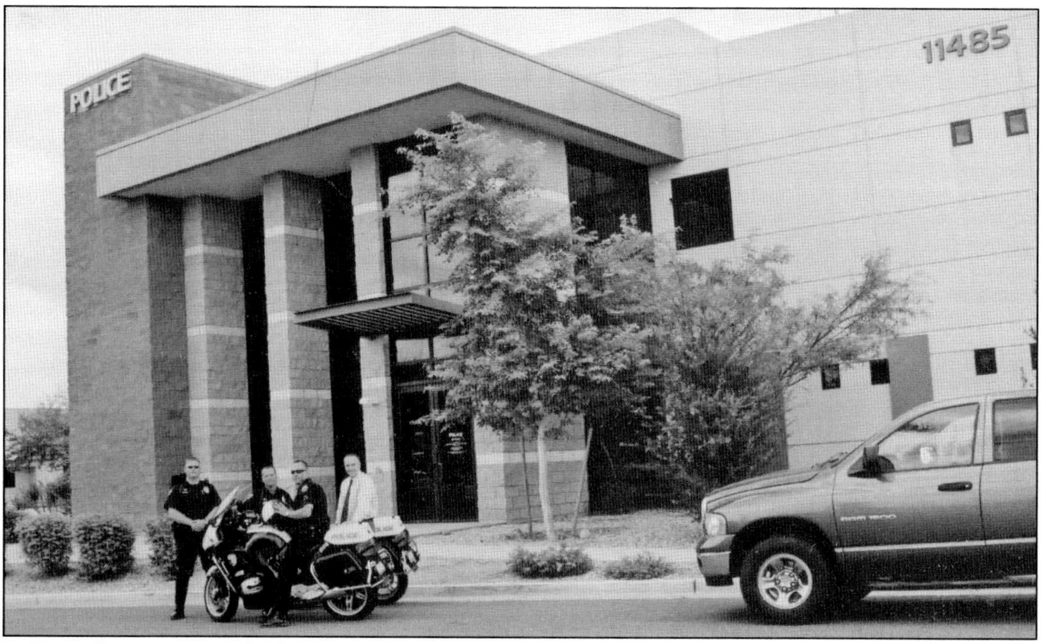

Police officers pose with the city prosecutor, Alan Kuffner, in front of the new Avondale police station. The motorcycles and new Dodge truck are the latest equipment used by the department. The truck has a siren and emergency lights hidden until needed. (Courtesy author.)

Some of Avondale's finest are pictured here. The officers, from left to right, are Eric Spano, Jeff Williams, and Jeff McGrath, and the city prosecutor is Alan Kuffner. (Courtesy author.)

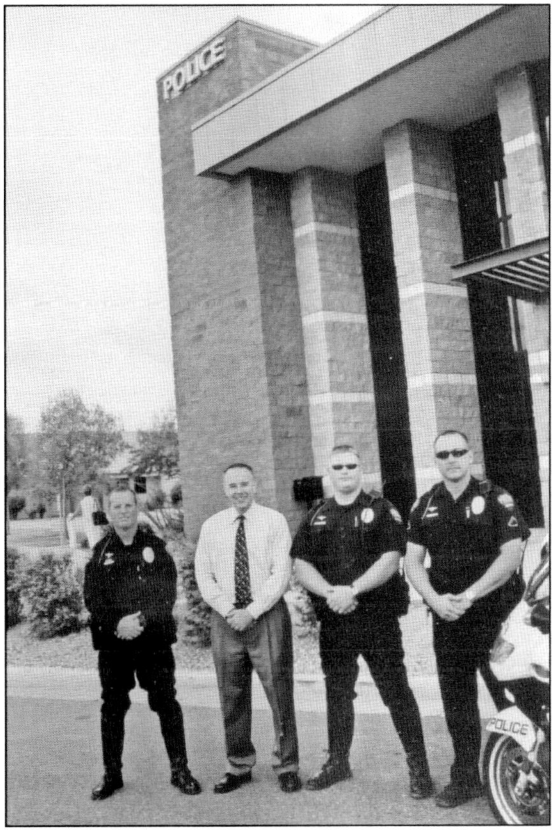

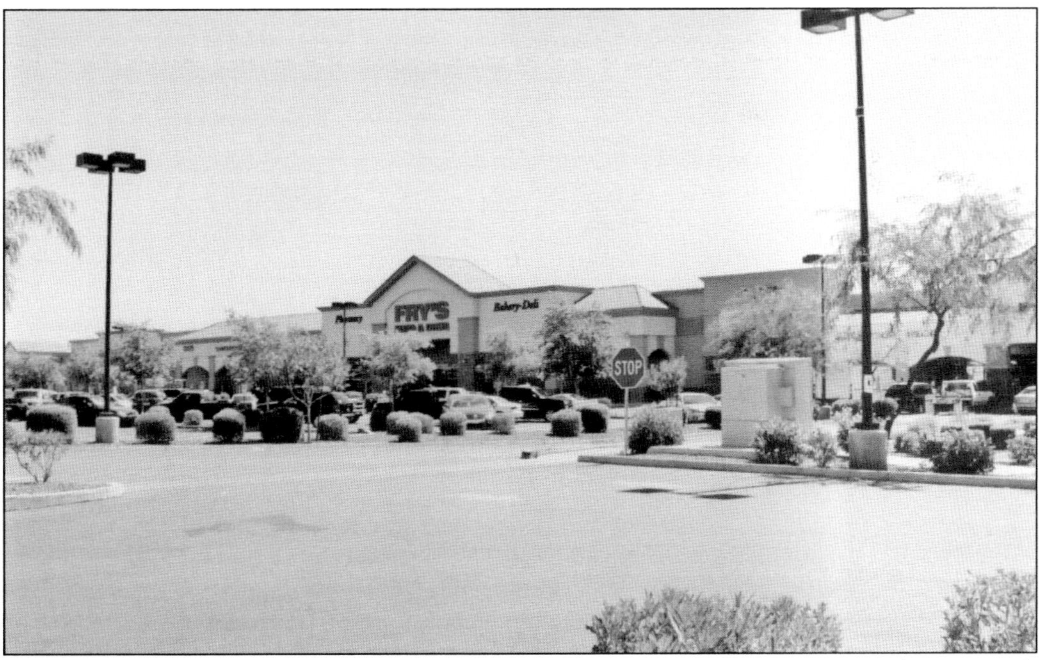

A century ago, the land provided for this Fry's shopping center once was a vast desert ostrich farm. (Courtesy author.)

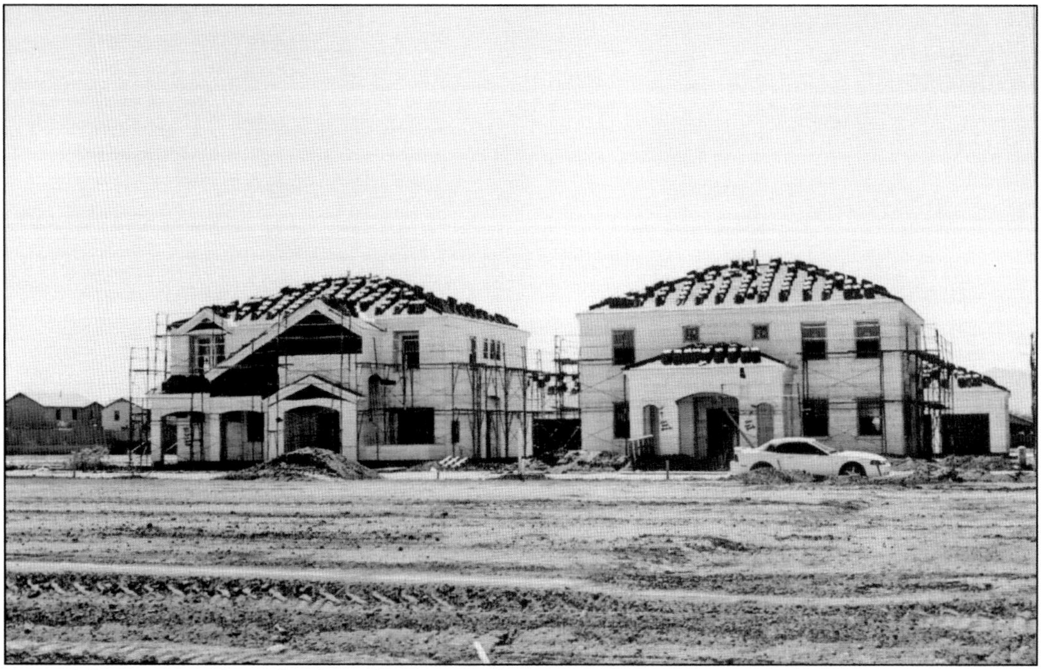

Avondale, Arizona, has a brisk real estate market. Since Maricopa County is the fastest-growing county in America, the future looks bright even in a slow market. (Courtesy author.)

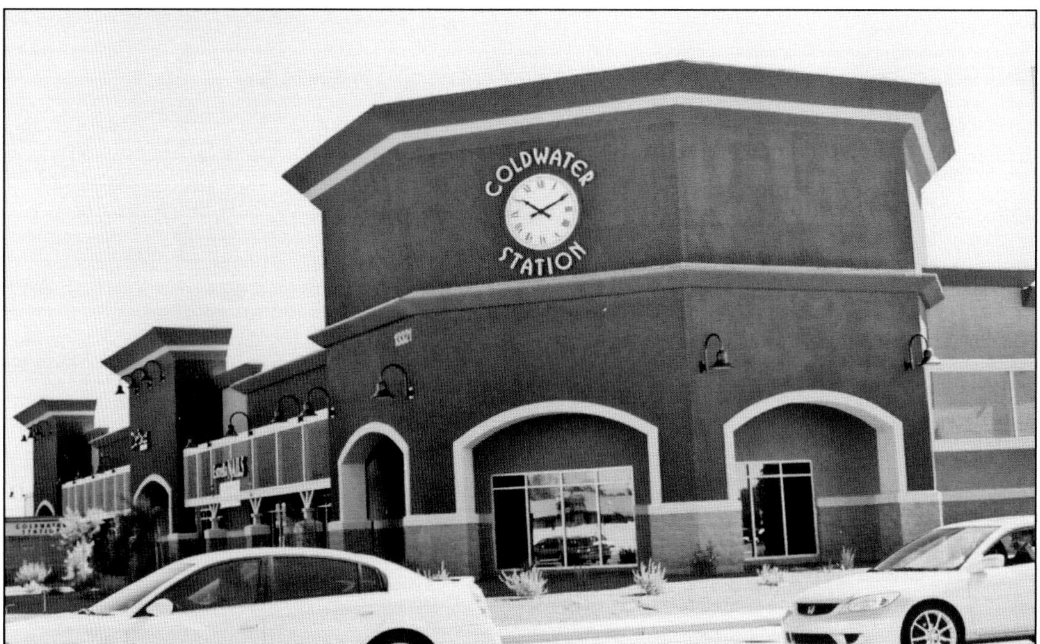

The Coldwater Mercantile building looks as if it resides in Litchfield Park, but the area is incorporated in the City of Avondale. It has a name taken from the past. (Courtesy author.)

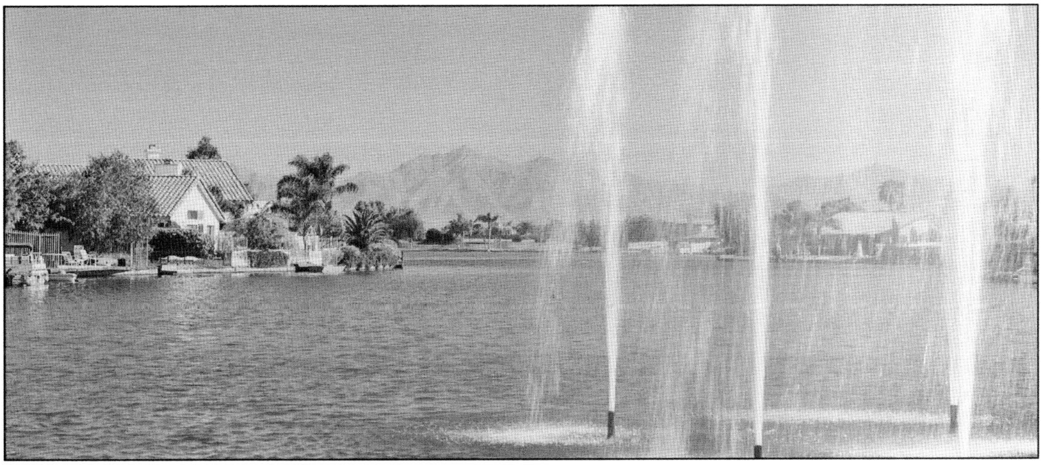

Garden Lakes was one of the first planned communities in the city. The land at one time was the place where an irrigation flume extended over the Agua Fria River. Today it is a beautiful lake community. (Courtesy City of Avondale.)

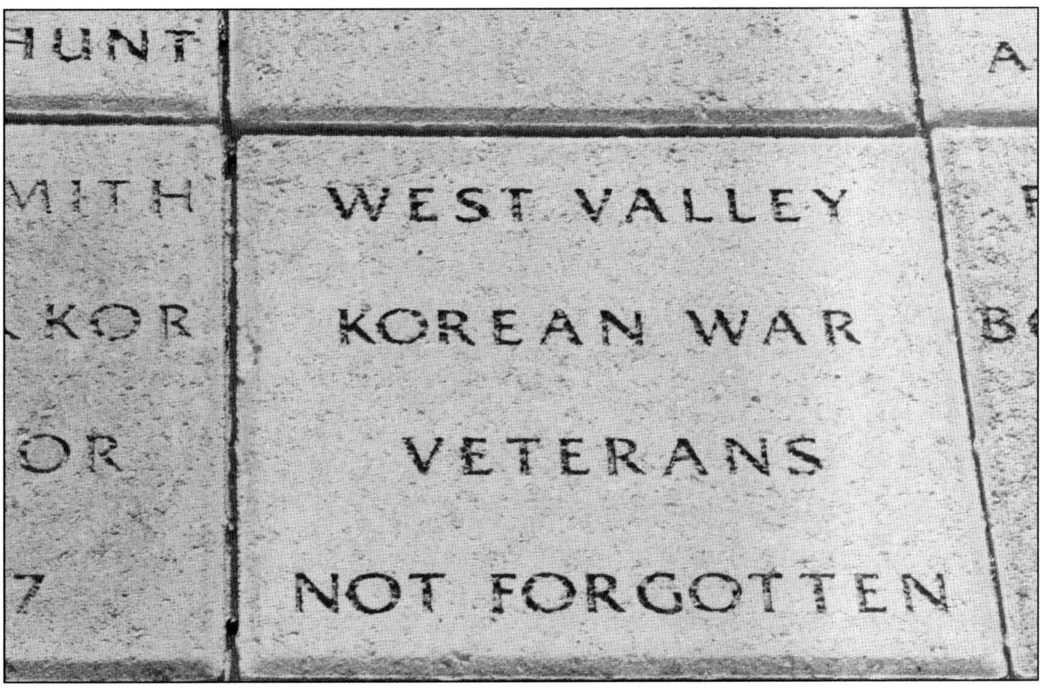

Avondale's veterans are honored with a memorial on the grounds of city hall. (Courtesy City of Avondale.)

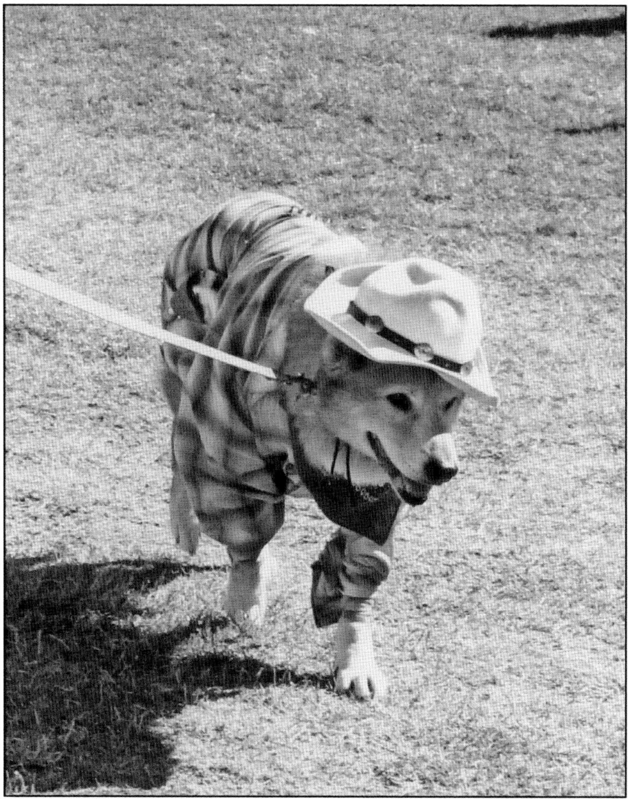

Avondale's dog park has many breeds prancing around. Maybe this pooch is clad as Billy Moore. (Courtesy City of Avondale.)

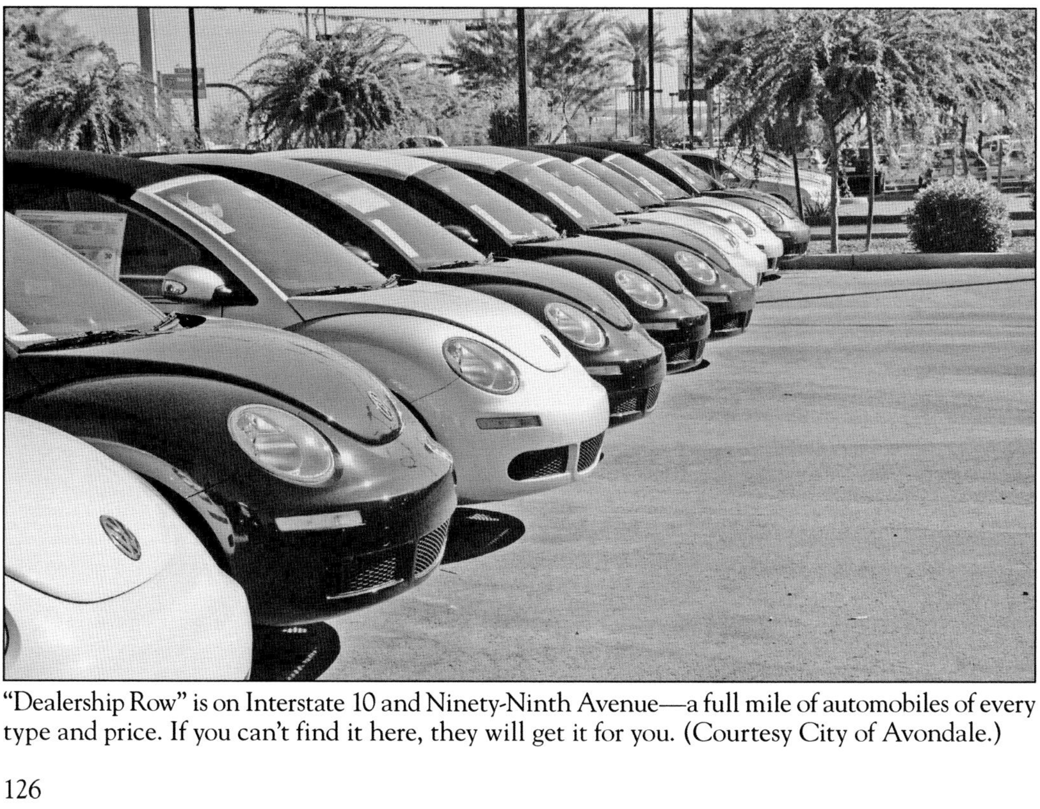

"Dealership Row" is on Interstate 10 and Ninety-Ninth Avenue—a full mile of automobiles of every type and price. If you can't find it here, they will get it for you. (Courtesy City of Avondale.)

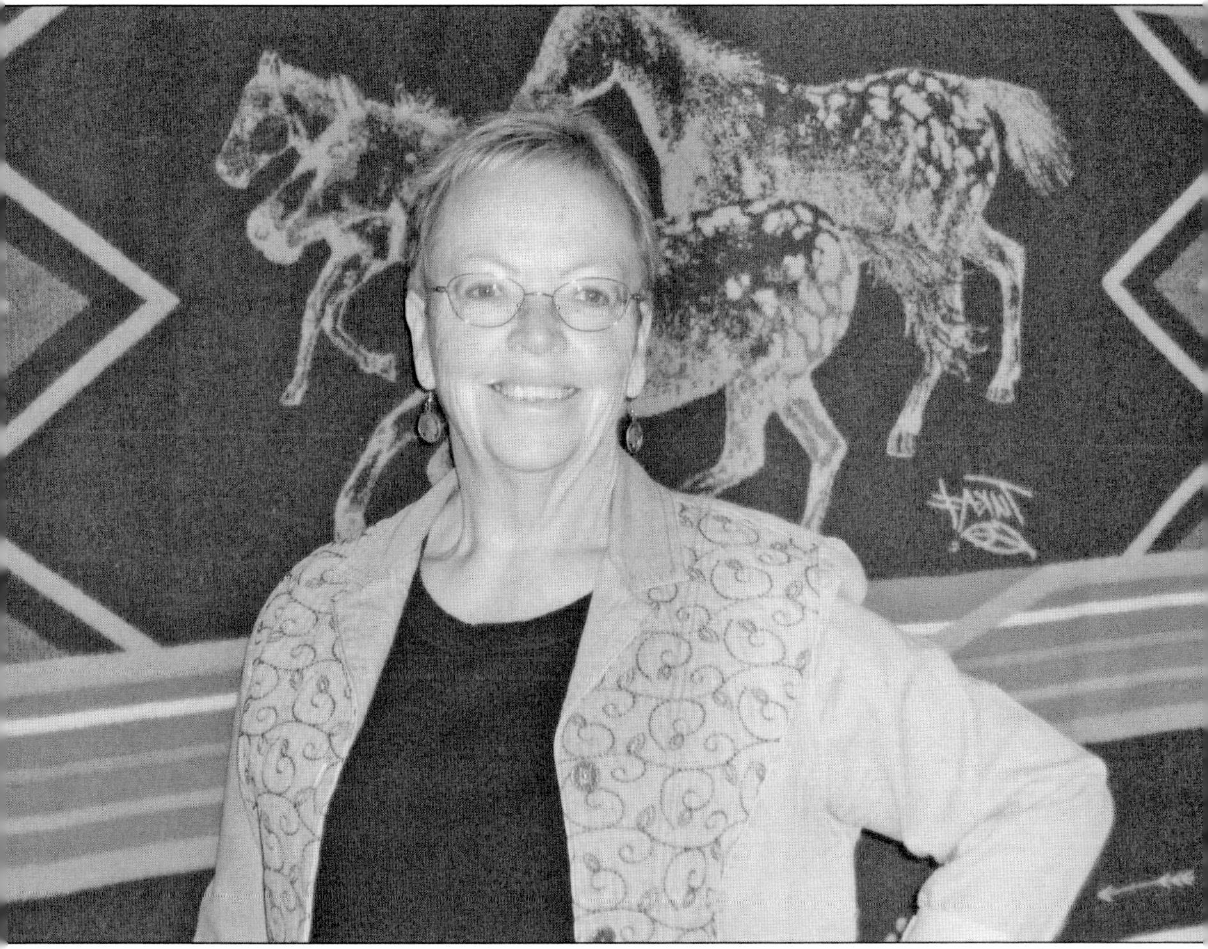

Jerry Squire is an Arizona native and accomplished pencil artist. She is enchanted with the folklore of Arizona, as many of her relatives experienced the Old West firsthand. She is the secretary for the Three Rivers Historical Society and is on the local planning committee for the upcoming Valley centennial in 2012.

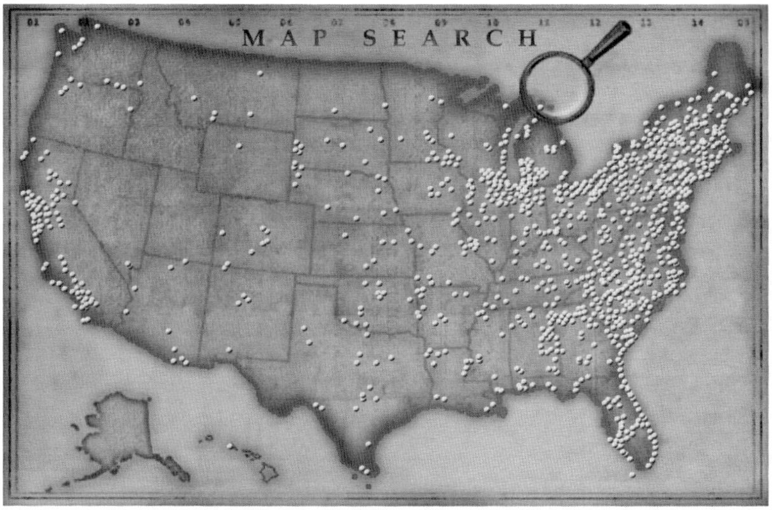
MAP SEARCH